MAKING MODERN MOTHERS

Rachel Thomson, Mary Jane Kehily, Lucy Hadfield
and Sue Sharpe

D0885846

First published in Great Britain in 2011 by

The Policy Press
University of Bristol
Fourth Floor
Beacon House
Queen's Road
Bristol BS8 1QU
UK
t: +44 (0)117 331 4054
f: +44 (0)117 331 4093
tpp-info@bristol.ac.uk
www.policypress.co.uk

North American office:
The Policy Press
c/o International Specialized Books Services (ISBS)
920 NE 58th Avenue, Suite 300
Portland, OR 97213-3786, USA
t: +1 503 287 3093
f: +1 503 280 8832
info@isbs.com

ISBN 978 1 84742 604 8 paperback
ISBN 978 1 84742 605 5 hardcover

British Library Cataloguing in Publication Data
A catalogue record for this book is available from the British Library.

Library of Congress Cataloging-in-Publication Data
A catalog record for this book has been requested.

Cover design by The Policy Press
Front cover: photograph kindly supplied by www.chrisclun.com
Printed and bound in Great Britain by Hobbs, Southampton

For our mothers and their mothers:

Anne & Blanche

Marcella & Elizabeth

Sue & Irene

Mary & Fanny

Contents

Acknowledgements

The research on which this book is based was made possible by support from the Economic and Social Research Council, grant RES-148-25-0057. The research team comprised the authors, with additional support from Lesley Henderson, Katy Prestedge and Karl Barr. Transcription was provided by Amanda Nicholas, Catharine Elliot, Linda Quantrill and Pat Dixon. The research formed part of the ESRC Identities and Social Action programme. We would like to thank Margie Wetherell, the programme director, for her consistent support, and our sister research project 'Becoming a Mother' (involving Heather Elliott, Wendy Hollway and Anne Phoenix), with whom we have enjoyed much parallel play, and all those who participated in the analysis groups. Mothercare helped us in securing access to our sample, and our policy collaborator, the Family and Parenting Institute, helped us to disseminate the findings. We would also like to thank Imogen Tyler, Jane Franklin, Jacqui Gabb, Julie McLeod and Sheila Henderson for reading drafts, as well as our research students (Ruth Ponsford, Naomi Rudoe and Jo Sanderson-Mann) for the conversations that form the background to the book. Finally, and most importantly, we would like to thank the mothers, grandmothers, friends, partners and children who contributed to the study.

ONE

Motherhood at large

People romance about their children long before they are born – long before and long after. They name them and rename them. They see them as their second chances, 'a chance to get it right this time', as if they were able to give birth to themselves. They have children to compensate themselves for the things they didn't do or didn't get in their own early life. They conceive because they feel compelled to make up, to a non-existent person, for a loss they have themselves suffered. Children are born because the parents feel the defects in themselves, and want to mend them; or because they are bored; or because they feel in some mysterious way, that it is time for children and if they don't have them their lives will begin to leak meaning away. Some women have babies to give a present to their own mother, or to prove themselves her equal. Motives are seldom simple and never pure. Children are never simply themselves, co-extensive with their own bodies, becoming alive to us when they turn in the womb, or with their first unaided breath. Their lives start long before birth, long before conception, and if they are aborted or miscarried or simply fail to materialise at all, they become ghosts within our lives. (Hilary Mantel, *Giving Up the Ghost: A Memoir* (Harper Perennial, 2004), p 228)

The idea of having a romance with reproduction has powerful resonances for the experience of pregnancy and birth in contemporary times. Pregnancy is no longer marked by a period of confinement – the very term sounds obscenely old fashioned – the relic of a bygone era when reproduction was private, constrained and hidden from view. In the new-fertile-world-order the pregnant body is everywhere and motherhood is never far from the headlines. It begins with the BUMP. The swollen tummy of pregnancy, once veiled in voluminous amounts of material, Laura Ashley dresses, polka-dot maternity smocks and outsize shirts producing a perverse dialogue with the body: 'I know you've had sex at least once and, for that, the next nine months must be spent looking as deeply unsexy as possible.' But not any more. At the level of the representational, the latest look, the new fashion accessory is the bump itself. Calling for celebratory forms of visibility, mothers-to-be are encouraged to emphasise it, contour it, show it off. Skin-tight T-shirts and low-cut jeans reveal the bump in all its gorgeousness.

But the mooning tummy of pregnancy is more than a stylish display of mellow fruitfulness. Pregnancy leads to birth and birth leads to parenting, just as it did for our mothers, grandmothers and great-grandmothers before them. So, apart from the bump-on-show, what else has changed for mothers-to-be? Becoming a mother can be seen as a profound moment of personal change which ties women to the past, the future and each other. Yet what it means to be a mother is shape-shifting in line with women's increased participation in work and education. The general trend is towards later motherhood, delaying the birth of a first child until education is completed and the career is well established. Emotional stability, financial security and the 'right' relationship are expected to fall in line with this life trajectory, making birth the apex of achievement for grown-up girls living the success-story narrative of contemporary times. Yet for some young women first pregnancy comes early. Marked by disaffection from education, lack of opportunity and poor socioeconomic circumstances, young motherhood may be the first act of adulthood rather than the highly prized goal of deferred gratification. Could it be that motherhood is becoming the site of a new social division between women?

In this opening chapter we contextualise the Making of Modern Motherhood study on which the book is based. This involves reviewing the ideas that have informed our particular approach, describing our research design and methods and outlining the structure of the book and the key arguments that we make.

Making modern motherhood

> Many, probably most, women feel that their range of choices is greater than that of their mothers with regard to work, marriage and reproduction. Yet ... in the post-war world an increasing gap has opened up between women in terms of opportunity and autonomy. One of the most significant differences of income and expectation in late twentieth-century society must be that between the teenage unmarried mother, unable to escape from dependence on state benefits, and the professional woman in her late thirties, married to another professional, having her first child and able to pay for a nanny. (Lewis, 1992, p 10)

The increasing participation of women in further and higher education and the labour force since the Second World War has transformed the shape and meaning of women's biographies (Lewis, 1992) – reflected in a trend towards later motherhood. Yet this change has been uneven, with stagnation in social mobility and widening inequality heightening differences *between* women – reflected in differential patterns of family formation, depending on educational and employment status (Crompton, 2006). The social polarisation of motherhood is one of the most distinctive demographic trends of the post-war period – reflected in a movement towards later motherhood for the majority, and early motherhood for a minority. In 2008 the average age of a woman giving birth in England and Wales was 29.3 years – an increase of 2.5 years over a 20-year period. The most obvious manifestation of this polarisation has been the intensive public focus on teenage pregnancy as a social problem, where a concern with age replaces earlier concerns around illegitimacy and marriage as markers of autonomy and respectability (Arai, 2009). Although later motherhood tends not to raise political concerns about economic dependence, it does become visible through popular concern over the availability and ethics of infertility treatment, the supposed 'intensification of parenting' and the commodification and delegation of domestic care.

—

3

The transition to motherhood in the contemporary era is an arena where socioeconomic differences between women are defined, compounded and inflated through the creation of distinct cultures of child rearing (Clarke, 2004; Byrne, 2006; Tyler, 2008) which then lead into divergent educational trajectories (Vincent and Ball, 2001; 2007). New motherhood constitutes a destination point for the social mobility of one generation and the departure point for another. Remarkably, despite concerted efforts on the part of feminist campaigners, motherhood in the UK continues to be 'sexed', with women taking primary responsibility for childcare (Breitenbach, 2006), including the thinking and planning of delegated care (Doucet, 2006), and after the birth of a child it is women rather than men who bear the financial penalty in terms of income and earning potential (Davies et al, 2000). The tendency in policy and popular culture to talk in terms of 'parenting' rather than mothering may communicate the veneer of equality, yet in practice elides the enduring sexual and class politics that shape the situation and experience of mothering (Jensen, 2010).

Rising birth rates in the UK provide the backdrop to the contemporary politics of motherhood. The Office for National Statistics (ONS, 2009) recorded the overall population in 1998 as having risen by 2 million since 2001, to a peak of 61.4 million. The increase is ascribed to a baby boom as fertility rates reached their highest level for 15 years.[1] Babies born in England and Wales in 2008 were most likely to have a mother aged 25–34, with over half (54%) of mothers being in this age group. A further 25% of babies were born to younger mothers, aged below 25, while 20% had mothers aged 35 or above at the time of birth. Fathers tend to be older than mothers. Nearly half of all babies born (47%) had mothers aged 30 or over, but nearly two-thirds (63%) were fathered by men in this age group (ONS, 2009). Almost a quarter of all births registered in Britain in 2008 were to women born outside the UK (ONS, 2009), and the politics of motherhood is increasingly entangled with the politics of citizenship (Bryceson and Vuorela, 2002; Erel, 2009).

Sociological studies of motherhood are products of their times, bearing the traces of the theoretical and popular preoccupations of their era. The key texts of second-wave feminism took issue with

–

4

the models of motherhood inherited from the 1950s – extricating practices of care from essentialist and oppressive ideas of maternity and femininity (Rich, 1976; Chodorow, 1978; Ruddick, 1980). An explosion of feminist social history and policy analysis in the 1980s and 1990s was central to recognising the role of the law, state and medicine in regulating and dividing mothers (Phoenix et al, 1991; Lewis, 1992; Smart, 1992), as were psychoanalytically and sociologically informed accounts of the ordinary nature of maternal ambivalence which acknowledged the subjective force of 'being loved so much and blamed so intensely' (Parker, 1996; Smart, 1996). The late 1990s witnessed a growing awareness of the ways in which the commodity frontier of global capitalism had transformed the private sphere, both replacing and intensifying the meaning of motherhood (Hays, 1996; Hochschild, 1997) and the disruptions that this causes to ideas of the heterosexual nuclear family (Van Every, 1995; Silva and Smart, 1998; Stacey, 1998). The current landscape is characterised by a new self-consciousness of maternal relations as shaped by intergenerational dynamics, both at the intimate level of the personal family biography (Bjerrum Nielsen and Rudberg, 2000; Lawler, 2000; Brannen et al, 2004; O'Connor, 2011) and at the cultural level of the intergenerational project of feminism (Everingham et al, 2007; Baraitser, 2009a; Woodward and Woodward, 2009). Mothers are understood simultaneously as daughters in familial and generational terms, with the effect of complicating feminist narratives of progress and solidarity with powerful emotions concerning ingratitude and disappointment. The question of whether women can or should be equated with ideas of reproduction was central to the radical feminist critiques of motherhood, inciting interest in science as an escape from biology (Firestone, 1970). Yet in practice, new reproductive technologies have not always realised their imagined transformatory potential (McNeil, 2007), often reiterating rather than destabilising traditional gender performances while also opening up new arenas of the body and intimacy to medico-marketised forces (Mamo, 2007). The 'queering of motherhood' is an important critical strand within and outside feminist approaches, destabilising taken-for-granted associations between biological sex and gender identity, and

–

increasingly, between people, objects and representations (Shildrick, 2009).

Contemporary research into mothering also takes cultural representation seriously, be that the new modes of seeing the foetus in 4D, the spectacle of pregnant beauty and abjection (Tyler, 2008) or the ways in which photographs and consumption constitute maternal practices (Lustig, 2004; Longhurst, 2009; Rose, 2010). With no sustainable division between the public and the private to rely on conceptually, documenting what mothers 'do' and where and how they 'do it' becomes a reinvigorated empirical project (Clarke, 2004; Baraitser, 2009b; Elliott et al, 2009; Sanderson-Mann, 2010). A further characteristic of contemporary research on motherhood is an interest in the mother as a subject in her own right, and in the maternal as providing new ways for thinking beyond the individual (Baraitser, 2008; Pollock, 2009). Inspired by phenomenological paradigms, we are asked to consider the mother as a generative ethical project rather than the empty subject of much psychological and psychoanalytic theory. Rather than reading the accounts of mothers back to universal models of pathology and development, we are invited to consider how their experiences push them into territory that confounds their own expectations and those of our theories.

Situations in a common culture

Our approach fits within this new landscape: informed by an intergenerational and cultural perspective. We take seriously the challenge of recognising social change and diversity as live and unfolding historical processes. We have found a conceptual framework for our approach in the phenomenology of Simone de Beauvoir, who conceptualised women in terms of a bodily 'situation' (1997) that is itself situated in terms of the particularities of lived experience (subjectivity), social arrangements and the norms and discourses that constitute the 'myths of femininity' (Moi, 1999, p 80). In thinking about first-time motherhood as a bodily and biographical *situation* it is possible to think about the commonalities of women's lives without ignoring the contingencies and differences. For some, reproduction is a struggle that opens the body to expert systems, technologies and collaborations in the form of infertility treatment, assisted conception, surrogacy and adoption. For others the body is taken for granted: a source of pride and wonder or an imposition to be eliminated or accommodated. The subjective experience of pregnancy and birth is dependent on the personal and economic circumstances of expectant mothers, their positions within families and the intergenerational legacies that come into play as maternal subjectivities are formed. Bodily situations combine with personal histories to locate women differently in relation to norms and discourses of the 'mothering advice industry', maternity services that exist within local and national mothering cultures. The coincidence of these constitutes the situation of mothering, which is itself articulated in and through time. The concept of the *situation* enables us to capture the differently materialised ways in which women of the same generation encounter motherhood, an approach suited to both the diversity of women's lives and the potential of new technologies to disrupt the terms of reproduction (Howie, 2010).

We also take seriously the need to locate motherhood within its cultural context in ways that reveal how it is routinely lived and occupied in women's lives. Drawing upon British Cultural Studies perspectives, we work with the cultural as a concept defined by *everyday social practice*, where elitism implodes in the erasure of distinctions between high and low culture or creative and mundane practices. Following Raymond Williams (1961; 1989), we recognise the radical gesture and simple beauty of *culture as ordinary* at work in the visible but often unremarkable activities of daily life. The everyday practices of mothering can be seen as constitutive of a maternal culture that is made and remade by successive and overlapping generations of women. Each chapter of the book can be seen as a site of practice for *structures of feeling* that accumulate and regenerate in the transition to motherhood: conception; the body; the family; expert discourses; work; commodities; and finally, birth. For Williams, the affective affiliations generated by structures of feeling refer to the largely unspoken shared values of traditional working-class communities. Applying this concept to the experience of new motherhood recognises the emotional forces that may shape the maternal landscape through other registers of belonging

–

7

and sharing in which class is present but not determining. Such structures may of course be open to charges of sentimentality as recuperative strategies formed in the absence of familial class-cultural connection. Our study found examples of women connecting and disconnecting around motherhood, suggesting that opportunities for newly contoured versions of the maternal and community may be possible in certain contexts.

To borrow another concept from cultural studies, we have used the idea of a 'common culture of motherhood' throughout to acknowledge the range of resources available to women in the shaping of a maternal identity and the myriad ways in which they can be integrated into the personal project of motherhood. We would include forms of embodiment, work and family connections as entwined in the 'common culture' in the blurring of boundaries between home made/mass produced, private/commercial, inside/outside. Willis's use of the concept of 'common culture' emphasises the aesthetic and 'sensuous possibilities' (Willis et al, 1990) of young people's own lives, in which the commercial world provides the raw material for the 'symbolic creativity' to be found in expressive youthful display. Our study is also concerned with what people do with things, and particularly the stuff of motherhood. Recognising that it is largely the market that offers new mothers a common culture, the study is orientated towards understanding the meshing of a common culture of motherhood with the diverse and situated everyday experience of mothering. By tracking individual journeys and patterns of consumption, we capture routine social practices and registers of affect.

Our approach is genuinely interested in what mothers have to say, but we do not simply take accounts at face value. Metaphors of communication are central to the ways in which theorists have attempted to capture the process of identity formation, and the relationship between the individual and the social (for example Volosinov's (1973)[2]). In recent work on the ways in which the performance of particular gender identities relates to broader configurations of class and gender, Judith Butler (2004) explores the 'social intelligibility of an action' (p 41) that allows for 'certain kinds of practices and actions to become recognizable ... imposing a grid of

—

legibility on the social and defining parameters of what will and will not appear within the domain of the social' (p 42). Identities, practices and performances that lie outside of the norm are unrecognised, illegible and, as such, unliveable, yet there is always potential for recognition, and in lying outside the norm such identities maintain a (troubling) relationship with the norm. Norms may not be obvious, but are most noticeable in what Butler calls an implicit *normalising principle*, 'difficult to read, discernable most clearly and dramatically in the effects they produce' (p 41). Echoing these themes of the storied and legible life, Plummer (1995) suggests that personal narratives remain an inherently conservative form, speaking to the past rather than the future. It is hard to tell new stories, which can emerge only in the confluence of developing identities and available resources that facilitate both the story-telling and its reception. The transition from private story to the generation of a public problem involves struggle and recognition of subjecthood, and the privilege to narrate oneself (rather than to be narrated by others) reflects wider dimensions of social, cultural and economic status (Kirkman et al, 2001; Adkins, 2003; Skeggs, 2004; Miller, 2005; Couldry, 2010). Working with the narratives of expectant and new mothers, we have sought to listen for and recognise these struggles for intelligibility, remaining sensitive to the operations of cultural and symbolic capital as well as to our own investments and defences as researchers (Lucey et al, 2003).

A comparative and dynamic approach

The Making of Modern Motherhood study set out to capture and relate two dimensions of social division – division that exists *between* generations (as captured in relationships between grandmothers, mothers and daughters) and division *within* generations (as captured by women becoming mothers for the first time). Recognising the complexity of this task, we maintained a substantive but relatively narrow focus on the experience of first-time motherhood and the transition into a maternal subjectivity. Located in the unique space of late pregnancy, our research encounters women as they approach birth, then follows a smaller number of case studies through into the first year of motherhood. A central objective of our approach has been to capture the paradoxical way that motherhood is both one thing and many, and for this reason we generated an initial sample of 62 pregnant women that was diverse in terms of age, social class, ethnicity, nationality, fertility history, disability and sexuality (see the appendices for full discussion of sample and methods employed). The particularly transient nature of pregnancy is located within the context of other temporal flows; the initial interviews were conducted in 2005 in the midst of the New Labour project of widespread change in social welfare, health and education. Subsequently, women and their families were revisited during the first year of the child's life. Two research sites, an inner city borough and a new town, generated a diverse sample of women linked by the common experience of becoming a mother.

In designing this study we were keen to capture and address two forces that hold the category of motherhood in tension (Thomson, 2010a). We wanted to engage with the question of diversity within the contemporary moment and the way that motherhood both provides the potential for identifications between women and the ground for women to experience differences in a heightened way. We wanted to add to this brew a temporal perspective on mothering as experienced by chains of women within families and between generations more collectively as, expressed through control over resources, institutions and representations. For us, this involves exploring motherhood as a historically located experience that is nevertheless mediated within families – between grandmothers, mothers and daughters, who in turn locate themselves as members of wider generations of women. In terms of our research design we have translated this into a desire to research motherhood in two directions: horizontally, as relations between women who share a historical moment; and vertically, as relations between intergenerational chains of women within families. It is an approach that seeks to move between an understanding of biographical time as experienced by individuals and within families and a more collective sense of historical time as experienced by generations and the relationships between generations (Mannheim, 1952).

Our understanding of generations draws on Karl Mannheim's classic essay in which he uses a musical metaphor to suggest that the *zeitgeist* of a period is not a single sound, but can be understood as 'an accidental chord' comprised of notes expressing the distinct *units* that exist within a generation. As with melody, the combination of these notes subtly changes over time. Through a shared social location, members of a generational unit are likely to share values and attitudes, and are in a state of constant *interaction*. Following Mannheim's musical metaphor, we wanted to capture the *zeitgeist* of contemporary motherhood, made up of the many different notes that are struck by distinct yet contemporaneous generational units. It was then a priority for us to map something of this diversity, at least for the contemporary generation of first-time mothers.

Another of our inspirations has been a study undertaken by Harriet Bjerrum Nielsen and Monica Rudberg (1994, 2000), who traced 22 intergenerational chains of Norwegian women in order to capture something of the historical changes in women's position within Norway in the post-war period and how change and continuity are mediated within families. Drawing on interview material, Bjerrum Nielsen and Rudberg suggest that at any one time there will be a lack of fit between gender identities (the kind of woman that one wants to be), subjectivity (one's sense of 'me') and the social and cultural possibilities available to realise these. The focus of their analysis was cross-sectional – identifying common themes in the accounts of the different generations (grandmothers born 1910–27, mothers born 1940–48 and daughters born 1971/72). This enabled them to characterise what was distinctive about the account of each generation and to suggest how successive generations could be understood as reacting to each other. Norway is a less diverse country than the UK, and we were aware that we could not assume such coherence within our generations, nor could we map family generation neatly onto historical generation.

Where Bjerrum Nielsen and Rudberg read across their generations to understand something about the historical periods during which these women were growing up, we were interested in our intergenerational chains as case studies. Our approach was influenced by work in the life-history field, where a family is taken as the unit of analysis and as a route into the wider social and historical landscape. An important example is Daniel Bertaux and Isabelle

Bertaux-Wiame's (1997) analysis of a single French farming family over five generations, which explores interdependency of destinies and the complex interaction of psychological and social factors over time. We are also indebted to Paul Thompson's adaptation of the family-systems approaches of John Byng-Hall, which conceptualises the family in terms of a continuous contractual relationship where unresolved emotional dynamics can be transmitted through the 'symbolic coinage' of family stories within which motifs, patterns and difficulties are repeated and the 'very phrases echo down the generations' (Thompson, 1993, p 30). Our hope was that, by collecting and juxtaposing the accounts of different generations of women about the experience of their first pregnancy and birth, we might capture the echoes of an unconscious family 'dialog' (Rosenthal, 1998) while gaining insight into how solidarity is maintained between women in the context of changing opportunities and expectations.

A third influence on our research design was an interest in capturing change as it happens. The arrival of a new generation in a family is a dynamic moment, where expectations hit realities, old roles are shed and new relationships are formed. Here we have drawn on Norbert Elias's (1978) conception of the configuration rather than the individual as the basic unit of analysis. The configuration is defined both by relationships and by temporal processes (coincidences, history), and the individual is understood as a point from which it is possible to have a perspective – a conceptual schema also found in child and family psychotherapy (Byng-Hall, 1995; Stern, 1998). We envisaged a longitudinal component to the case studies, designing the research around a critical moment of personal and family change (Thomson et al, 2002; Holland and Thomson, 2009). The prospective dimension of the research brings with it a new range of methodological and epistemological questions arising from how respondent accounts change over time, the significance of the researchers' subjective responses and reflections as a source of data in their own right and the impossibility of analytic closure (Thomson and Holland, 2003; McLeod and Thomson, 2009). Our approach contributes towards the development of a configurational perspective on family lives, stressing the importance of time, place and timing for how interdependencies play out and through which

—

resources and meanings are communicated between generations (Widmer et al, 2008).

Outline of the book

In the chapters that follow we synthesise this diverse data set in a range of ways. Our analysis of popular representations of mothering finds various expressions. Sometimes we reflect on how different women responded to particular visual images used as prompts in the interviews, sometimes we draw on the ways in which particular aspects of mothering are represented in popular texts such as magazines, books and television. Overall, we attempt to capture how women must always negotiate and position themselves in relation to a range of common cultural resources that do not simply include commercial products and advertising but encompass state and other services and different forms of expert advice. The interviews with the 62 expectant mothers provide the core of the book, enabling us to conceptualise patterns in our data such as the salience of 'age', which we suggest operates as a canonical narrative (Kirkman et al, 2001) through which women locate their own autobiographical narratives as mothers, with the youngest talking about their impending birth as marking the 'end of childhood', the oldest talking in terms of 'the last gasp of fertility' and the middle age group talking in terms of 'effective biographical planning' (Thomson et al, 2008). This argument is first set out in Chapter Two (Conception) through a close reading of three narrative fragments, but is reiterated and expanded in successive chapters in relation to different substantive fields.

Although we emphasise the salience of age we are also interested in other axes of difference, including social class, ethnicity, bodily capital, sexuality and locality, and we seek to demonstrate these as relevant. The way in which individual mothering situations come together in time and in social and geographical space is demonstrated most effectively through the analysis of the 12 case studies. These are employed strategically through the book, sometimes in order to capture incongruities between expectations and practices (for example Chapter Eight, Birth), sometimes to reveal differences within what appears to be a homogenous group of 'middle-class women' (Chapter Six, Work) and sometimes to explicate complex processes of identification and change (Chapter Three, Body). The voices of the grandmothers and significant others collected as part of the case studies feature throughout the book, the former providing commentaries on processes of continuity and social change in relation to work and the material 'stuff' of mothering, the latter contributing to our understanding of birth and fatherhood. The overall focus of the book is matriarchal, with men appearing through the narratives of women or when invited by the women to contribute. Something of the material culture of motherhood is captured in the photographs featured in the book, taken as part of our initial meetings with expectant mothers and reflecting their preparations for birth, capturing something of the way in which objects mediate and bridge the passage into a new experience and mode of being.

The book is organised into seven substantive chapters which enable us to move through our rich data set. We begin with conception and end with birth, capturing both the anticipation of our 62 initial interviewees and the hindsight and reflections of case study participants. Chapter Two invites the reader to focus on the narratives that women shared with us about discovering their pregnancy and sharing the news with others. Pregnancy involves the exposure of self to others, calling upon stories to do the narrative work of bridging a personal biography which changes personal relationships. The accounts demonstrate the ways in which experience is 'already storied' and how stories become ensemble performances through the repeated activity of telling. Here we identify common features of conception narratives and juxtapose the accounts of three women in ways that reveal the extent to which the situation of motherhood expresses inequality and the extent to which a woman's experience is 'intelligible' to particular and generalised others (Plummer, 1995; Butler, 2004). Despite the different circumstances in which women become pregnant, all three stories are highly moral tales, constructed (heteroglossically) in relation to broader narratives of pregnancy as a potentially shameful event requiring some justification. Finally, the chapter demonstrates the importance of narrative as a family practice, showing how relationships are claimed and brought into being, but also denied and refused (Strathern, 1992; Carsten, 2000;

Chavkin and Maher, 2010). Such narratives are generally forged in pregnancy before taking their place within family cultures, revisited by the next generation at key biographical moments.

In Chapter Three we move from talk to flesh, attempting to engage with the embodied dimension of pregnancy. Here we privilege the visual, tactile and existential dimension of pregnancy and breastfeeding, moving between analysis of the representation of 'pregnant beauty' (Tyler, 2008) and the ways in which the discipline of the pregnant body fits with women's intensely personal body stories. The chapter considers the maternal body as a temporary state for individual women and a carrier of meaning on the larger scale of class, culture and community. Illustrating how the embodiment of pregnancy is mediated by popular culture, pregnancy magazines provide an example of the 'bumptastic' approach common in media discourse, inciting women to become 'me' centred, to indulge and pamper an expanded, attention-seeking version of self. Yet this representation is at odds with the ways in which women describe their experience. Women in the study lived the pregnant body in a myriad of ways, some feeling inspired to embrace the performance of femininity while others mourned the loss of their pre-pregnant selves. Women commented upon their evolving relationship with a corporeality that gave them an exterior visibility and public presence that appears to invite dialogue and touch, even from strangers. Simultaneously, pregnancy prompts women to consider how they feel about themselves and the boundaries between self and others. Breastfeeding, in particular, highlights the vulnerabilities of the maternal body, manifest in the anxiety and loss of confidence women feel in the ability of their body to do what it is supposed to do. For most women, pregnancy becomes part of a body story, fitting with or disrupting a narrative of embodiment that is uniquely personal and keenly felt.

Chapter Four explores the ways in which familiar relationships change and regroup in the face of new motherhood. Reflecting on developments in family studies, the chapter is concerned to explore matters of practice and highlight what families do, as well as what they are. We consider the relationship context of new motherhood, mapping the ways in which motherhood is contoured by age-specific biographical trajectories. We discuss birth as an intergenerational act bringing an intensive traffic of conscious and unconscious meaning within the family. The chapter begins by counterposing the youngest and the oldest of our interview subjects, before exploring the ways in which relationships between couples, mothers and daughters, siblings and friends can be reconfigured by the arrival of a new generation. We demonstrate how the timing of motherhood defines possibilities and limitations that have consequential affects for the maternal landscape of women. Couples draw upon a range of imaginative, affective and material resources to adapt to changing circumstances and new horizons. Alongside the 'work' of the couple, mothers and daughters may re-evaluate their relationship from both sides. We found that mothers and daughters looked to each other to bridge the transition to motherhood, to personalise the experience and *make it real*. The connection could produce intense moments of identification, particularly in the recognition of a shared bodily inheritance. Moments of disconnection were also possible, as mothers-to-be might desire a break with the past. Both positions call upon new mothers to engage with their own mothers in order to fashion their own maternal identity.

Chapter Five focuses on expert advice aimed at pregnant women and new mothers, in order to identify components of the common culture of motherhood, including magazines, advice books, websites and networks such as the National Childbirth Trust (NCT). Here we show the ways in which these texts speak the contradictions of contemporary mothering, appearing to offer options that can be enjoyed in theory, if not in practice. By attending to the ways in which expectant and new mothers engage ironically and rebelliously with these texts, we suggest that, rather than seeing these texts as disciplinary in a Foucauldian sense, we should see the plethora of expert advice as operating as a commentary on the impossibility of getting motherhood 'right'. The growing phenomenon of the 'display' of maternal ambivalence through 'Mom-oires' (Cusk, 2001; Enright, 2004; and so on) and websites such as Mumsnet points to important shifts in the relationship between the expert and the mother. Engaging with experts, taking advice and building a personal knowledge base can be seen as part of the *work* of motherhood. The chapter suggests

—

that acts of engagement are not simply a matter of discovery or fact finding: it is more a case of positioning and recognising the self within the maternal culture.

Chapter Six reveals the context for contemporary motherhood as work becomes a ubiquitous feature of the contemporary female biography. Beginning with women's accounts of being pregnant at work, the chapter considers the argument that work has been feminised and women have been labourised – considered as workers first and mothers second (Power, 2009). In this chapter we reveal the extent to which a symbolic separation between working and mothering may be a middle-class phenomenon (Duncan, 2005). Through four examples of middle-class working mothers, it becomes possible to grasp the logic through which women seek out individual and couple solutions to what might be understood as collective or political problems. The twin figures of the glamorous 'yummy mummy' and the impoverished teenage mother exist as representational examples of how women may be differently positioned in relation to work in ways that suggest some of the difficulties of articulating a coherent politics of motherhood. For young mothers, paid work is commonly not a feature of their maternal practice, while for most middle-class women, career and mothering continue to be constituted as conflicting projects that must be 'balanced'. The relationship that a woman strikes in relation to work appears to be highly consequential to the kind of mothering project that she subsequently embarks on, including how she orients to expert advice, consumption and childcare. Women's initial attempts to seek out work-based support for pregnancy and childcare generally turn into local and individual solutions involving family, partners and the market. This is the post-feminist contract conceptualised by McRobbie (2007, 2009), where the right to assert sexual difference is traded for the right to be treated as a genderless worker. Yet sexual difference continues to exist in workplaces, as our case studies illustrate. Working and mothering remain entangled and entwined. Workplaces rarely allow for the materiality of the pregnant or lactating body, and the micro-politics of employment, domestic labour and childcare remain important to the moral terrain of maternal practice. Thinking about women as workers forces us to recognise the politics of class that fragments

—

women's biographies, inhibits relations of solidarity and isolates women from each other, even from those who are most like them.

In Chapter Seven we attend to the ways in which the material culture of mothering constitutes a marker of generational change. We begin by exploring commodities as preparatory, expressive and identity producing, with maternal subjects wanting things to furnish and make sense of the maternal project. New motherhood can be understood as a sustained and dynamic stretch of the commodity frontier. It may be productive to ask where the extent and limits of the market lie in relation to new motherhood. Is it boundaried by the needs of the new-born, or does it extend to housing, childcare and education, for example? The chapter takes an exploratory approach in which new motherhood can be understood a politically important moment in which relations between the state and the market are reconfigured. Despite the anti-consumerism of some of our participants, we suggest that, as in other spheres of consumption, alternative practices become incorporated into the commercial, leaving little space outside the market for doing motherhood differently. This can be seen most vividly in significations of *the natural*. Originally a challenge to the medicalisation of birth, ideas of the natural have been added to an ever-expanding choice menu of products and practices deemed good, pure and close to nature, regardless of the manufacturing involved in their production. Through material culture and consumer 'choice', mother and baby are brought into being as socially connected and emotionally realised actors in the drama of having a family. Rather than decry the losses associated with this extension of the commodity frontier, we explore the potential for the generation of new forms of sociability, recognition and connection.

Chapter Eight focuses attention on the extreme embodied struggle through which the child and mother are constituted and separated. We focus on the ways in which birth stories circulate in maternal cultures, asking how birth is made 'intelligible' and noting the cultural silences that continue to exist. This unfolding story reveals birth as a serious business which undoes the body work of femininity and remakes the woman as a mother. The chapter begins by mapping a feminist politics of birth and the formation of a contemporary discourse of 'choice' associated with the creation of individualised

—

birth plans and the promise of consumer choice in maternity services. Focusing on women's hopes and expectations for birth, we suggest some of the ways in which 'designing' birth forms part of a wider commodification of motherhood which leaves out the 'scary bits'. As an initiation into motherhood, birth is only partially narrated within the common culture. Drawing on case studies that include reflections on birth experiences by new mothers, grandmothers and partners, we build a picture of the ways in which maternal experience takes women into new forms of knowledge and connection and which question some of the taken-for-granted hierarchies between mothers that are associated with social class and age. In this chapter, as in others, we attempt to bring together sociological insights concerning social divisions, institutional processes and cultural representations with an awareness of the affective dynamics that bind generations and intimate relations. Each mother is situated uniquely in relation to a personal and family biography, but this biography is synchronised with those of others in generational terms that implicate her within a common culture of motherhood, with potential for solidarities and dis-identifications.

In the final chapter of the book, Chapter Nine, we revisit women after birth, capturing something of the transformations that becoming a mother involves. From this foundation we reflect on the question with which we embarked on this research, the intersection of two axes of difference which in turn shape the contemporary politics of motherhood – divisions between generations of women and divisions within a generation of women. This final chapter attempts to imagine mothers as a political constituency – existing in and through their enmeshment with NHS and maternity services, maternity and paternity leave, education and care.

A new politics of motherhood?

During the five years that we have been involved in this research we closely followed media coverage of motherhood, observing the way in which mainstream discourses of motherhood are more or less split into either/or debates (Hadfield et al, 2007; Franklin, 2008). So, for example, the core issue in discussions about working mothers is whether the place of mothers is in work or at home. If they try to do both, they are not fully appreciated in either place. Discussions about birth and pregnancy are increasingly framed around medicalised or home birth, peppered with issues of safety, risk and choice. Present in these debates, however, is also the desire to 'rethink' or move beyond, or to incorporate both sides of the argument. Social change influences new, perhaps more pragmatic, ways of thinking about motherhood. Women who stay at home argue that this is an independent 'choice', that being with children is not oppressive, but interesting and challenging. This is not a surprising choice, when we read that even professional women suffer discrimination at work and feel undervalued and demeaned.

Discussion of poverty among mothers, including low birth weight and the lack of maternity leave, seems to be marginalised, while the dominant discourses are about choice. Risk is discussed in relation to technology or the absence of it, whereas the risk of social exclusion for mothers is dealt with through Sure Start. New motherhood or parenting movements are generated daily on the internet, and are gradually filtering through to mainstream policy and media discourses. The debate over Gina Ford's 'no nonsense', routine-based approach to baby care is indicative of the strength of feeling women attach to their identity as mothers and the styles of parenting they adopt. The split between rational, organised parenting and 'natural', instinctive, unconditional mothering is pronounced across issues of birth, work and parenting. Women who take the 'trust yourself and your baby' route are accused of 'eschewing modernity'. In challenging modernity, they unsettle accepted ways of doing and being a mother. What is striking is that debates about motherhood tend take place between women, who are often bitingly critical of each other. Motherhood, then, is still a gender issue.

We write this book at a moment of potential change. After 13 years of a New Labour government which brought with it a commitment to supporting vulnerable children (realised through family tax credits, Sure Start, extension of maternity leave to 1 year, right to request flexible work, basic paternity leave, child trust bonds), we are faced with a Coalition government intent on remaking the welfare state. Although, in the general election, both leaders of the new parties in government courted mothers as a constituency, self-consciously presenting themselves as involved fathers, the future looks tough for mothers. Initial impressions suggest a greater reliance on the commercial sector and social entrepreneurism, including an expansion in private health care for those able to afford it. We can predict that trends towards the privatisation of childbirth are set to continue and accelerate, with the Momtrepreneur as a key figure in pushing forward the commodity frontier into the lucrative domestic interiors of middle-class families. We can also expect social class-based divisions between women to harden as families seek to defend their children against downward social mobility, monopolising the best in state provision or opting into private provision if necessary and possible. The spaces in which mothers mix are likely to diminish as state provision is reduced and is targeted on the most disadvantaged. As in previous generations, we can expect women to bear the brunt of the recession, both in terms of occupying the most precarious positions in the labour market and in terms of absorbing the radical cuts in the welfare state.[3] Yet we are also witnessing a renewed stirring in feminist activism among a new generation. Currently, attention is focused on sexualisation and pornography, reflecting perhaps the interests of a middle-class group of twenty-something young women, most of whom are postponing reproduction.

Historically, the relationship between feminism and motherhood has been generative yet complicated, providing a focus for activism yet also raising divisive issues concerning the centrality of biology to women's oppression. For example, there continues to be controversy over whether and how motherhood might contribute to women's self-actualisation, creating enduring tensions as to how to conceptualise and distinguish maternal and child subjectivity and well-being. In 1997 Arlie Hochschild wrote about a 'stalled revolution', suggesting that the historical shift constituted by women's entry into the workforce had not been matched by a shift in the division of labour at home. She subsequently characterised feminism as 'escaping the cage' of its radical origins, increasingly put into the service of an expanding form of neoliberal global capitalism that seeks to enter and make business out of domestic spaces that women have escaped (Hochschild, 2003). Over time, the commercial substitutes for family activities 'often turn out better than the real thing ... in a sense, capitalism isn't competing with itself ... but with the family, and particularly the wife and mother' (2003, p 37). Thus a 'cycle is set in motion. As the family becomes more minimal, it turns to the market to add what it needs and, by doing so, becomes yet more minimal' (2003, p 37). In commodifying care, the market incites forms of excellence and achievement that go far beyond the standards of 'good enough mothering' but which increasingly set a benchmark for new forms of distinction in a wider context of downward social mobility. This 'slicing and dicing' of the mother's role is not entirely new: the delegation of care has a long history in upper-class households. The contemporary market for commercialised care is created by middle-class working women and serviced by poor women often involved in global chains of care, where mothering is displaced and reconstructed down the line (Chavkin and Maher, 2010).

Writing about Silicon Valley at the turn of the century, Hochschild captures something of the state of things to come for many developed western economies. Motherhood is ripe for another round of politicisation, constituting both a singular and multiple experience, connecting and dividing women as daughters, mothers, non-mothers and grandmothers, as well as employers and employees. We hope that this book contributes to the project of forging a new and invigorated politics of motherhood, providing insights into why solidarities are so difficult yet potentially so rewarding and necessary.

Notes

[1] www.guardian.co.uk/world/2009/aug/27/population-growth-uk-birth-rate-immigration.

[2] Volosinov's (1973) concept of 'speech acts' in his study of language as a struggle for meaning embedded in the social world. For Volosinov, all speech acts are addressed to another's word or to another listener; even in the absence of another person, a speaker will conjure up the presence of an imaginary listener. In an evocative and much-quoted passage Volosinov conjures up the reciprocal relationship between speaker, listener and their social world: 'the word is territory shared by both addresser and addressee' (Volosinov, 1973, p 86). Arguing that all

—

forms of communication and social experience are dependent on social context, Volosinov identifies two poles: the 'I-experience', which tends towards extermination as it does not receive feedback from the social milieu; and the 'we-experience', which grows with consciousness and positive social orientation. From this perspective, self-confidence, for example, can be viewed as an ideological form of the 'we-experience', deriving from positive and affirming social relations rather than individual strength and personality.

[3] www.hmrc.gov.uk/budget2010/individuals.htm#4; www.fawcettsociety.org.uk//index.asp?PageID=1198.

TWO

Conception

Memory (and its corollary, forgetting) is integral to our research, and we found that late pregnancy and early motherhood are suffused with powerful evocations of the embodied practices of mothering and being mothered. The preservation and passing on of special objects (books, baby clothes, health records, toys, cots, blankets, talismans to ensure safety) can be seen as a memorialising and materialising of these intergenerational connections. Yet the staging of memory through such material practices always also involves an editing out: what is remembered is not simply a record of the past but rather, a representation of the past in the present, shedding light on the identities, anxieties and situations of those involved. Riceour (2004) talks in terms of a 'reciprocal relationship between remembering and forgetting' which shapes both the perception of experience and the production of narrative.

The stories that we tell about important life events form the fabric of our biographies and are a medium through which families communicate and bridge historical and biographical time. Yet these stories are not straightforward, literal accounts of what happens. Rather, they are records of what is sayable and what is not, examples of the ways in which we seek to make ourselves intelligible within the world, visible to each other, and through which connections are forged and refused. The exploration of narrative has been a productive tool in the study of motherhood (Bailey, 1999; Kirkman et al, 2001; Miller, 2005). In this study of motherhood we have invited people to tell us stories: the story of their life, or their pregnancy, or their births. This has included asking people to tell us stories that they have been told by others as well as those that they tell themselves. In collecting these accounts we have gained a sense of their slipperiness, sensitising us to the challenges that may be involved in hearing as well as telling (Layton, 1998). Most of us think that we know something of our own birth. We have probably asked and been told something of the when and where of it. We may know the location and who was there to witness the event. If this information is unavailable to us we may long for a narrative that secures our origins and locates our entry into the world. When women are approaching their first birth they tend to revisit these stories, asking again, but for different reasons, finding a new sense of urgency to questions about the length of the labour and the relative difficulty of the birth and breastfeeding. At this moment we may be open to a bodily inheritance of 'child-bearing hips' or a 'fast recovery'. Yet what are we told and what do we hear in these situations? Think, for example, of the expectant mother who shared with us her hopes of inheriting the 'short, sharp labour' that had been a familiar motif in family stories, imagining that her partner would be present in the same way that her father had been for her. But the story that circulated in the family was quite different from the more difficult account of her first birth that her mother shared with us in an interview, involving a long confinement and an enduring sense of trauma – an experience that her daughter was to repeat.

We first met with mothers towards the end of their pregnancies – at a point when they had begun to slow down, to rest and to prepare themselves for what was to come. For most of our participants it was a good time to talk, and they readily accepted our invitation to tell the story of their pregnancy and to share their preparations for birth. We tried our hardest to be good listeners, to not interrupt these accounts and to witness them as evidence of the work in which women must engage in order to make themselves intelligible to us and to themselves. The overriding aim of our research was to capture the simultaneous singularity and multiplicity of motherhood. We met and spoke with 62 women who were having their first child at the same historical time in two distinct geographical locations, yet whose lives were diverse and divergent. Although the predicament of pregnancy was shared, the way in which the situation of motherhood was constituted for these women differed profoundly. Age, wealth, fertility, migration, disability and sexuality all combined to shape the situation of motherhood for individuals, yet in becoming mothers they were also exposed to common cultural resources encountered through the ways in which motherhood is represented and regulated in popular culture, public services and expert advice.

In this chapter we begin our exploration of the singular yet shared situation of mothering by attending to the accounts that women shared with us at the beginning of the first interview, when invited to tell the story of the pregnancy. We anticipated that women's accounts of their pregnancy might take the form of discrete narratives within the interview, defined in terms of having a beginning, middle and end and by the sense that they had been forged and told outside the interview encounter. Our analysis confirmed our initial hunch that this aspect of the pregnancy is already 'storied' prior to the interview and that these stories are an important source for understanding the project that motherhood represents to individual women. We approach these stories as a record of the 'situation' that pregnancy poses for the women concerned. We have thought of these stories as 'conception narratives' with common components – recounted in different orders and to different effects: finding out and 'knowing' that you are pregnant; reconstructing and remembering the moment of conception; and going public by sharing the news with layers of significant others. Remembering and forgetting are explicit tools through which a narrative is forged, setting out the parameters of the project of motherhood and the characters included in the endeavour. In our approach we have sought to maintain a focus on what people claim in terms of relatedness to others, understanding the process of storying pregnancy as central to the ways in which families are named and brought into being at dynamic moments such as the arrival of a new child (Strathern, 1992; Carsten, 2000). Yet we have also attempted to think about how the women in our study are differently positioned in terms of securing recognition for their pregnancy from others. Here, as elsewhere in this book, we draw on the idea of 'intelligibility' as a way of capturing the extent to which personal biographies synchronise and resonate (or not) with culturally shared discursive formations of what it is to be 'normal', 'successful' and 'sensible' (Butler, 2004). The chapter begins by a consideration of issues that arose from an analysis of the full data set of 62 interviews, followed by a closer examination of specific conception narratives which give insights into the work that such narratives perform and the very different ways in which potential mothering situations configure and play out.

—

Storying conception

A recurrent theme in this book is the significance of age in shaping the situation of mothering – both in terms of the salience of embodied age, and more profoundly in the way that age acts as a marker for socioeconomic inequalities. To be a 'young mum' or an 'old mum' is to be positioned as outside of the norm, demanding elaboration of the consequences for the child and the mother. Being too young is defined in terms of an interrupted education, inadequate maturity and a lack of economic autonomy giving rise to dependency and 'poor outcomes' for the child (Rudoe and Thomson, 2009). Being too old is more likely to be conceptualised in terms of physical capital, having insufficient energy to fully engage with a child, bringing an overly psychological mode of parenting and potentially shaming one's child, and in a range of ways putting one's own interests first. Between these is the terrain of the normative, neither too young nor too old, but 'just right', characterised by complex reckonings of 'readiness' in terms of biographical maturity, economic autonomy and relationship security. In our research, 31-year-old Kate talks in terms of a "fierce", "emotional" feeling emerging at the moment at which she is "ready to let go of – or give up certain things" associated with an extended phase of youth. This means being "ready to give someone else a life and still have my life, but not be as sort of selfish about it". Others, such as Carly, conceptualised readiness in terms of a couple relationship, explaining that "we're both in our late 20s, we're not children any more and it's something that can be really good for the pair of us and we love each other very much so we thought yeah, let's just do it".

Timing is also constituted within a family, with sibling order interacting to create a second-order synchronisation. Lorraine, for example, explained that her pregnancy caused trouble within her family, as older childless sisters felt displaced within the natural order of the family. Tina, whose younger sister became a mother before her, also sees the disruption of the sibling birth-order status as a being a bit "strange". She explains that people have always tended to think her sister is the older one because she "settled down a lot earlier" and is more "sensible". Beyond the family, women's sense of timing is connected to the timetables of their peers, collectively forming a generational unit that shares aspirations, values and life-style. Some of the younger mothers expressed concern that by becoming a mother they would lose touch with a peer group making their way through school, college and a landscape of youthful leisure. In contrast, 32-year-old Alice felt that becoming a mother enabled her to move with her peers into a new and shared life-style. Not having a baby at this point would mean being left behind.

> "I feel like I have two groups of friends, and I've moved from one into the other. And I have the married or stable relationship, and in the last two years most of those have added a small child to it. And then I have the single and childless couples sort of friends ... who are telling me about the party they went to, and the galleries that they went and saw, and this and that and the other. And I feel like I'm – you know, I'm moving from one group to the other. And I'm quite happy about that, because I feel like I've been in the first group for quite a long time. And I'm pleased I'm not left in the first group as one of the single ones, because I think I'd be bored with all that stuff." (Alice, 32)

The place that the pregnancy takes in the unfolding biography of the individual, the couple and the family is central to the way in which conception stories are narrated, with pregnancies constituted variously as surprises, mistakes, decisions, miracles and rebellions. The project of making a pregnancy intelligible involves a number of tasks and stages, including recognising the pregnancy oneself, positioning it within webs of relationship and demanding recognition from others. These stages closely parallel the component stages of successful story-telling outlined by Ken Plummer (1995), including the ability to imagine, articulate and to be heard by others. Although a few women reported an immediate bodily awareness of conception, for others the failure to recognise pregnancy was a central and comic element of their narrative, emphasising the rupture between the pre- and post-pregnancy self. For example, 27-year-old Heather, who was on the pill, misrecognised her pregnancy as constipation. Following a scan:

> "it turned out that I was 19.5 weeks (laughs) and didn't KNOW.... And that was 100% the turning moment for us … that little soul is in there, and he's been fighting away for 19 weeks without me knowing. And I'd been exercising hard and thinking, you know, maybe I'm becoming sluggish and, you know, need to exercise more, and playing squash …"

Even when pregnancies were planned, women talked about the shock of conception, wryly replaying their recent past from their new position of pregnancy and reframing everyday self-destructive habits such as drinking as behaviour that might have been risky for the foetus.

If missed periods and sensitive breasts were the signals of an unplanned pregnancy, confirmation was generally secured through the pregnancy test kits which, again, were used as comic props within several narratives. For example, 32-year-old Hannah sends herself up by counterposing her professional role as a nurse with her incompetence in deciphering the meaning of two thin blue lines of the pregnancy test that she secretes from work. Where women had struggled with infertility, knowing that you were pregnant and feeling that the pregnancy was secure could be a fraught process. Lyn, 31 years old, describes how, after years of infertility and miscarriage, she struggled to believe the accumulating evidence of a missed period and positive pregnancy test and her doctor's confirmation. She explains that:

> "it was a really strange feeling, I suppose it was … it was, it took us a long time before we, but I suppose it was like the first one, we lost the first one around 13 weeks so we couldn't like, kind of enjoy it and say yeah I'm pregnant again, because it was the worry and the fear of losing it again that kept us, actually the second time around we hadn't really told many people. The first time around it was like telling the family first and then the really close

friends, the worst bit was actually going back to tell them that we'd lost it, so with this one we couldn't even, like with my, I think it was around the first scan when we kind of really officially told the families, but before with the first one we just told them immediately, you know, so it wasn't exciting as we thought we would be, when we did fall pregnant. People were, you must be over the moon, I was like, I don't know, yeah it was a strange feeling, really strange feeling."

Several women remarked on the necessary reorientation towards the body that was involved in shifting from a habit of avoiding pregnancy to the pursuit of conception. The potential for infertility marked the narratives of most women, including the youngest, who might couch the non-use of contraception in terms of testing their fertility. When women became pregnant quickly they tended to describe themselves as "lucky", and many had contemplated the possibility of infertility in advance of planning their pregnancy, expressing fears of "going down that road" and becoming "desperate".

When researching motherhood, it can be easy to forget the centrality of sex to the project of conception. Maternity plays a central and paradoxical role in the heterosexual matrix through which sex and gender are subject to a myriad forms of splitting along axes of good and bad, male and female, sexual and asexual, the sacred and the profane. One of the central tasks for the conception story is to negotiate the moral status of the pregnancy through the locating and claiming of paternity in a specific act of sexual intercourse. The way that this is negotiated varies, with some accounts more coy and confused than others – sometimes reflecting the relative challenge involved in making the pregnancy in question respectable in social terms. Questions of agency and causality lie at the heart of these accounts, yet are couched in a language of 'fate', 'falling', and 'letting things happen'. Where a teenage mother might admit to 'doing nothing to not make it happen', an older mother might 'leave it to mother nature to decide' the outcome of unprotected sex. Both may find it hard to articulate a desire for pregnancy and the commitments and changes it entails.

—

Securing approval from others for a pregnancy is the third crucial component of the conception story. Ideally partners, parents and friends reveal themselves as being 'over the moon' in response to the news – confirming the pregnancy as secure, recognised and welcome. The journey to this destination may be complicated, with layers of careful revelation associated with fears of miscarriage and the politics of family allegiance. However, the revelation may be as unplanned and equivocal as the pregnancy, with accounts emphasising how others 'found out' rather than how they were told. For example, 18-year-old Amber explains that she had mistakenly left the wrapper of her pregnancy test in the bathroom at a family barbeque for all to see. For some women, telling a partner was difficult, anticipating that paternity might be denied or they that they might be encouraged to terminate what for them was a wanted baby. Where a couple had deliberately set out to become pregnant, confirmation could be held as a 'delicious secret', intensifying a sense of intimacy until it was agreed exactly how the news would be shared. Age and relationship status often made a big difference to whether a pregnancy would be welcomed, and several although not all of our youngest mothers reported very negative responses from their families and others. The order in which parents, in-laws, siblings and friends are told constitutes an affective map of the relationships into which the child will eventually emerge. Several women were caught between the urge to tell their mothers or their partners first, and couples often negotiated complicated procedures for guarding against snubs and perceived disloyalty on the two sides of the family. The 12-weeks' scan operated as a key milestone for many, who either held back from sharing the news or shared it with those whom they judged sufficiently intimate to also share the burden of a miscarriage. In some cases, as illustrated below, women lost control of the news of their pregnancy, finding themselves the object of gossip and rumour – revealing the extent to which the process of becoming a mother is also a process of being interpellated within a category that exposes the self to potential mis-recognition, regulation, ridicule.

In the following sections we present three examples of conception stories, each a strong narrative involving an explicit staging of memory. The first is told by a Jade, a 17-year-old woman, and is an ensemble piece involving many characters and detailed yet obscure plot lines. Here, remembering and forgetting are staged to achieve ambiguity in terms of agency, causality and outcome. The second story is told by 33-year-old Deborah, whose pregnancy is planned and desired yet also involves complex negotiations with her partner and friends. Although her story appears at first sight to be polished and contained, we can also see the intensive work that her narrative is doing for her as she negotiates boundaries between the private intimacy of the couple and the public declaration of pregnancy. The third narrative is from 42-year-old Orla, who became pregnant as a single woman through donor insemination. Again, this is a highly moralised account that claims respectability for her choices, locating the pregnancy within a web of supportive family relations. In each narrative there is a staging of remembering and forgetting that is integrally related to the exposure of the self to others that pregnancy involves.

Conception as survival

We met Jade at an educational project for young mothers. She was four months pregnant and had been evicted from her mother's house following conflict arising from her pregnancy. As her account indicates, the project of becoming a mother is contoured differently, depending on resources and circumstances. Jade provides a detailed account in which agency and the sequence of events are dissected and confirmed to moral effect. It is important to know who did what, to whom and when. Yet Jade has relatively little economic, social or interpersonal power and struggles to be heard and believed by others. She is faced with the problem of transgressing norms, thus becoming an object of gossip and rumour within her wider peer group. Her conception story has to do some very particular work, to establish her integrity as the narrator of her own life, in the face of both popular discourses that might pathologise her as 'too young' and, more immediately, local discourses within which her 'story' becomes subject to the normalising effects of local value systems.

Jade's story was not 'typical' of the accounts that we gathered from the younger mothers, which were in general rather taciturn and cautious. She tells her story in a flood of words, episodes of uninterrupted narrative. The interviewer (Lucy Hadfield, herself a young woman) provided an audience; Jade addressed her as a supportive 'bridge' for the reception of the tale. The story of conception is marked by an intense and continuous flow of narrative detail. This part of the interview is framed by two episodes: first, an account of her mother's violent reaction to her pregnancy and her resulting homelessness, and second, a romantic description of how she met the baby's father and developed a sexual relationship. She then embarks on the following complex account, explaining how he disappeared for three months after she had told him that she was pregnant, and how her mother had intervened to inform his family. Unusually, Jade's conception story begins with 'telling others' rather than the story of conception:

> "when I first told him I was pregnant he wasn't there for me for three months and I was very very upset and I was like, I wanted him there and stuff, but because we wasn't together it was just a casual thing, er … he was too interested in his life and he didn't want anybody to know. And one night I went round to my mum's house, me and my mum spoke for quite a few hours which was quite shocking. And er … she asked me for his house number so I gave my mum his house number and she spoke to his step-mum and told his step-mum because he hadn't told his parents, and an hour after she spoke to his step-mum, his dad rang, and his dad said I'll get Darren to ring so … an hour after that he rang and then he started coming in to me and the baby's life basically for three months, well six weeks. And then he told me he was going into the army, went three days after my birthday, I didn't know he was going he just disappeared, and I rang up his dad and his dad told me he's gone into the army, and I've not, I've only just recently got hold of him and that was two weeks ago…. his dad was lying for him saying he was in the army … and then two weeks ago I thought, oh I'll try and ring him because he'd

always, his phone was always on, but he doesn't answer the phone to me. So I tried ringing him and he answered to me and he goes ring me back in 15 minutes, so I left it 20, 25 minutes and ring him back and we had a good conversation, because I was actually falling in love with him, and I was like really upset how he was treating me, and I told him on the phone that I'm not in love with him any more, I just really care for him and I don't want anything to happen, and er … he'll try turning it around and say he could change that and I turned round and said what do you mean you can change that? He says I can change you falling back in love with me. … Because he knows how to work my mind and he knows what changes me cos if he was to turn up he would know, that the way I was with him before, because that's what used to happen, we never used to see each other for months on end and then I'd meet up with him and I'm like I'm glad he's here and he knows that, that's why. … But he's just, he's too interested in his personal life … I don't count any more, I don't rely on him any more, so I don't need him now. I just want the baby to know he's got a dad, because he didn't grow up with a dad, from 5 years old he didn't grow up with a dad so if he wants to be the same with his child then let him. But rumours were going around that it wasn't his kid, it wasn't his baby."

This is an incredibly dense passage of speech, including a great deal of crucial and conflicting information. Although it does not have narrative slickness, it does manage to convey all the key characters involved (herself, Darren, her mum and his dad); the problems (her lack of influence, his own ambivalent feelings about fatherhood); and the context (a situation devoid of privacy in which communication is difficult and mediated by rumour). Jade's narrative communicates a very personal story: the patterning of an intense but intermittent relationship and the chaos of conception as she forges an account that speaks to an imaginary audience of parents and peers likely to comment on her pregnancy and speculate on matters of paternity.

—

In keeping with many other women in our study, men are central to the shaping of a maternal identity, even when marginal or absent. For Jade, Darren is the absent centre; his role as the baby's father counts but cannot be counted upon. The final comment, that Darren might believe that the child was not his, provides the 'complication' on which the narrative turns. It is at this point that remembering becomes important and Jade's account turns to a reconstruction of the past.

> "I fell pregnant on the 17th April, and I slept with someone two months previous. And she [friend] thought she worked out the dates and she thought I was pregnant with the other person's baby. And I was like no, because I fell pregnant on this time and I know I fell pregnant on this time because I had a period whatever, and I thought I could trust her and I told her and then she went back and told him that I'd slept with someone a month before I slept with, so basically I slept with someone in March, so it looked like it was the person's I slept with in March and not his, but I didn't sleep with no one in March if you know what I mean, so she made it out as if, I didn't know who the baby's dad was. So I asked him and he said no he's not heard anything about it whatever, but he turned round and said if the baby isn't mine, keep it quiet. And that was ticking over in my head, and I put the phone down to him and it was ticking over in my head what does he mean by that, does … if the baby isn't his, does he still want anything to do with it, do you know what I mean? And it was like, confusing so I rang him back a couple of days later, and I asked him and he just said if the baby isn't mine to keep it quiet. But, I said, the baby is yours."

It is not until this point that Jade tells the story of finding out that she was pregnant. The story that emerges suggests that from the very beginning the experience was 'public', 'shared' and contested. As with many other conception stories, her account begins with mistaken embodied symptoms.

Jade: I'm just being sick cos I've still got a hangover and it comes up positive and I'm crying and I'm really upset cos I'm saying I don't know what my mum's going to be like, and er … I got my mate to come in, so the lady went and got my mate, and my mate's cuddling me and I'm crying more because she was cuddling me and comforting me. And I was just worried about what my mum would say. And then the lady at the clinic advised me to get rid of the baby. And I was really angry because I was shocked, just found out, worried, and she was advising me to get rid of the baby.

Interviewer: What did she say then?

Jade: Well me and my mate were sitting there and she turned round and said, if you're so worried about your mum, or my parents cos I still weren't speaking to my dad, if you're so worried about what your parents are going to say I really do recommend, advise you to have an abortion, and she goes come back in a week and let me know and then we'll sort it out from there.… I need a fag, so I had a fag and I was like how am I going to tell him? How'm I going to tell the baby's dad? And I was thinking it over and over in my head, how'm I going to tell him? And I went to my best mate how'm I going to tell him I don't know what to say? And she was like I'll tell him, I was like alright then, I was shaking and I was crying, and all upset.… I text him saying, just casually hi what are you up to? We need to talk. And he didn't text me back … So we rang from the pay phone and she turned round and said er … Jade's just been to the clinic and he went yeah, she goes she's just found out she's pregnant and he goes you're joking … he thought she was lying and I turned round, I was angry and I was

really mad, I says does he think I'm lying? And she goes
yeah, so I said give me the phone, so I took the phone
and he goes stop crying, I says I'm upset, I just found
out I'm pregnant. And I said we need to meet up and he
says alright I'll meet up on Saturday, three months later
he finally met up with me and that's what's shocking
because I was like, he's going to be a dad and he left it
three months to meet up with me and I was always on
his back saying come and meet me and stuff. Yeah …
I'll never forget the day I found out.

This final episode in Jade's conception story can be seen as a
condensation of what has come before. The setting and the
conversation are described graphically, almost cinematically. As
readers, we can also imagine being there, or at least watching. The
difficult decision of whether or not to keep the baby is dispersed
and Jade's ambivalence is expressed in several ways: shocked by the
counsellor's advice, having the fag, insisting on telling immediately
yet passing responsibility to her friend. In observing that she would
"never forget the day" that she found out, Jade is also positioning
this story as emblematic of the way in which she is imagining her
project of becoming a mother: with herself as an ambivalent yet active
agent within a wider dramatic landscape, with a present yet absent
father and grandmother. Almost by default, the counsellor plays a
critical yet 'off stage' role. In voicing the possibility of a termination,
it becomes possible for Jade to turn away and engage in the drama
that is the pregnancy.

Conception as inevitable

The second conception story is told by Deborah, a woman who
is well resourced and secure. Unlike in Jade's case, the conception
described was planned. Nevertheless, the core components of the
narrative: finding out, 'knowing', remembering and telling still
structure the account. Deborah was nine months pregnant with
her first child when we met her. Until that point she had been
working full time as an information worker in a large public sector

organisation. The pregnancy she describes was a shared project between herself and her partner. Deborah's conception story begins with the relationship:

> "Bit disorganised really because we have been together eleven years, well seven years before we got married erm and we were engaged for about six years something like that, just not very, we didn't really have any big plans or anything like that about where we wanted to be or whatever but I think we always knew that we wanted to be together, we wanted to have a family and then I guess a couple of years ago, about a year ago probably, we said 'Right are we going to do this baby thing?' And so, I came off the pill and erm we said 'Right in the next two years we will see what happens and if it is meant to happen it is meant to happen and if it doesn't happen it won't'. So we were sort of using other forms of birth control while we were trying to come to terms with the fact that if we do it now we might have a baby in nine months' time and erm ended up getting really drunk one night and forgetting! (hearty laugh) That was really the first time that I could have got pregnant because I had been secretly doing the maths and counting the days so yes in September within about two weeks of trying properly it was just the first time (laughs) really funny!! ... I didn't find out that I was pregnant for about six weeks and it was a really big shock. And then I thought, oh ok, well it is meant to be then, that's fair enough. My mum had had problems conceiving my sister and she said to me, 'Well if you are going to do it you better get on with it because if you take as long as I did to have your sister, if you have the same kind of problems ...', erm, I think she had a blocked fallopian tube or something like that so there is a six-year age gap between me and my sister, erm, 'You better get on with it'. So we did and it took six weeks instead of six years! (laughs) But there you go! That's just one of those things."

Deborah's description of herself and her husband as "disorganised" appears ironic, in that the pregnancy is planned and appropriately synchronised within the norms (that is, after marriage, in stable emotional and financial circumstances). Yet as the narrative unfolds, the "disorganisation" emerges in the form of uncertain communication between the two. The initial narrative episode articulates a simple story that allows both for them to be planners (coming off the pill) and to be more romantically caught by fate (forgetting one drunken night). Yet in her mentioning of "secret calculations" and her mother's warnings about infertility we get a sense of a more anxious and individual account beneath the surface. On Lucy's prompting, Deborah airs some of these feelings in a much less articulate manner:

> *Interviewer:* So you came off the pill but you still kind of backed it up a bit?
>
> *Deborah:* Yeah, yeah (coy). I mean my husband was not … I mean did I make him aware that I was doing the counting? I mean (laughs nervously) I was thinking 'Do we need to use a condom now or do we not?' And then sometimes I would go, 'Yeah I think it is alright', but then sometimes I would go 'I am not quite ready yet, not quite ready.' So we had some kind of …, it was kind of … I don't know really. I think, well I am just trying to remember, we didn't really ask questions about are we really going to do this now, it was just kind of we will see what happens, but I knew in the back of my mind when wasn't a, when it was like days 14–17 I was thinking, 'Well, maybe not'. Not that anything really happened between days 14–17 anyway because we were both too knackered (both laugh).

She then goes on immediately to narrate the experience of discovering that she was pregnant. Despite all the secret calculations, this is constructed as a story of shock, and returns to a more assured and rehearsed story-telling style.

Interviewer: So you say you felt really shocked when you —

Deborah: Yes I was really, really shocked. Erm I think I was shocked because I had been out on several drunken weekends (laughs) in the first sort of five weeks which was erm, and actually we were away for a weekend with friends and one of my friends, she had her baby in December so it was last October, that's right. She said to me, 'Are you sure you are not pregnant you have been to the loo about six times in the last hour.' She said, 'I have got a pregnancy test upstairs go and do it.' And I said 'No I am not doing it, I am not doing it. I feel fine!' Oh yes I am about a week late but I think my period is coming you know and I've got the cramps and whatever and she said, 'You should probably do a test you know. I had that when it was like an implantation so you should probably do a test.' So I thought well you know I better do one and I did it and I didn't tell my husband I was doing it and I came downstairs into the kitchen and I just handed him the rest of the bottle of wine and showed him the test. And we were both standing there in the kitchen going, 'Oh my god, oh my god, oh blimey, oh my god!' I don't know, I felt kind of caught out. I mean I am 33 (laughs) and I felt like how I would imagine a 17-year-old would feel cos it had just been the first time and I hadn't thought it would happen. But it did and it was like, blimey and I have got to do something about this. So I did, I made an appointment with the doctor and erm we confirmed it and did all the dates and it was just a question of keeping it all quiet then from work because I think I was about six weeks, something like that."

In contrast to the earlier 'we'-ness of her account of planning to get pregnant, Deborah's story of finding out is characterised much more by a sense of herself in relation to her peer group. She talks of friends having babies and encouraging her to think that she might be pregnant. Again, alcohol features prominently: and a drunken weekend with the girls is juxtaposed with the drunken night when they had not used contraception. It is fascinating that Deborah describes herself as feeling like a 17-year-old when she realises that she is in fact pregnant: citing the well-worn clichés of feeling "caught out" and it "not happening the first time". This both gives us insight into the extent to which women are aware of and fluent in a wide range of narratives of motherhood, and also might help us to see how exposed Deborah feels by the experience of becoming pregnant. It is instructive then, to see how Deborah's narrative turns, and relates the experience of pregnancy back to the couple and the private. The care that Deborah and her partner take in regulating who is told, when and in what order, suggests that 'telling' involves important work in the process of constructing a new identity and relationships. Perhaps the most important part of this is to forge the pregnancy as shared enterprise for the couple. Lucy asks Deborah why she waited to tell everyone.

> "Well, just the 12-week thing really. I wanted to leave it just to be safe erm cos … I mean a few of them have had miscarriages and whatever and I just thought I knew that for my parents it was their first grandchild. For my husband's parents it is less of an issue because it will be their third erm and I thought when I start on the whole I am pregnant thing I am going to get the phone calls like every second day like, 'Are you all right? Are you okay? Are you feeling sick?' And I thought, 'I think I will just keep this special time just for me and Partner to tell everyone'. We would sort of grin at each other and make excuses about why we are not eating pâté and whatever (laughs). Which was quite hard actually."

The final episode in Deborah's conception story is the stage at which she is ready to 'go public' to the group of girlfriends who form the audience for her account, all now mothers, egging her along, waiting impatiently. Here she returns to the opening motif of organisation/ disorganisation:

"I think I did a mass e-mail to everyone actually saying, 'We finally got ourselves organised and Junior is on its way.' And the particular friends, the weekend I think it happened, the friends that were here, we were having a girly weekend and I sent my husband to bed and we were [doing here] watching Bridget Jones and drinking several bottles of Chardonnay – it was dreadful and I had to e-mail them and say, 'You know that weekend when you were here and I got really, really drunk well I think it may have been then. That could be too much information for you but' (laughs)."

This final sentence serves to tie all of Deborah's key themes and characters together, and implicate them in the moment of conception. It is a moment of deliberate and controlled exposure of the self to others, the intimate to the public and the sexual to the social. If conception is a moment in which individual agency is relinquished (and marked as such by alcohol), then the restaging of this memory, both in the e-mail and in its subsequent retelling can be understood as an articulation of a new identity settlement, the beginning of the project that is motherhood.

Conception as earned

The third example of a conception story comes from Orla, who was one of 10 women in our study aged 40 or more at the point of having their first child. Typically, these older mothers had struggled to become pregnant, generally because of the difficulties involved in synchronising a shared desire for parenthood and fertility. Several had assumed that they had "left it too late", expressing wonder, amazement and delight in their bodies and often reporting highly emotional responses from family members who had "given up", "stopped asking" or assumed "that would never happen". There were several women in our study who were approaching motherhood as individuals rather than as a couple. In most cases these were the youngest women in our sample, whose pregnancies were unplanned or whose relationships were not well established. Yet in two cases women set out to become pregnant outside of couple relationships. For one woman this involved the decision not to terminate a pregnancy resulting from a casual fling. For Orla, it involved seeking help to become pregnant using donor insemination at the age of 42. Orla's conception story evolves from a dense monologue that encompasses her entire fertility history. It is a highly moralised account that locates herself as a thoughtful agent.

> "I got pregnant years ago in a relationship with a man who had two kids … I don't know quite how that happened but anyway I got pregnant. And he was not keen at all on the idea, and I was quite keen, I was quite planning it on going alone and then I just … I just worried about this child and having to say to him or her you know, that cos he just basically said I'm not having anything to do with it, and I just thought that's a terrible, how can I say yes your dad really adores his other children but he doesn't want anything to do with you, and I just thought it's just too, it's awful, so I had a termination which I think was the right thing to do, but then I had this whole kind of, oh god I'm never going to have another baby, that was my one chance then, I don't know, I've just never been in a relationship where it's, that we've got to the point where we've talked about having children … I think I was 31 when that happened, but every single relationship since then in my 30s has been about, has broken up basically because I've wanted to have kids and my partner hasn't and so, I mean it's you know with men it's much easier for them because they don't have the time pressures happening."

Orla locates her pressing desire for motherhood in a family history of infertility. She explains that her mother and grandmother both started their menopause when they were 38 and her sense of urgency increased when her older sister began to report menopausal symptoms:

"so there was this real you know time pressure thing hanging over me … And then er … and then I got pregnant accidentally at the beginning of 2005 … a casual fling, a drunken thing, and literally I've had unprotected sex three times in my entire life and every single time I've conceived, it's quite scary. So in fact I should have a brood of about 10 children around me, so I was just delighted, I was thrilled to bits, I was amazed. I was convinced it was a miracle baby and it was … fantastic."

Orla explains that she felt able to pursue single motherhood at this point because her upbringing was characterised by her father working away for long periods of time, leaving her mother with sole responsibility for the children. She recounts that her immediate response to the unplanned pregnancy was to go to her family.

"I told my mum and she was very … 'oh God' about it, and she said how are you going to cope, and I said I'll cope cos I will, cos I always cope, it's fine, I know it's going to be hard but … and then my mum, when I told my mum she was very negative about it and then she was really … 'God what are we going to tell your father', you know she really worried me about how he was going to react. I didn't have any idea, I just didn't know, I thought he'd probably react in a similar way to her, so I went down there, probably best face to face, that's what me and my mum decided and er … I told him and he burst into tears and was just like 'oh that's wonderful darling', you know? I was amazed and she was amazed, so I don't know. … Anyway and then, I had my first scan at 11, 12 weeks and I thought everything was fine and they said oh … the baby's … its died, and I was just, devastated is the only word, I just fell to bits it was absolutely awful …"

The experience of losing the baby and sharing this loss with her supportive and involved parents galvanised Orla's resolve to pursue the objective of motherhood as a single woman. At this point in her narrative she represents herself as a remoralised agent who takes responsibility for her maternal desire and has the capacity to negotiate access to donor insemination.

> "Anyway, so yes I lost the baby and then I just kind of, I don't know I was in a state for ages then, er … and then I don't know, I just thought I've got to … I can do this and how am I going to do it and I thought about just going to a club and picking up some random bloke and having a shag and I just thought, oh I don't know, it all just seemed very distasteful and I thought oh God, then I'll catch something horrible, I don't know. I just thought no that's not a very good idea so … then I started looking into the idea of donor insemination and I tried to research it, there's not that much information out there … I mean I think there are an increasing number of women doing it on their own but … there's not much data about it and trying to find stories and my friends would tell me about articles they'd read in magazines and you know interviews with women so, I read those and er … and so I started looking into clinics and quite a lot of them actually it turned out won't treat single women. Which I suppose is their prerogative anyway, so I found a clinic that would and I did a, I wanted to have enough time … I contacted the clinic at the end of January. I decided that I was going to have one very big party, so I did party very hard over the last Christmas and New Year, knowing thinking well that's going to be it now, then I led a very virtuous life."

The juxtaposition of hedonism and the virtuous life that characterises so many women's conception stories is replayed here in an almost ritual form, marking a transition from good-time girlhood (however extended) to mature motherhood. Orla's staging of the moment of conception appears at the end of the account. She begins with the "technical" merger of egg and sperm in which agency and causality are held in tension:

> "it was all just textbook really it worked first time, I had three good eggs and they er … I had two goes the sperm I decided, they said oh you know it's up to you, you can have as many tries or goes with it as you want, actually separate days one after the other, and it's really because the whole process is really lengthy and then the actual IUI bit takes about 30 seconds, literally just look at the vial put it in, and then they go away and you lie there for 5 minutes and it's just like, oh God is that it?"

Her account then turns immediately to a negotiation of paternity in which Orla comically juxtaposes her 'choice' of donor and the clinic's formal procedures for information sharing, going on to imagine a future where the identity of the father may have deep emotional resonance for a child not yet known.

> "I chose the father … they gave me, oh you had to describe, you had to write down what you wanted, in terms of er … the donor, and all you can do is obviously talk about looks because they don't tell you anything else about them. And she said to me, I said how do people … I was like I don't know, how do people normally choose? Well quite usually they pick someone who looks like their partner, but obviously that isn't applicable. Or if someone on their own they'd pick someone that looks like them, and er … and I said what about my ideal man and she laughed and she said alright then, it seemed as good a method as any. So the father of my baby is 5 foot 10 and has black hair and green eyes and is Irish and he obviously looks a bit like Aiden Quinn in my head, he's incredibly lovely and gorgeous. So you know I might end up having this dark-haired baby, which would be very bizarre … And when the baby's born they give me a pen portrait which is something that this guy has

written a bit more about himself. ... And then when the baby's 18 then he can go back to the clinic and get some more information about him and then he can decide if he wants to contact his ... this guy or not."

Making sense of this new ethical territory is not easy. Orla assumes that she is part of something that will only grow, and "it will be interesting to see whether children do decide to make that contact". Her account suggests that by pursuing donor insemination Orla has made a responsible choice that takes the question of paternity outside of discourses of forgetfulness and shame.

"I think I would be very uncomfortable saying I don't know who the father is, this is all I know and they can never get in touch with them, it's just ... it seems ... less, er ... selfish way of doing it."

Orla's conception story ends with an ambiguous evaluation of herself as a moral actor, noting a dissonance between the subject who chooses motherhood and notions of motherhood as selfless and beyond choice

"Cos I think it is, what I've done is selfish, it's about me, and wanting to have fulfilment of my maternal urges. I'm not saying that I don't think I'll be a good mum, I like to think I will be you know, but I'm sure all women that deliberately go into motherhood think that of themselves, you know maybe I'll be crap. But you know I am kind of denying a child knowledge of their natural father which is you know, it's not ideal, but then in some ways I kind of think it's better than just a kind of, if that other baby had come to term, you know what am I going to do? Am I going to tell this guy, when I've seen him since and he still has no idea about what has happened which is very weird. So he'll probably never know. I don't know, I'm kind of ... I don't really know the answer to that one I suppose."

—

Research into the social dimensions of new reproductive technologies has drawn attention to the significance of naming, claiming and narrating as fundamental to the bringing into being of families, involving exclusions and forgetting as well as inclusion and remembering (Strathern, 1992; Edwards and Strathern, 2000). It is contended that these narrative practices may be amplified by challenges posed by technological mediation, yet are a common feature of kinship networks, themselves the result of such narrative and symbolic practices. The 'heterosexual imaginary' that invisibly underpins our understandings of conception is remarkably resilient, given the extent to which the process can be mediated by technology (Nordqvist, 2008). By juxtaposing these three examples, we hope to have revealed the ways in which the 'event' of conception and the 'situation' of pregnancy pose a set of challenges to subjects that are negotiated through narrative work. These conception stories, though reflecting the radically different situations of the three women involved, must nevertheless achieve certain tasks, bridging a personal biography with a speculative future in which a new subject is situated within a meaningful and intelligible network of relationships which, in turn, reciprocate these claims.

The identity work of new motherhood

Remembering and forgetting are part of the substance of these tales, pointing to the moral work involved in securing paternity and locating reproduction in a normative sequence of life stages that is deeply tied up with notions of respectability in contemporary western culture. Forgetting also plays an important role in the way that women narrate the profound change in their situation. Alcoholic confusion, fatalism, incompetence and misrecognition are all performed in these stories, enabling the self and the intimate to be opened to the view of others. 'Telling' can be a way of seeking to control this exposure and to regain control. Selective remembering is the process through which a narrative is forged. Yet what is not told can still be present in its effects, a lingering feeling left with the interviewer and the reader.

Conception stories are part of the identity work of new motherhood and give insights into the necessary features of the changing identity and the nature of the project. The ways in which women narrate this situation have common elements: with recurrent motifs around 'knowing', 'remembering/forgetting' and 'telling'. Yet each also shows how women encounter motherhood in extraordinarily different circumstances. While it is productive to read these examples against each other, comparison should remain cautious. We are not seeking to identify ideal or typical narratives of early/late or planned/unplanned motherhood. Rather, we want to capture something of the paradoxical nature of motherhood that is both one and many things. The women in these examples are fluent in the popular narratives of motherhood. Each is aware of the need to construct an acceptable narrative that is recognised in the local culture of her life and the wider cultural community to which she belongs. Their accounts are highly moral tales, constructed heteroglossically in relation to broader narratives and normative expectations as well as personal fears and individual circumstances. They are aware of and position themselves in relation to the 'shame' of pregnancy and work to narrate themselves within the boundaries of normalising principles. Irrespective of their situations, each of them struggles to make motherhood intelligible and their narratives bear the marks of a search for audience and for others to witness, affirm and react to this change.

Understood in narrative terms, these are extraordinarily rich and inventive accounts – harnessing and shaping meaning, attributing responsibility, inventing causality. Their comparison is productive, enhancing an appreciation of form as well as the ways in which context shapes the narrative challenge. Yet reading these accounts together can also be uncomfortable, revealing a stark inequality of security and resource between the women. It is hard to hear these voices without also evoking a wider welfare discourse that places Jade's story safely beyond intelligibility and recognition. This does not mean that Jade does not claim recognition – her account is dominated by such claims, yet these claims have no purchase on public morality. Where Deborah's story employs the ironic comic form of Bridget Jones's diary, Jade's story can too easily be stripped of pathos by hearing it through the voice of *Little Britain's* Vicky Pollard[1] – the increasingly acceptable popular portrayal of the 'undeserving'

—

poor. Orla's decision to embark on motherhood as a single woman demands that she defend herself from charges of selfishness. She manages this by positioning herself as sensible and careful, opting for donor insemination as mediated by the regulated machine of the clinic rather than the unrespectable leisure spaces where she might meet a man for sex. A theoretical focus on intelligibility such as that argued in different ways by Butler (2004) and Plummer (1995) encourages us to understand the cultural realm as a site of politics, and potentially of social change. Yet a focus on norms and normalisation can also impoverish our understanding of the social world. To call certain lives unintelligible or unliveable may well reveal the operation of normalising principles and the paradoxical contingency and continuity of privilege, yet it does not provide us with many tools for appreciating the forms of recognition and sustenance that are always in play, however marginal and fragile.

Note

[1] Vicky Pollard is a comic character who appears in the television show *Little Britain*, a caricature of a working-class teenage girl, played 'in drag' by a male comedian. Distinctive features of the characterisation include her dress (track suit, gold jewellery and high ponytail) and her fast, breathless speech. The iconic status Vicky Pollard quickly achieved has been attributed to a widespread reviling of working-class 'chav' culture during the New Labour administration in the UK.

THREE

Body

"Pregnancy does not belong to the woman herself. It is a state of the developing foetus, for which the woman is a container; or it is an objective, observable process coming under scientific scrutiny; or it becomes objectified by the woman herself as a 'condition' in which she must 'take care of herself.'" (Young, 1990, p 160)

In the course of researching modern motherhoods we found ideas about gender and femininity to be habitually embodied in pregnancy. The expanding pregnant body appears as a visible sign of who the subject 'is', a performance underscored by bodily change, deportment and style. Like the young people that Connell characterises as developing a form of '*gender competence*' (2002, p 81), the first-time mothers in our study expressed a feeling of growing into their bodies in ways that defined them as a woman:

> "A pregnant stomach is quite a satisfying thing. It's firm and round and I felt quite, I mean proud of it isn't the word – but I definitely felt it as a positive part of my body, rather than something that was not connected to me as a woman, as a sexual human being." (Eleanor, 26)

Integrating pregnancy into a sense of self as gendered, sexual *and* maternal is a recurrent theme in women's accounts. While Eleanor's pregnancy appears to enhance her sexual subjectivity, other women struggle to blend a maternal self with other aspects of their identity, particularly the sexual. For these women, taking on a maternal identity has the effect of overwhelming a pre-pregnant sense of self, producing a profoundly changed subject:

—

"I just feel like 'mummy', I suppose it's what you wear and how you dress yourself and now everything seems like I'm slowing down and I'm feeling tired all the time and I feel much older … like moving on to another stage, it's not just the body, your mind kind of changes and you feel a lot more mature, that's how I feel." (Lyn, 31)

These contrasting accounts indicate that pregnancy can provoke intense and potentially conflicting forms of identification, marked by a desire to accommodate the self within the maternal experience and a sense that in taking on the identity of *mother* we enter a distinct stage in emotional maturation that leaves behind the former self. The potential for disruptive and unresolved feelings can be seen as a haunting feature of women's accounts of their pregnancy, alluded to and occasionally fully articulated in late pregnancy. In this chapter we consider the embodied experience of pregnancy, how it is lived, understood and narrated by women themselves. In doing so, we pay attention to the spaces where the body is discussed in relation to women's experience – in theoretical conceptualisations such as performativity and phenomenology as well as in normative discourses found in the representational field of popular culture, particularly pregnancy magazines and advertisements. Following a discussion of maternal embodiment, subjectivity and popular culture, the chapter focuses on themes that bring the pregnant body into focus: the bump; touch; and breastfeeding, before finally considering pregnancy as part of a body story in which women integrate pregnancy into a uniquely blended narrative of embodied selfhood.

Reading the body

The embodied experience of pregnancy presents a challenge to feminine subjectivity manifest through a temporary state where notions of selfhood and bodily boundaries are compromised by an emergent other (Rubin, 1977; 1984; Young, 1990). Following the idea of gender as a performative bringing into being (Butler, 1990), impending motherhood appears to occupy shifting terrain as a *more than* constitutive space for the birth of another. Seemingly more persistent than a performative conjuring, pregnancy appears to come with its own bodily manifestations and emotions that require subjective re-evaluation, identity work and accommodation.

Butler develops Foucault's insight that even the human body – that fleshy and seemingly most 'natural' of beings – is constituted in the discursive capillaries of medical, educational, judicial, military and religious technologies. Foucault has argued that the body is subject to a historical and discursive genealogy, being part of what Butler (1990, p 141) describes as a 'social temporality'. The body is, in Foucaultian terminology, the product of a unique 'bio-power' subject to levels of regulation including, most effectively, self-regulation (Foucault, 1978, p 143). While Foucault (1978), in his early work, has been criticised for neglecting the materiality of the body, Butler (1993) emphatically contends that bodies matter. Her concern has not been to discount bodily experience, but rather in 'initiating new possibilities, new ways of bodies to matter' (1993, p 30). There is little discussion in Butler's work, however, of the anatomical constraints engendered by such bodily regimes as puberty, menstruation, childbirth, lactating, dieting, ageing, disease or disability, to say nothing of such racialised markers as colour. Instead, in deploying the notion of embodiment, Butler has sought to reconcile the historically conceived signing of the body with an active notion of the performative. The way we style our bodies is neither a matter of sex (nature) nor simply an adjunct of the prevailing gender order (culture); rather, it is one of the techniques through which we perform, enact and 'do' gender. In this respect, Butler regards sex and gender as 'illusions of substance – that bodies are compelled to approximate, but never can' (1990, p 146). In this reading, gender identity is an embodied action that does not exist outside of its 'doings'; rather, its performance is also a reiteration of previous 'doings' that become intelligible as gender norms.

The idea of the maternal body as performative suggests a certain lightness that is rarely noted in women's accounts of their pregnancy. In an anthropological study of four centuries of childbirth, Gelis comments that 'being pregnant means losing one's freedom of body and mind: every gesture, every word spoken, every movement of a pregnant woman also involves the child. She has to live for two' (1991, p 66). The heaviness of pregnancy is experienced both as a physical grounding, gaining weight and slowing down, and as an emotional weight of responsibility realised by mothers-to-be in the acceptance of a position as intermediary between the foetus and the world outside the womb. The relationship between inside and outside becomes central to the embodied experience of pregnancy, defining women's way of being in the world in the transitional period from conception to birth. Phenomenological perspectives embrace the in-between-ness of pregnancy as an intense, uncertain and emotionally rich experience that opens up new ground for feminine subjectivity (Young, 1990). Central to this perspective is the recognition that consciousness resides within the body and 'the lived body has culture and meaning inscribed in its habits' (Young, 1990, p 14). In the development of an analysis of the pregnant subject as 'decentred, split or doubled in several ways' (Young, 1990, p 160), Young poetically describes the bodily conundrums of being 'with child'. A woman's relationship with the foetus unsettles the integrity of the body as she is both 'herself and not herself'. Feeling the movement of the foetus in the womb as *hers*, while knowing it is *not hers* invokes the strangeness of transition; occupying the indeterminable status of non-unitary subject, bodily boundaries break down in a process of bodily change that produces a profound split between past and future.

Building on phenomenological insights derived from a position of living and thinking through the body, other feminist writers have explored the creative potential of feminine subjectivity as *fluid* (Kristeva, 1980; Grosz, 1994). Grosz's concept of 'volatile bodies' defines subjectivity as a constantly shifting form, moving between inner psychic worlds and exterior forces of power. Using the analogy of a Mobius strip to capture the seamlessness of this movement between internal and external, Grosz stresses the capacity of bodies to 'act and react' as centres of desire and agency. Also concerned with the affective realm of desire, Kristeva (1980) focuses on the way in which culture separates pregnancy from sexuality. Exploring the liminal reaches of the maternal, Kristeva suggests that the heightened experience of pregnancy and birth can provide women with access to the repressed, preconscious self, attained through a state of 'jouissance' in which the maternal and the sexual can come together again. Making sense of pregnancy and birth through embodied experience remains a generative approach, used in this chapter to consider the body as the nexus of an inside–outside relationship that gives shape to the maternal project.

The maternal body in contemporary culture

Popular culture can be seen as a canvas for the display of the pregnant body, providing one of the contexts within which pregnancy is made intelligible. There is an intense focus on all aspects of the pregnant body in popular culture, reflecting, to some extent, the body-beautiful visibility of women within that culture more generally. Marking a shift from previous generations, pregnancy is no longer regarded as a period of 'confinement', a term that in itself suggests restriction, constraint and time spent away from the public sphere. Grandmothers in our study who became mothers in the 1950s and 1960s confirmed this generational shift. Commenting on the sociability of contemporary motherhood, including ways in which pregnant women become the centre of attention, grandmothers reported that their generation 'just got on with it' without the fuss or back-up that women appear to get today. In noting the difference, grandmothers indicated that pregnancy for them was more of a private affair, to be accommodated within the domestic sphere and the extended family. Some women in this generational cohort envied the life-style choices available to mothers now, and particularly the availability of a range of domestic appliances that made life *easier*. For their generation, being a mother involved domestic labour that was both hard work and time consuming. Unlike mothers today, they had little time for fun activities such as playing with their children and enjoying leisure time together, as they were preoccupied with the demands of cooking, cleaning and servicing the family. Changes over time, from the grandmothers' perspective, minimised the work of running a home and having a family, giving mothers more choice and the capacity to combine motherhood with work outside the home and other activities (Hadfield, 2009). While pregnancy makes visible key differences between mothers and daughters, many of them also acknowledged an intergenerational link that was embodied and deeply felt (Lawler, 2000; Pines, 1997). Mothers and daughters commented on a shared physicality which they expected (and sometimes feared) would structure analogies between their experiences of reproduction. Daughters generally looked to their mothers for an intimate account of how pregnancy and labour could be for them, and even where there was no biological link between mother and daughter (as in cases of adoption) claims were made between generations to establish similarities and continuities in the corporeal experience of mothering. The idea of claiming *bodily inheritance*, discussed further in Chapter Eight, provides a residual and emotionally charged connection between generational chains of women. Yet shared corporeality extends beyond ideas of inheritance, involving ongoing practices of recognition, observation and care (Kehily, 2008). Mothers noticed the small but significant bodily changes that marked their daughters' transitions to new motherhood. For example, Erica observed that, since becoming pregnant, her daughter had lost her comforting childhood habit of simultaneously touching her tummy when she put her fingers in her mouth. The bodily traces of childhood, habitually occupied and known intergenerationally, were breaking down, signalling the shift to a new relationship with the body as a connected but reconfigured mother–daughter bond.

In contrast to the experiences of the grandmothers' generation, pregnancy in contemporary times is presented in the representational field as something to be publicly celebrated and enjoyed. The aestheticisation of the bump and the ubiquity of celebrity culture contribute to a glossy ideal of 'pregnant beauty' (Tyler, 2001, 2008), to be observed, admired and emulated beyond the pages of a magazine. Pregnancy magazines can be seen as sub-genre of women's magazines, a form imbued with bodily concerns and regulatory imperatives. Regularly used phrases and strap lines in pregnancy magazines such as 'bump-tastic', 'blooming marvellous' and 'it's the time of your life' suggest to women that the pregnant body should be shown off. The burgeoning fashion industry for pregnant women, profiled over several pages at the back of each magazine, incites women to see pregnancy as a nine-months catwalk in which style and high fashion remain uncompromised by weight gain and the loss of waistline. Furthermore, pregnancy is seen as an additional reason to look good, pay attention to appearance, to continue to inhabit the feisty, successful, eye-catching and head-turning persona of pre-pregnancy. A feature in *Pregnancy* magazine entitled 'Sex in the city' explains:

> OK, so you're having a baby (admittedly your greatest achievement to date), but that doesn't mean your smart sassy work wardrobe has to suffer. Show them what you're made of with these killer outfits that will have the office gossips gawping over the coffee machine. (*Pregnancy*, September 2004)

Pregnancy in contemporary times is publicly celebrated and enjoyed

Across the glossy pages of the magazine, the body can be viewed as *surface*, a site of consumption and display. Women are encouraged to develop a narcissistic relationship to their pregnant selves. Believing that it is all about *me*, self-centredness is presented as normal. The preoccupation rests with the exteriority of the body – looking good and becoming self-absorbed to the point where the foetus is seen and claimed as part of the woman's body. Featherstone (1983) notes the narcissistic pleasure of looking good and adhering to a bodily ideal within consumer culture that promises to reward sexy bodies. Bartky (1990) suggests that women internalise the ways in which women are read through their bodies and their bodies are routinely evaluated and judged by others. Narcissism, she argues, is a strategic response to the widespread appraisal of female bodies. As a defensive manoeuvre, women's narcissistic relationship to their bodies can induce self-hate as well as pleasure. Importantly, through the process of internalisation, women become self-regulating subjects of patriarchal culture. Young (1990) contributes to the idea of the maternal subject as narcissistic in her comments on the 'innocent narcissism' that prompts women into admiring bodily change:

> As I undress in the morning I gaze in the mirror for long minutes, without stealth or vanity. I do not appraise myself, ask whether I look good for others, but like a child take pleasure in discovering new things in my body. (Young, 1990, p 166)

Inside out

The narcissistic, product-hungry maternal body appears to occupy two different positions in the pages of the magazines: one highlighting the externality of the body to be cared for by the maternal subject, the other focusing on interiority to be looked after by the medical profession. Of the former, there is the appeal to the fashionable, confident mum-to-be as a unique individual, celebrating her fecundity and enjoying the me-time of pregnancy by pampering herself because she *is* special and this is a special time in her life. A regular feature of *Pregnancy and Birth* entitled 'It's all me, me, me' profiles the latest pamper products for mothers-to-be with the introductory line:

> You're pretty amazing. We reckon that growing a baby is the best excuse ever to spoil yourself or get someone else to do it. (*Pregnancy and Birth*, September 2004)

Magazines call upon pregnant women to indulge themselves as part of the preparation for birth, to write themselves into their to-do list with care-of-the-self activities such as 'go to the movies, spend time with the girls, get your hair cut, get pampered' (*Prima Baby*, August 2005). Spa breaks and treatments are widely advertised, many of them specifically targeted at mothers-to-be. In an elaboration of this position, many features also suggest that pregnancy is the time for women to strike up a new relationship with their body. Women's magazines tend towards a Foucaultian view of the body as a project for discipline and self-improvement, commonly promoting a range of new regimes in the form of diet and exercise programmes, beauty products and the clever use of clothes and make-up to gain control over an ever-wayward corporeality. Magazines aimed at pregnant women talk back to the regulated body of pre-pregnancy. In a feature calling on women to make 10 pregnancy resolutions, loving your body is top of the list:

1. Love your body.

> Hate your big bum, lardy thighs, tiny boobs? Well this is the year you should be celebrating your amazing body and its ability to grow a baby ... pregnancy gives us all a break from diet tyranny and while we're not suggesting that you hit the pies, this is the one time in your life that you'll want to see your stomach getting bigger, so enjoy it. (*Pregnancy and Birth*, January 2006)

Loving your body, maintaining pre-pregnancy activities and being kind to yourself become part of a package of advice and care widely promoted by the magazines. One feature drew heavily upon the idea of maternal narcissism and notions of the pregnant woman as an object of fascination. Likening pregnancy to having celebrity status and claiming that everyone loves a pregnant woman, 'It's your 15 minutes of fame' when attention is showered upon you:

> Ever wondered what it's like to be famous? Well, you're about to find out. Having a bump tends to put even the quietest of wallflowers in the spotlight. Okay,

we can't promise there'll be paparazzi hiding in your rhododendrons … but one thing you won't be short of now you're pregnant is adoring fans. (*Mother and Baby*, March 2005)

Loving your body and delighting in getting bigger, however, is short lived. Features on the post-natal body exhort women to 'get your body back in eight weeks', exercise regularly and regain control of weight and shape. The trick to regaining a pre-pregnancy figure is to kick-start the body project as soon as possible after giving birth, focusing once again on regimens of diet and exercise, control and regulation. In these features the ideal of losing the baby weight ('jelly belly' as it's touchingly referred to in some titles) and getting back to 'normal' shortly after birth becomes the marker of a successful pregnancy and an accomplished new mother. While concerns with body weight may appear to be an overblown anxiety of consumer culture, Gelis's (1991) study documents a pervasive interest in getting your body back in 18th- and 19th-century France. Throughout the 19th century it was common for pregnant women to bathe in 'blessed springs' to bring protection on the child and enlist the help of certain saints charged with helping women to regain their figure.

Working in conjunction with the 'me-me-ness' of pregnancy and focusing on the interior rather than the exterior, there is the idea of the pregnant body as a biological wonder requiring medical attention. Viewing the interiority of pregnancy as an object of medical intervention is largely assumed in the magazines. Early pregnancy signals a visit to the GP, the scan, antenatal check-ups, classes and the formulation of a birth plan in preparation for birth. Labour is commonly treated as an interface between the pregnant women and medical professionals within a hospital context. Health and medical advice feature prominently in every issue of pregnancy magazines. Much health advice appears to be driven by the need to protect mother and baby from harm, often focusing on foods and medicines it is safe/not safe to take during pregnancy. Additionally, health concerns that increase during pregnancy such as heartburn, constipation and gum disease become the subject of discussion.

Common to all magazines is the intense focus on the 'miracle' of pregnancy, summarised as 'nine magical months'.

The week-by-week guide to pregnancy, with a description of the bodily changes and foetal development during each week, is a mainstay of all publications. These features are amply illustrated with pictures of women at different stages of pregnancy, alongside pictures of the developing foetus.

Week-by-week guide to the 'miracle of pregnancy'

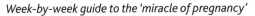

Readers are encouraged to chart this journey for themselves in pregnancy planners that outline the changes, followed by a space for women to record their feelings. Of paramount importance is the birth plan. As a testament to the medicalisation of pregnancy in the West, the birth plan exists as a document of negotiation, encouraging women to think about what kind of medical encounter they would like during labour. In the birth plan matters of pain relief, type of birth and birthing partner offer women preparatory moments of 'choice' within a medical framework. However, the birth experience may not correspond to the plan, as many women testify. The final words of a pregnancy planner given free to readers of *Practical Parenting* are:

> You've done it! No matter what kind of birth you have, focus on the health and well being of you and your baby – that's all that matters. Things may not go as planned – there may be moments when you feel you can't cope. But when you hold your child in your arms for the first time … worries and fears will fade into nothing.

Living the pregnant body

First-time mothers in our study echoed, challenged and elaborated on the ways in which pregnancy was represented in popular culture. A recurrent feature of women's accounts drew attention to the bodily inconvenience of pregnancy. One woman referred to this as "the minor indignities that make you realise that YOU don't matter". Many reported a growing litany of ailments that derailed the representational ideal of looking good and becoming the centre of attention: sickness, sleeplessness, stress, incontinence, constipation, piles, indigestion, swollen feet, tiredness and heartburn in different combinations produced a body that felt heavy and uncomfortable, especially in the last few weeks before birth. While some women tolerated the discomfort with some stoicism in the belief that it was "for a good cause" and a "beautiful reason", others lamented the loss of their former selves and the bodily accomplishments that were now out of reach. "I saw my trainers the other day and nearly wept (laughs) because going running to me was very much an evening activity, a way of relaxing and everything else," remarked one respondent who was simultaneously upset, amused, and resigned to giving up the exercise she loved.

The ways in which the pregnant body was lived and experienced were heavily marked by age. Young mothers in our study enjoyed the physical capital of being young, having energy and having a body that effortlessly did what it was supposed to do – conceiving, expanding, going into labour and bouncing back into shape – with seemingly little intervention or encouragement. For them, the body was a taken-for-granted holder of youthful femininity. For a middle group of women in our study (age 25–35), pregnancy and the body became a more self-conscious project. Consumed with maternal desire and the biological imperative of a ticking body-clock, these women were keen to synchronise pregnancy with career, relationship and financial security. As so much rested upon the successful coordination of different biographical domains and biological events, women in this group *needed* it to work and often put considerable effort into manipulating events that would make pregnancy possible, forward-planning work commitments and leave arrangements with a knowledge of their ovulation cycle and a purposeful consumption of folic acid, for example. A third group of women in our study (age 35+) presented themselves as having an anxious relationship with their bodies. Often following a difficult fertility history, many older first-time mothers regarded their bodies as vulnerable, unruly and prone to let them down. Against the backdrop of miscarriage and failed conception experienced by many women in this age group, they felt "lucky" to be pregnant just as they were at the point of giving up.

The bump

For *all* mothers in our study the bump remained a defining feature of their maternal selves, the key signifier of pregnancy itself and a subject that aroused strong feelings in respondents. The biologism of living the bump appears significant in the development of a maternal identity, giving women preparatory time to grow and know their foetus while adjusting to the idea of motherhood, and revealing their private selves to public gaze and recognition.[1] The implied consequences of embodying pregnancy as the preparatory state for motherhood are challenged in situations where women become mothers without going through pregnancy. Adoption and surrogacy provide examples of different routes to motherhood, raising questions that may challenge the status and identity claims of maternal subjects: How do women become mothers without going through pregnancy? What counts as an 'own' child and how are these meanings established? (Lesnik-Oberstein, 2008). Cathy experienced pregnancy as both intimate and estranged when she became a mother through surrogacy. Negotiating for another woman to carry and give birth to her baby involved Cathy in establishing bonds of connection that were both emotional and legally binding. As far as possible, she and her partner attempted to share in the experience of pregnancy, yet contractually specific roles which made Cathy a mother only following someone else's birth prompted her to consider her claim to motherhood through the eyes of others. Before the birth of her child she was anxious about what neighbours would say when she appeared with a baby, having never been pregnant. Should she explain the situation? Would she look like a baby snatcher? Could she pass and be accepted as a *real* mother? Once the child was born and legally hers, Cathy gained confidence in herself as a mother, yet the narrative work of establishing corporeal connections continued, involving an ongoing intensive awareness of her connection with her child as seen through the eyes of others.

While pregnant, women commonly referred to the aesthetics of the bump, with the "football bump" being preferable to the "kidney bean bump". Whether the swollen tummy was attractive or not and whether it should be on show were matters of concern and debate. Echoing Tyler's notion of 'pregnant beauty' as a regulatory ideal haunting the maternal subject, one respondent articulated her experience of the visual codification of the pregnant body as:

> "It seems to me that there's a kind of hierarchy of bumps
> – you know, bumps that are beautiful and bumps that
> aren't ... I also find myself, you know, looking at other
> women's bumps and thinking, 'Oh they've got a proper
> lady bump and mine isn't as elegant as hers'." (Valerie, 42)

Resonating with ideas of 'reflexive embodiment' (Crossley, 2006), many women, implicitly and explicitly, commented on the importance of acting on one's body, particularly to maintain the body. Such maintenance work was premised upon efforts to preserve a recognisable version of femininity that finds reference points with internalised versions of self and identity. For some women this involved the self-discipline of bodily regimes such as pilates and yoga, defending against the loss of bodily integrity associated with pregnancy and birth. In preparing for labour, Tina Wagland followed her mother's advice to shave her legs and have a bikini wax: practices that bespeak her investment in the aesthetics of bodily presentation, redolent with notions of human autonomy and respectability. For many others it was addressed as a more generalised notion of looking after yourself and *not letting yourself go*, a phrase that captures the concerns of the present with resonances of a moral order of the past.

Issues of respectability were imbued in women's accounts. This can be seen most clearly in talk about how to wear your bump. Skeggs (2004) develops an analysis of the ways in which femininity can be understood as a class-based property premised upon appearance – what you look like serves as a shorthand for who you are, defining at a glance feminine identity, behaviour and morality. Skeggs argues that appearance works as a condensed signifier of class in which negative value is attributed to working-class forms of embodiment and adornment. Seen from this perspective, class exists as a process that works through evaluation, attribution and authorisation. Within this symbolic economy, working-class women are commonly assumed to embody a style of feminine excess denoting an overly abundant and unruly sexuality that places them dangerously close to the reviled figure of the prostitute. The fecundity of working-class women in particular is viewed as excessive and morally reprehensible. Skeggs claims that the respectable/unrespectable binary that served to evaluate the working class in industrial times now works in different ways to construct certain vices as marketable and desirable while others retain little exchange value. Young working-class mothers provide a striking example of a group whose embodied vice is not recoupable for exchange:

> Even in the local context her reproductive use value is limited and limits her movements ... white working-class mothers are yet again becoming the abject of the nation. (Skeggs, 2004, p 23)

Women in our study appeared reluctant to speak of social class in direct ways, often hesitant to position themselves or others in socioeconomic terms. Rather, they spoke of class indirectly through celebrity personalities such as Jordan and the *Little Britain* character Vicky Pollard. From the safe distance of spectator, women commented upon the class-coded behaviour and value systems prompted by these two public figures.

Blending celebrity and maternity, Jordan/Katie Price

In an image shown to all our mothers-to-be, glamour model and reality TV star Jordan is pictured in the final weeks of pregnancy wearing a cropped, see-through top and size 6 jeans, leaving the bulging tummy fully exposed between the micro garments. Many of our respondents expressed a deeply felt abhorrence as they distanced themselves from Jordan's style of celebrity and maternity:

> "I hate her so much. You don't understand how much I hate her. I just hate her. I don't know why I just can't stand her. I mean she is SO – oh I don't even KNOW how to put it in words ... because I feel sorry for her kids ... I'm sorry, but you know, as a mother there's only – there's an extent to how much modesty you should have and she's just – she's just bang out of it." (Cody, 20)

While some women struggled to find the words to express their distaste, other women drew upon a lexicon of respectability commonly applied in the appraisal of working-class femininity. "Inappropriate", "tart/slapper", "ridiculous" and "bonkers" sum up many of the responses which comment more broadly on her borderline status as a celebrity and a mother-to-be. The invocation of notions of propriety and reputation become recognisable themes in many women's responses to Jordan, indicating a need to for women to position themselves in relation to these discourses that have an impact upon feminine subjectivity in a general sense (Skeggs, 2004) and appear to find renewed focus in pregnancy. In addition to charges of sexual looseness, Jordan's style despoils the state of pregnancy itself. For 32-year-old nurse Hannah, "Being pregnant and carrying a baby is such a precious, beautiful thing I just think she makes it look cheap and nasty." The exception to the generally held views on Jordan came from an older respondent:

> "In a modern world I'm delighted that Jordan can go out with that much cleavage and that much tummy on show. And yes, it's her choice and actually, you know, there's nothing wrong with that ... Who cares what she looks like ... it's not for anyone else's benefit, it's for hers ... obviously I know it's trying to say, 'I can be sexy and pregnant' and of course you can, why wouldn't you be able to be? I do think, largely speaking it's a good thing."
> (Belinda, 42)

Aware of the constraints young women may be subject to, and possibly of the feminist critique, Belinda asserts Jordan's right to flout convention and please herself. In doing so she blends a feminist sensibility with the 'can do' discourse of new femininities which emphasises individual choice and personal freedom, particularly in the sexual domain. It may be interesting to consider whether the moral condemnation of Jordan/Katie Price that we encountered would prevail in the light of her media profile since the fieldwork period. In the last four years Price has moved beyond the glamour-model image to establish herself as a ubiquitous media personality, an astute, hard-working business woman, mother of disabled son Harvey and an aspiring A-list celebrity. Price has her own equestrian business, reality TV show, advertising and commercial contracts and a series of publications, biographical and autobiographical. Through the reality TV series *What Katie Did Next* and innumerable 'exclusive' features in *Hello* and *OK* magazine, every aspect of her life has been lived, and sold, for public consumption. Having met Peter Andre in *I'm a Celebrity Get Me Out of Here*, Katie is now divorced from him following televisual scenes of marital disharmony in the unfolding drama of a one-woman soap opera. Katie's image has evolved to blend 'sexy' with millionaire media star, dedicated mother of three and champion of campaigns to support children with disabilities. As we finish this book, Jordan adorns the cover of the January 2011 edition of *Now* magazine, ready to fight her next battle in the politics of motherhood under the headline 'Jordan warns Alex: I'll have a baby – with or without you!'.

A further image arousing strong emotions among respondents was a photograph of the *Little Britain* character Vicky Pollard.[2] This image produced immediate peals of laughter. As an instantly recognisable parody of young motherhood, the image generated expressions of humour, derision and disgust. The aggressive, shoplifting, pram-faced girl in the maelstrom of a troubled life has become associated with excessive working-class femininity and particularly 'chav' identity (Nayak, 2006; Tyler, 2008), a ubiquitous signifier for the unrespectable poor whose profligate ways define bad mothering and locate it within the realms of social exclusion or underclass status. Responses to Jordan and Vicky Pollard provide glimpses into the class-inflected perspectives and practices documented by Skeggs (2004). A 42-year-old respondent living in a rural area comments that there are many young women in the county town that "look just like" Vicky Pollard, pushing prams, smoking and shouting at their kids, indicating that, for her, while the media character may be a caricature of comic excess, the reality is recognisable and is not so far removed from the media portrayal. Many younger respondents, however, found Vicky Pollard "funny" but unrelated to reality, being quite unlike them or anyone they knew. Such contrasting views suggest that the fault lines of gender and class, while structurally significant at so many levels, can also shape-shift at the level of the local, creating scope for multiple acts of recognition and misrecognition.

Young women in our study, having their first child in their teens, demonstrated an acute awareness of how their pregnancy was viewed by others. In a societal context where normatively appropriate behaviour resides in expectations of delayed pregnancy, teenage mothers-to-be can be made to look and feel aberrant. For them, the bump was not about looking good and feeling sexy as promoted by the pregnancy magazines. Rather, the pregnant tummy was a potential source of shame and something they had learned to be defensive about. Many young women reported feeling judged by other people's responses to their pregnant body:

> "Some people look at you funny because you're young and you've got a bump … two ladies were sitting on the bus the other day talking about how young people were getting pregnant and how it was a disgrace and all this lot. And I wanted to say something but I couldn't because I didn't want to be rude … some girls cover their bump and some girls don't. I usually do but sometimes my tops do rise and I think that's what they were shocked about cos some of my tummy was hanging out." (Sophie, 17)

Sophie is aware of the shock value prompted by being young and pregnant, without saying anything herself, and her swollen belly talks back to the women on the bus. Displaying the tummy can act as a gesture of defiance, a 'what you gonna do about it?' flash of resistance designed to unsettle adults around her. As a young mother-to-be, Sophie has embodied resources associated with youthfulness: enhanced health, energy, elasticity and renewal that give her a certain physical capital. These physical resources, it could be argued, enable her to cope with the demands of motherhood in ways envied by older first-time mothers. Sophie is attuned to these differences and offers a counterpoint to contemporary discourses by suggesting that age may not be the most significant factor in first-time motherhood:

"What's the difference between having a baby now and having a baby when you're older? There's still the knowledge, you can't change the fact that you're gonna have a baby for the first time. No matter how old you are it's the same set of issues, you know, sleepless nights, breastfeeding, changing the baby and you're not gonna know any different because you're 17 or you're 30. Older people don't think like that. They judge you because you're young and having a baby … I love being pregnant. I absolutely love it. I'd go through it again and again."

In claiming new motherhood as a universal experience, Sophie demonstrates her command of the knowledge necessary for her new role. Keen to assert that youth should not be a barrier to motherhood, she has enjoyed the embodied experience of pregnancy and feels prepared for the transition to parenthood.

Touching and dressing the bump

The visibility of the bump creates a meeting place between the pregnant woman and others. Its unassailable presence brings with it the filthy looks and instant judgement encountered by Sophie as well as more positive responses. Pregnancy magazines refer to the visibility of pregnancy as a gloriously benign form of stardom in which the pregnant woman takes centre stage. Pregnant women themselves, however, do not report occupying this kind of space. A key observation, much remarked upon by women in the study, is the feeling that their bodies become public property as the pregnancy advances. The growing bump gives everyone, it seems, licence to transgress normative body boundaries, to comment on women's changing shape and act on desires to touch the bump. Touch, that most intimate of senses protected by mores of privacy and body space, is given new meaning in pregnancy as a lightning conductor of interest, amazement and care. Viewing it historically, Gelis (1991) points to the symbolic power of touch as an essential part of rituals to keep the foetus safe. Visiting shrines and sacred statues, pregnant women in Brittany would touch their naked navels against the statue to ensure a trouble-free pregnancy and birth. As pregnancy relates to the abdomen, this part of the body becomes the site of ritual practice, despite the Church's condemning it as 'licentious behaviour' (Gelis, 1991, p 74). These ritualistic elements may have disappeared from contemporary practices of touching the bump, yet contrasting feelings of comfort and indecency remain.

Women were mixed in their responses to touch in ways that reflected a combination of feelings they had about their bodies, their pregnancy and the circumstances of the touch. One younger respondent worked vigilantly to establish her body, and particularly her tummy, as an entirely private, no-go zone:

> "I don't let people touch my belly, people always want to see my belly, it's like, I turn round and say to them, only my midwife sees my belly because I was so insecure about myself, I would never wear shorts or go swimming so when people come up and try and touch my belly, I'm like, no you're not touching my belly … My baby's dad touched my belly once and I hit him for it, I slapped him round the head." (Jade, 17)

Other women felt less strongly, having more equivocal responses to their bump being touched, as one older respondent commented:

> "Complete strangers come up and – just don't do it. I wouldn't come up and touch your stomach so don't come and touch mine … it's quite intrusive but you have to be nice to them because you know, they've got the best of intentions … I've not been particularly, 'oh look, you know, I've got a kick' … I mean, can we just get on with it." (Carol, 39)

The impatience with other people's interest in her pregnancy has to be met with a forced tolerance that politely acknowledges their kindly regard. Other older respondents echoed this pragmatic approach to pregnancy, suggesting to others than there was no need to make such a fuss. A surgeon, in particular, noted that it was nurses and auxiliary staff who took an interest and most wanted to touch her tummy, in contrast to her peers, who barely registered her pregnancy. Such differences point to some of the class-coded and situated ways in which the pregnant body may be viewed and treated. Among professionals, the etiquette was to observe no change, whereas other workers effusively embraced the changing body and most wanted to touch (this is a theme that we explore further in Chapter Six, Work). Between couples, however, touching the bump could be reclaimed as private:

> "Oh beautiful! I don't mind at all … it's all so good, like, 'allow me to share this miracle with you' or, 'allow me to feel such a beautiful thing' … it's like feeling a hug." (Mercedes, 43)

Pregnancy as a time of heightened intimacy

This image of soon-to-be parents was shown to pregnant women whom we interviewed. Choreographed in black and white, the beautiful couple place the rounded stomach of late pregnancy at the centre of their intimate exchange. The visibility of his wedding band raised a few critical comments from women who didn't identify with "that within marriage aspect of it". Although some women glossed over the image or criticised it as unreal or exploitative, it evoked a significant number of responses, most of which were positive. Most women recognised the encoded message of the image: pregnancy as an eroticised time of heightened intimacy for the couple. Women's responses varied according to their situation, and they interpellated the image to find points of identification with their own experience or how they would like their relationship to be. Some women made a positive connection with their own embodiment, saying, "it reminds me of my bump"; another recalled telling her boyfriend that he didn't touch her stomach enough; while others disliked being touched there.

For a significant number of women, the image highlighted the closeness of the couple, reflecting the way they felt perhaps it should be between a pregnant woman and her partner. Marion West (49) said she thought it was "lovely", "Because that's the sort of sensual, um element, and the jointness of pregnancy, so I really, really like that one. Because it's the partnership, it's not hers, it's theirs." Natasha (17) also liked it: "to me that shows the love between a mum and dad to be", but admitted that it had not been quite like that for her. For some it represented a special link between them and their partner, and Adwin (26) said "that's how I feel at the moment, more connected to my husband than I did before". Mary (33) identified strongly with the image, as her partner loved touching her stomach when the baby moved, and "it's like he's going through it with me". Pauline (40) liked it because she thought it was good for making pregnant women more visible and to "let people know that it's fine for them to still feel sexy when they're pregnant". This sentiment was echoed by Melina (32), who commented "you know, there is still life for pregnant women (laughs)". The sensual aspect of the image sometimes made a space for the subject of sex within pregnancy to be discussed. As always, the diversity of views and experiences was evident, some saying they certainly didn't feel sexy when they were heavily pregnant, while others quoted their partners as finding them more sexy, although they often admitted that sex was less comfortable, or that their partner was reluctant or afraid of this hurting them or the baby.

Clothing the bump and developing a wardrobe suitable for late pregnancy presented a challenge for most women, producing moments of rupture between how they saw themselves and what they were supposed to wear. The very idea of maternity wear and specialised garments for pregnancy had little appeal. Women spoke of readily available high street maternity wear as lacking in style and aesthetics, "frumpy" being the most-used word to describe the garments on offer. Designer maternity wear, as featured in the pregnancy magazines, was prettier and more chic, but expensive and impractical for everyday purposes. Some women reported frustrating and abandoned trips to shopping malls to buy suitable clothing that was comfortable, affordable and fashionable. Other women gave up on the idea of modelling 'blooming' maternity wear, adapting and stretching their usual clothes instead. Pregnancy for some women, however, presented an opportunity to develop a new relationship with their body, to engage in a playful experimentation with their changing shape:

> "I found most of the maternity clothes in the shops very boring … I've got some maternity clothes that I like but I haven't enjoyed clothes in the way I usually do. Actually, the thing I noticed, I've got used to it now but the thing I noticed early on, I felt OK wearing slightly more feminine clothes than I usually would because I felt my shape was so outrageously feminine." (Laura, 35)

> "I'm wearing tighter-fitting clothes than I've worn before. I'm not concerned about my weight at all. I've never worn clothes that are cling fit but I have with my pregnancy. And I've been showing off my midriff a little bit, mainly because my T-shirts have been shrinking, but I wouldn't have done that before and I've never in my life been excited about putting on weight but I have

been with this, every morning I'm like, I've put on a couple of pounds, it's fantastic ... I'm just happier with my body." (Karen, 30)

Breastfeeding

Of all the subjects discussed with first-time mothers-to-be, views on breastfeeding produced a consensus. Most women concurred with the generally held medical view that 'breast is best'; the most convenient and nutritious way of feeding your baby. NHS leaflets given to pregnant women promote breastfeeding as the most 'natural' way of feeding your baby. The Breastfeeding Network, a national organisation to encourage and support breastfeeding, places emphasis on the health benefits for the child, claiming that, in addition to the short-term benefits, breastfeeding can help reduce health inequalities in the long term. Aware of the work of other organisations such as La Leche League and the National Childbirth Trust (NCT), some women in the study also accepted the widely circulated idea that breastfeeding is the ideal way of developing a bond between mother and baby, essential for the psychological well-being of the child. Collectively, medical and support services reiterate the message that breastfeeding gives your baby the best start and can be seen as part of a 'positive parenting' repertoire (NCT, www.nct. org.uk/parenthoodpolicy, accessed 29 September 2010). Feminists and sociologists have absorbed the health messages while pursuing a different approach that considers the sensual and erotic pleasures of breastfeeding as a celebration of female sexuality and women's capacity to nurture (Sichtermann, 1983; Blum, 1993).

Relatively little attention has been paid to the ways in which breastfeeding relates to women's sense of self and embodiment (Schmied and Lupton, 2001). In most accounts the decision to breastfeed is regarded as a matter of personal choice and bodily aptitude, though some empirical studies suggest that social context is most important to women's decision making (McIntosh, 1985; Hoddinnott, 1996). In their study of Australian first-time mothers, Schmied and Lupton (2001) found that women's experiences of breastfeeding divided them into two distinct groups. First, those who

—

found breastfeeding pleasurable and a source of intimate connection and interdependence with their baby, to the point where mother and baby blend into one to the exclusion of all others. A second group of women (two-thirds of a sample of 25) responded very differently to breastfeeding. Experiencing the baby as Other to them, these women found breastfeeding disruptive and overly demanding. Women described feeling enslaved by their baby's needs and the enforced domesticity of it all, culminating in a loss of self and personal agency. Many of these women found the physicality of lactation disturbing. Heavy breasts, sore nipples and leaking breast milk, for example, are experienced as bodily distortions, causing distress and embarrassment, prompting a need to separate from the infant and retrieve a sense of selfhood marked by clearly defined bodily boundaries between mother and baby.

While pregnant, most women in our study expressed a desire to breastfeed, often followed by an acknowledgement that they may bottle-feed as a fall-back position. Most women had also bought bottles and sterilising equipment as part of their preparation for childbirth – a purchase that could signal either comprehensive readiness or a lack of confidence in their ability to breastfeed. If the bump makes pregnant woman visible and exposed to the public gaze, it is breastfeeding that marks new mothers as visible and different. The idea that breastfeeding is natural is largely unsupported by the organisation of facilities in the public sphere. Neither is there widespread tolerance of breastfeeding as a normal babycare practice. Some women reported that breastfeeding was difficult within the extended family. Feelings of embarrassment and vulnerability imbued women's accounts. This is especially true of the younger women in our study, who felt their status as young mothers was subject to scrutiny:

> "Yeah I think that's [breastfeeding is] the best thing cos it reduces a lot of things. I wouldn't do it when I'm out. I'd always have bottles with me ... I just don't want everyone staring cos that's what people do. And you can't argue with every person that stares at you cos there's gonna be a lot of people." (Fiona, 15)

Having an acute awareness of the way in which others position her, Fiona does not want to attract attention by breastfeeding in public. While she may muster a combative response in some situations, she feels, in this case, that the weight of public disapproval would be against her. Other young women locate a different set of fears. In this example the young mother-to-be expresses internal anxieties that breastfeeding might transmit something bad from her body to her baby:

> "I don't even wanna talk about breastfeeding. It makes my head spin. I don't know what it is about breastfeeding, it just scares me. I don't know. Maybe it's because in a way, maybe it's just exaggerating or hallucinating about the fact that because I've smoked so much, and I don't feel as if I'm totally healthy, and my baby could be feeding off something off of me. I don't know, I don't want anything going wrong. Do you know what I'm saying? So therefore it's one of them, you know, clean conscious feelings where if you're feeding them proper milk then they're not – at least you're feeding them proper milk. But knowing if you're properly healthy inside and feeding your baby this, how's it gonna affect them, how's it gonna affect you?" (Jade, 17)

Here the very personal health concerns of the young mother question the pervasive notion that breast is best. Feeling that her body may be contaminated leads her to think of formula milk as "proper milk" for her baby, inverting the normative discourse of medical professionals and support services.

The middle and older group of mothers in our study were more likely to subscribe to the 'breast is best' discourse and make great efforts to realise it as a practice. As accomplished adults who had approached their pregnancy as a project, many women in this age range had encountered NCT materials and were open to medical advice premised upon a recognition of *the natural*. Breastfeeding provided an opportunity to connect with the timeless biological miracle of pregnancy and birth:

—

"I think it's amazing. I can actually feed the baby with what I produce, you know, and that's true for centuries … that's amazing, it's just milk, you actually produce your own food for another human baby, it's really bizarre, I think it's amazing … The breast, it's not like a sex object, when you've got a baby and you're breastfeeding I feel it's a natural thing." (Lyn, 31)

Other women in this age range express a politicised commitment to breastfeeding:

"Being a middle-class sort of anti-consumerist, I don't want to get, you know, embroiled in buying loads of baby formula and all the equipment that goes with it, I resent that. But I particularly resent the fact that's it's, you know, there's no way, by all accounts, it can possibly be as good as breast milk … on the one hand, it [breastfeeding] seems much more convenient and better for the child, why would you not want to do that? … But I'm slightly daunted by whether I'll be able to … maybe I'm the first person in existence whose breasts are just UNABLE to produce milk, for example. There's that sort of fear, or I just won't be able to get my head around it. But it's certainly what I've opted for." (Valerie, 42)

In this account and many others, the commitment to breastfeed is haunted by a lingering uncertainty that it will work for them. Taking on the idea that breast is best does not necessarily abate the personal worries women have that their bodies may let them down at the moment when they are called up to perform the seemingly most natural of acts.

In the case of Marion West, at 49 the oldest woman in our sample, the inability to breastfeed causes severe distress. Marion expressed a desire to breastfeed throughout her pregnancy. Favouring natural practices as far as possible, Marion had taken a research-orientated approach to her pregnancy, reading widely and seeking out a range of information to understand the pregnancy and birth process. Her desire to breastfeed was based on a deep commitment to doing the right thing for her baby and, importantly, to forge the mother–child attachment that breastfeeding is reputed to bring. Finding herself unable to breastfeed shortly after giving birth has a devastating effect on her emotional well-being in the postnatal period:

> "I wasn't myself when I came home, very aware of that ... it was affecting me mentally ... I was very cross, very cross about the contradictory advice and the breastfeeding because that was something I really wanted to do and I got very upset about not being able to do that because I felt it wasn't giving her what she needed ... the morning after she'd been born they [nursing staff] wanted to give her formula and they did ... I just felt she was contaminated. I felt she should have natural. She should have what she should have, not formula milk and I didn't understand why they were in such a hurry to give it to her and that again made it feel like she wasn't mine. It's like they'd broken some connection and taken over. Just taken over what was right for her."

By her account, it took Marion several weeks to "get things in perspective", adjusting to the fact that her daughter was bottle-fed, not breastfed, and that this in itself did not inevitably result in the despoilment of her daughter's health or the breaking of the mother–child bond. As the mirror image of the young mother's experience of herself as potentially harmful to her baby from smoking too much, Marion positions *herself*, her womb and her milk as natural and connected. Contamination, for her, is a by-product of contact with the outside world, and particularly the ingestion of formula milk. To the mother wanting to hold on to the antenatal experience of ownership and connection, the post-partum world appears strewn with the hazards of separation, literally populated by the objects of matter-out-of-place (Douglas, 1966).

Pregnancy as part of a body story

For many women in the study, pregnancy is articulated as part of a body story they tell about themselves. As feminist scholars have documented, narratives of embodiment exist as productive sites of dialogue in an evolving conversation to understand the relationship between personal experience and broader social relations (Haug et al, 1999). Situating the pregnancy within a more elaborate story of embodied selfhood becomes a common trope for making sense of the physical changes and their relationship to the pre-pregnant and post-pregnant body. The issue of weight gain and body image is never far from the surface. In many ways the body stories can be seen as recuperative narratives to absorb and contain some of the emotions involved in dramatic bodily change. They can also be read as attempts to resolve or make sense of the messiness of bodily boundaries and the unruliness of the pregnant body, commonly experienced as the expanding abdomen, leaky breasts and the confusion between inside and outside. Confirming pregnancy as a watershed for all things bodily, some women alluded to their pre-pregnant bodies as a time of lost innocence, a corporeal Garden of Eden before being permanently marked by stretch marks and childbirth. Asked how she felt about getter bigger during pregnancy, a younger mother-to-be responds:

> "It's uncomfortable, it's heavy, it's tiring, it's just different. I used to be slim but (laughs) them days ain't coming back ... it's beautiful the way the baby grows and stuff, I find it quite nice. Not – I know it's – you ain't got your figure any more, it's gone, but it's worth it." (Amber, 18)

In this account the feelings of loss are stabilised by the joy of growing a baby. For other women, however, the gift of a baby is not enough to offset the difficult emotions raised by the bodily disruption of pregnancy. Another, younger, respondent reflects upon her body and her pregnancy as a site of struggle and the object of self-blame:

> "I used to be quite big. I was a big girl and I was wearing about size 20 clothes, and when I come down here I lost

all my weight and I was 13 stone and I found out I was pregnant and then I just cried and cried because I knew I was going to be putting on weight and I spent all my time and effort to lose it and I've not bought no new clothes since I was pregnant, cos I didn't see the point cos I'm going to get bigger ... I've gone up about two sizes ... obviously the belly, it's like getting all stretch marks and stuff and it puts me off, and I look at it and I think, I'm going to blame my kid, and it's always like – my mum blamed me but – I don't really care to be honest. I've got myself into the position I'm in now and basically it's my fault, well it's our fault that I'm the way I am. I can't say, oh I feel horrible because I'm getting fat whatever, because I put myself in it, if I'd have thought more I wouldn't be in this position in the first place." (Jade, 17)

In both cases pregnancy appears to amplify feelings women have about themselves, and particularly their relationship to their body. Women spoke of feeling less attractive while carrying extra weight and simultaneously feeling more exposed in bodily terms, as pregnancy appears to license others to routinely comment upon their weight gain, shape/distribution of weight and physical well-being. Developing a sense of perspective that accommodated feelings of loss, change and the relinquishing of control over one's body could be a difficult emotional journey. For a small number of women in our sample (n=5), the bodily dimension of pregnancy tapped into long-standing health difficulties concerning weight and body image. These women had a history of disordered eating, often from childhood, and had previously received medical treatment for anorexia, bulimia and/ or obesity. Anastasia (26) reports "having a problem with my weight – always". At age 4 she was overweight. Her mother put her on a strict diet, and at age 11 she was diagnosed as anorexic. This was followed by a long period of bulimia during her teens, which lasted until she met her present partner at age 18. Anastasia recounts that her partner made an important intervention to interrupt the eating disorder: "He caught me (laughs) I was throwing up and he sort of said, 'This is no good. You either have me or the toilet', so I had to make a choice there". Now pregnant with her first child, Anastasia is overweight, describing herself as having "two bellies", one pregnant and one fat, that seem to be competing with each other for dominance. While still unhappy about her body, she is pleased to be free of the mood swings and unhappiness of the past, and for this reason could not go back to her former practices. Post-natally we learn that Anastasia's troubled relationship with her body continues, culminating in her having surgery for a tummy tuck, carried out privately at great cost to the family, who borrow the money for the procedure. Despite the cost, Anastasia felt that the tummy tuck had been worthwhile, building her confidence and helping her to feel comfortable in a swimsuit when she took her son to the pool.

To further illustrate the ways in which pregnancy may be woven into a narrative about the body we focus on Carly, whose story of body, self and pregnancy serves as an illustrative example of many of the themes discussed in the chapter.

"I'm not going to be forever like this, am I?"

We make contact with Carly through a local NHS Health Centre she is attending for antenatal care. She is 26 and living with her partner and dogs on a desirable, suburban housing estate in the New Town. She has a full-time job as a sales administration supervisor for a large car sales company.

Carly's mother is the absent centre of the interview. In the early stages of the interview Carly establishes that her mother died from a rare form of cancer when she was 18. Her father was not in her life – he left the family when she was 5, leaving her mother to bring up her and her younger brother. The death of her mother had a devastating effect on Carly that she describes as a shutting down, losing trust in others while simultaneously building barriers to keep people at bay. Early adult relationships were troubled and short lived. Carly lost patience easily and would cut people off if they displeased her – friends, boyfriends, even her brother. She also hints that she went off the rails as a young adult – clubbing, smoking, drinking, thinking "What the hell, life's so unfair anyway". Her main aim was to be independent, holding down a job in car sales and looking after her dogs. Later she describes the dogs as her family: they offer her unconditional love and did so at a time when she felt everyone had abandoned her and she couldn't trust anyone. The person who broke through the barrier of her highly defended early adult self was her present partner. She met him at work and they have now been together for three years. She talks of him as safe, providing her with security by just being there and being himself. Her brother took a different path. They fell out and he became a father at 17 while in a relationship with a 16-year-old girl. The couple are no longer together but they have a good relationship, share childcare on a half-weekly basis and he provides financial support. Carly and her brother have since rebuilt their relationship. Having a baby, in the light of this personal history, is a "massive" leap of faith for Carly, a life-affirming act that responds to the trauma of the past. The pregnancy is wanted, but unplanned. They had talked about having children but had not planned anything. She talks about Mother Nature having her own plans.

The body is a key theme in her account. Carly has always been slim and pretty. Working in a male environment, she has enjoyed attention from men, basking in their flattering comments and shamelessly exercising her femininity to get what she wants. When speaking of her work environment, Carly refers to herself as "evil" and uses a range of aggressive phrases such as "stick to your guns", "standing your ground", "fighting your corner", "firing back" to describe her strategies for coping in the workplace. The language of conflict draws attention to the combative culture of car sales companies and her competence in this arena, displaying a constant readiness for the fight. Pregnancy has changed work relations, and particularly her ability to use her sexuality to enlist the cooperation of male colleagues. She has been upset by "fatty" jokes and less-than-complimentary comments and is not at all happy about the loss of her old identity. Asked how she felt about her pregnancy, she responds:

> "The only thing that I say it has affected me mostly which I didn't realise, was how I've taken it emotionally with regards to the change of my figure, I did not accept that very well at all, I'm fine now that I'm getting to the

end, but I just … but I'm looking forward to getting my figure back. I didn't realise how vain I was about how slender I was, because I did work, before I fell pregnant I worked really hard going to the gym four times a week, not necessarily just to lose weight but I ran the race for life for cancer for my mum and … I lost a shed-load of weight and got down to my figure how I really really wanted it and then I fell pregnant and I just didn't realise how hard I took it emotionally, with my changing figure and not being able to fit in my normal clothes and it … I feel that it changed my identity to myself because I have always thought that in myself I'm quite an attractive and slim kind of nice-figured person and er … then all of a sudden I just started putting all this weight on and I just felt very unsure of myself as a person, because I'm not this flirtatious sexy character any more, I'm this great big wobbling weeble and will people still react the same to me, cos I've worked in a very male environment for most of my working career, and a lot of the times to get on in a male environment you do have to have a certain persona, it gets you through on a daily basis and I just felt very vulnerable having my figure changing and people noticing all this going on about me and sometimes people make not very nice remarks. They don't mean to upset you and people are just doing it in jest but people feel that when you're pregnant they think it's quite acceptable for them to go 'alright fatty', and it's just not nice, even though you know you're pregnant and it's for a lovely reason but it can still affect you very much consciously if people are going 'alright fatty', 'look at the size of you', you're putting some on, and it's just … you really want to tell them where to go because you don't want to hear it."

Carly has not bought much maternity wear because she doesn't like it and it doesn't fit with her image of herself. Outside of the professional sphere, within the safety of her relationship, Carly has found it equally difficult to adjust to her changing body shape:

"I remember I did get quite tearful because we went out for my birthday in January and I wore a maternity skirt and top and even though they were nice clothes, I looked at myself in the mirror and I just cried because I just didn't feel like me. I said to my partner 'I'm not going to be like this forever am I?' and he said no you're having a baby and it just didn't feel right looking at myself in the mirror and it really broke my heart but … people accept it differently, I know, there's a girl at my work and she's pregnant as well and she's absolutely loved being pregnant and loved having her great big bump and she's worn beautiful clothes and it just suits her, I think sometimes pregnancy just suits women and sometimes it just doesn't suit others. And I don't think it suits me."

Concluding that pregnancy simply does not suit her glides over, but at the same time reveals, the emotional struggle of wrestling with the strength of her investment in a pre-pregnant identity. Carly's difficulties with the embodied experience of pregnancy, however, do not necessarily imply ambivalence to motherhood. As a couple, they are excited and well prepared for parenthood. They have bought a dizzying array of baby things and have decorated a bedroom as a nursery. It's bright and colourful, with early years toys all around. There is a framed picture of her mother on the windowsill in the nursery. Magnetic letters on the radiator spell, 'Mummy and Daddy love you'. Carly wants to keep her mother's memory alive and wants her daughter to know her. She has well-developed plans to achieve this, which include visiting her mother's graveside, teaching her daughter the things her mother taught her and having imaginary conversations that give her mother a presence in routine domestic life. For Carly there will always be a loss, which is more pronounced now she is pregnant. She particularly regrets not being about to ask for those "little bits of wisdom" that mothers provide. Carly wants to know her own birth story, what she was like as a baby and was she breastfed – questions of bodily inheritance and parenting practice that other respondents come to know and take comfort from.

—

A persistent theme in Carly's account remains the importance of bodily resources. Being slim and attractive, looking good and feeling feminine, especially in the workplace, suggest that her physicality is a central part of her identity and ability to 'perform' in various settings of her life. Pregnancy disrupted her internalised version of who she was, producing dissatisfaction with her body and the way others responded to it. If it were possible to suggest a link between her physicality and her mother's death it might point to her self-reliant investments in the body as a response to loss. Her self and her body becomes the thing she can count on, the thing that enables her to get what she wants in the job market and the thing that does not need others. Carly's mournful self may, at some level, be aware of distancing others as a strategy to prevent further loss. Developing a relationship and having a baby can be seen as a renewed act of faith in herself and in the world. Simultaneously, becoming a mother exists as a magical solution poised to make a settlement with the trauma of the past, or to rework that trauma in a new time, place and body. Interestingly, pregnancy facilitates an intergenerational conversation with her late mother that is live, active and infused with fantasy, imaginatively recreating her presence beyond the point where Carly knew her.

Conclusion

Focusing on the embodied experience of pregnancy, this chapter discussed the bodily changes that mark pregnant women as visible and the meanings that may be ascribed to them. The chapter considered the maternal body as both a temporary state for individual women and a carrier of meaning on the larger scale of class, culture and community. The representational field of mass communication and popular culture showcases a burgeoning of interest in the maternal body, suggesting that pregnancy is a time to display and celebrate the wonder of fertility. Pregnancy magazines incite women to become me-centred, to indulge and pamper an expanded, attention-seeking version of self. Concurrent with the me-me experience, magazines promote the idea of pregnancy as a biological miracle to be managed by medical experts. Yet this representation is at odds with the ways in which women describe their experience. Women in the study lived the pregnant body in a myriad of ways, some feeling inspired to embrace the performance of femininity while others mourned the loss of their pre-pregnant selves. The bump defined the maternal self and was read within an aesthetic register that positioned women as respectable or otherwise. The hierarchy of 'pregnant beauty' encoded in the bump (Tyler 2008) is imbued with class-cultural ascriptions, drawing attention to the aberrance of young mothers, as represented by the comedic Vicky Pollard character. Through the corporeal experience of pregnancy, women develop an exterior visibility and public presence that appears to invite dialogue, touch and meaning-making. Simultaneously, pregnancy prompts women to consider how they feel about themselves and the boundaries between self and others, a dialogue that may be redolent with tensions never fully resolved, as Jade and Carly illustrate. Breastfeeding highlights the vulnerabilities of the maternal body, manifest in the anxiety and loss of confidence women feel in the ability of their body to do what it is supposed to do. Like the bump, breastfeeding carries class-cultural baggage, most acutely felt, in this case, by middle-class new mothers. Finally, the chapter considered pregnancy as part of a body story, pointing to the ways in which pregnancy fits with and becomes part of a narrative of embodiment that is uniquely personal and keenly felt.

Notes

[1] Gelis (1991) documents a recurrent invocation of the stomach through pregnant women's devotion to patron saints and ancient rites aimed at protecting pregnancy in Northern Europe. Citing the example of Saint Mamart in Western France, who was commonly portrayed holding his own intestines as they emerged from a wound in the abdomen, Gelis's study suggests that the stomach has a long history as the locus of pregnancy, particularly generative in conjuring up the inside-outside permeability of this part of the body.

[2] For more detail on Vicky Pollard, see note 1, p 51.

FOUR

Relationships

"When I actually told them I'd got pregnant they were just completely over the moon, and my mother in particular I think is – is just beside herself (laughs) with excitement." (Nadia, 36)

"We chose to go out for a meal, and his brother and wife and Mum and Dad were there, and um we were sort of all round the table in this restaurant and told them our news, and she promptly burst into tears, the brother's wife, and got up from the table and left." (Hannah, 32)

Becoming pregnant for the first time can be a well-kept secret or an immediate public announcement, but at whatever time it becomes public, it sends a ripple through all surrounding family and close relationships. The effects of pregnancy are not restricted to the female body or even the balance of the couple relationship. Partners, parents, siblings and other relatives and friends observe the expanding bump and may participate in advice and the gradual accumulation of baby clothes and baby things (see Chapter Seven, Commodities). With the arrival of a new generation, the whole configuration of interpersonal relationships is disrupted and forced to change to accommodate the need for new roles and additional resources. Birth is an intergenerational act, resulting in an intensive traffic of conscious and unconscious meaning within a relationship network. Mothers and daughters may re-evaluate their relationships from both sides, daughters may come more 'into focus' and mothers are rediscovered in one's own embodiment (Pines, 1997). The psychotherapist Daniel Stern rejects the term 'regression' to conceptualise this intense experience of connection, emphasising instead the 'pervasive present remembering context' that new mothers experience, where 'old schemas of being-with-mother tumble out' (Stern, 2008, p 183).

—

From a psycho-social perspective, Hollway describes new mothers as 'generational pivots – positioned in the middle of three generations' and acting as 'powerful transmitters of culture transgenerationally' (Hollway, 2010, p 11).

New motherhood incites new forms of sociality. Couple relationships are subject to radical new demands, and relationships with siblings can be re-energised as parallel projects of parenting unfold and interact (Mauthner, 2002; Mitchell, 2003). Grandparents may take on a new kind of role (Wheelock and Jones, 2002; Chambers et al, 2009) and new mothers find themselves seeking out relatives and friends with babies rather than those without (Ferri and Smith, 2003). The duration of the existing couple relationship also has implications for the perceived challenge represented by parenthood. Well-established couples might fear the loss of life-style or intimacy, or embrace the new situation as a shared adventure. Some come together around a shared desire to parent, while others might part as nascent relationships are overwhelmed by its demands. In all cases, the situation of mothering is characterised by the challenge of *synchronisation*.

In this chapter, this reconfiguration of relationships is explored through the experiences of a selection of first-time mothers from different backgrounds and circumstances. Interweaving through the chapter are the ways that couples are constituted and change through first-time motherhood, and how this impacts on what families do, as well as what they are. We do not assume that the heterosexual couple will always be found at the centre of a parenting project. Our findings suggests that there are various other sorts of 'couples' being formed, dependent on women's age, situation, sexuality, social class, ethnicity and the nature of relationships. So who actually makes up the 'couple' when a new baby arrives? Grandmothers, sisters, surrogates, child minders and absentees may each play a part. The chapter is divided into three sections. In the first we counterpose the situations of our oldest and youngest mothers, exploring the dynamics of 'coupling' that are in play and their implications for parenting practice and the 'place' of the baby within the family. In the second section we contextualise new motherhood within a framework of detraditionalisation, asking whether it is possible to think about

—

new motherhood beyond the normative couple. Drawing on case studies again, we observe some of the contingent practices that arise from new parenthood, as well as teasing apart ideas of normality and diversity. The third part of the chapter explores the significance of intergenerational dynamics. It begins by discussing the changing experience of mothering as articulated by the grandmothers in our study, before focusing specifically on mother–daughter relationships and the matrilineal conversations that new motherhood makes possible. In tracing the impact of the arrival of a new generation on personal and family relationships, the chapter covers a great deal of ground, yet returns always to the singular yet diverse experience at the heart of our study, the transition to motherhood.

The approach that we employ in this chapter, as elsewhere in this book, involves a focus on the diverse situations of new motherhood and the distinctive logics and practices that these give rise to. In terms of a broader sociology of the family, our approach sits within a phenomenological turn associated with a shift away from defining the form and functions of 'The Family' and towards an interest in family practices (Morgan, 1996; 2011, Gabb, 2008), the claiming of family connections (Edwards and Strathern, 2000; Mason and Tipper, 2008) and the negotiation of obligations (Finch and Mason, 1993; Arber and Attias-Donfut, 2000; Irwin, 2003). We are particularly interested in the ways that changing material circumstances are mediated through intimate and affective practices (Bertaux and Bertaux-Wiame, 1997/2003, Smart, 2007; Charles et al, 2008; Widmer et al, 2008; Walkerdine, 2009) and how new motherhood operates iteratively as a profound yet linking event within personal biographies, demanding creativity in the form of individual and collaborative responses (Baraitser, 2008; Thomson, 2008). Within the social sciences a great deal of attention has been paid to the ways in which egalitarian relational practices can 'undo' tradition, facilitating new forms of intimacy between couples and generations (Giddens, 1991; Beck and Beck-Gernsheim, 1995). Such practices are not simply 'invented' anew, but travel across the affective connections that span the past and present, and bear the traces of the class journeys traversed. Our aim in this chapter is to communicate a sense of how new motherhood

—

impacts on intimate networks in ways that reveal the diversity of our sample, and the multiple perspectives that it enables.

Couplings

The importance of age is exemplified in the first in a series of comparisons of couplings. While most of these teenage mothers had been in some sort of couple situation when conception took place, the pregnancy tended to destabilise the relationship. Chantel (16) and Serena (17), who both live with their families, described how their relationships with their boyfriends have gone downhill since they became pregnant, and Melissa (18), turned out of home by her mother when she found she was pregnant, still lives in her boyfriend's family's house, although she and her partner have separated. Mumtaz was living with her family when she got pregnant with her 17-year-old boyfriend. Fearing the reaction of their parents, they married secretly on the day she took her pregnancy test and put themselves in a hostel, only to split up after a few months. When interviewed, she was living alone in the hostel but visiting her mother at home every day. For most of these teenage mothers-to-be in our research, the main intimate connection is with parents and siblings, rather than friends or the wider world. In this situation, the couple that counts is not the heterosexual unit of mother and father of the baby, but a member or members of the close family, usually the mother. In the two examples that follow, we can see what a critical part age has to play in the biographical narratives of these two mothers who are both having their first child, and its impact on their coupling and the rest of their family lives.

Kim was born in the late 1980s and brought up in Zimbabwe until the age of 10. Following a period of civil unrest and political turmoil, the ethnically white family returned to the UK (where the grandparents remain) and Kim's mother remarried and had another child. At school in Zimbabwe, Kim had been academically successful and the family had been relatively affluent. She had plans to become a lawyer and declared to her family that she would never have children. The move from Zimbabwe to the UK was traumatic for Kim. Her identity as high-achieving, can-do girl made her unpopular with peers in her new social context. She was bullied at school and left formal education. While she was on a home schooling programme, Kim's bedroom became her personal space, her classroom and the site of her sexual initiation with her stepfather's nephew – an event that was subsequently treated as taboo within the family. Kim describes the experience of finding she was pregnant as "overwhelming – there were loads of tears". The news was not well received by her family. Her mother, Gillian, was angry, physically attacking the young man and throwing him out of the house. Kim's sister was, according to Gillian, "shocked and disgusted and said, 'I will never do that and I refuse to be called Auntie.'" Friends were also shocked by Kim's pregnancy – she "didn't seem the type". Kim gave up formal schooling and completed a parenting course for young mothers while pregnant.

Putting her anger aside, Kim's mother took charge, outlining the options to Kim and supporting her decision to have the baby. As in other family matters, Gillian is at the centre of this family drama; it is a real crisis to take control of and there's so much to do. She buys pregnancy magazines for Kim, has found out about benefits and allowances she will be entitled to, and has started to stockpile baby things.

Gillian tells us:

> "I said to her, well you've got three options, you can keep it, you can have an abortion or you can put up for adoption. Whatever decision you make, make sure it's the correct one, and I will stand by whatever your decision is."

The choices, however, are haunted by the lingering trace of Gillian's own experience as a pregnant young woman forced to leave the parental home by her father. Having experienced the shame of early motherhood and the struggle to recover from it, Gillian does not want the moralism of the past revisited upon her daughter. Kim becomes contradictorily positioned within the family as a child with a child. Gillian refers to her as "still a child", adding, "I brought her into the world, she's my responsibility until the age of 21." As the pregnancy progresses, Kim begins to imagine herself as a mother, saying that she wants to make sure the baby has everything it needs, before anything else. She doesn't express an identity shift, but feels that others treat her differently. Kim tells us that she "lost contact with a lot of my friends, I don't hear from a lot of them now that I'm pregnant".

Gillian's mother, Nancy, came down from Scotland to help with the baby's birth and aftercare. Since Gillian moved to England, Nancy has been in regular contact with her and particularly enjoys seeing her grandchildren. Like Gillian, Nancy felt that Kim was too young to have a child but, as a Catholic, believed that termination was not an option. The birth, like the family situation, was turbulent, and Kim appropriately named her daughter Tempest. Her mother and grandmother attended the birth, after which Kim passed out and could not look after Tempest for several days. She tells us that she discharged herself from hospital,

> "and came home and my mum and my gran did the night shift with Tempest so that I could get some sleep … So after about the third day then my mum went back and said 'you know you've got to start now, it's your baby, it's not my baby'."

Kim was subsequently diagnosed with post-natal depression. Gillian comments: "she was very depressed and sitting crying and one minute she'd want the baby and next minute she didn't want the baby, so all very emotional and so she had lots of support and people coming helping her …". Kim is happy for Nancy and Gillian to see to Tempest and they are caught between supporting Kim and taking over. Living with contradiction appears to be woven into the fabric of the family, as the researcher observed in field notes documenting the emotional dynamics of the research encounter:

> Gillian sits down next to Kim and is clearly intent on presiding over events. Her body language tells me there is no shifting her. I'm feeling chilled and resign myself to living with it. Also this seems part of the family dynamic – mum knows everything, nobody has any privacy, the

living room is a public stage for family dramas and mum has the last word … Lots of contradictions emerge during the course of the interview. Mum is orchestrating events, present at birth and, with help of grandmother, takes over care of the baby immediately but also says that Tempest is Kim's baby and they had to hang back to make Kim realise this. At later point says that Kim is still a child, she has a responsibility to her as a child even though she has a baby. She could never throw her out like other mums did. Mum says that Kim won't meet a nice boy on the estate where they live, it's too rough, then proceeds to name a couple of boys whom Kim should have her eye on. Kim says that one of them has a girlfriend but mum says he's not happy with her and hints that Kim should consider stepping in. Lots of othering throughout the interview to establish the family as different: us/the estate; us/healthcare professionals; us/other young mums; us/ Tempest's father; us/drug users. (Field notes, 4 April 2007)

Tempest's birth has had a subtle but significant impact on family dynamics. After a year, Gillian is more in charge than ever, taking responsibility for Tempest, as Kim still has to be reminded to feed her daughter and attend to her needs, so much so that Kim claims that her mother relates to Tempest as a daughter rather than a granddaughter. Tempest has bonded with Gillian and with Kim's stepfather. Kim and her sister still have their differences, but her younger brother is jealous of the baby and appears to resent the attention she gets. Kim continues to rely on her mother, counts on her support on all matters involving Tempest and goes to her first when things go wrong. A year after her daughter's birth, she is planning to take a course in floristry. State support enables Kim to use childcare while she is at college. She and her mother choose a child minder together, visiting locally registered women and deciding jointly what is best for Tempest. Her mother provides additional support by giving lifts to and from the child minder's and looking after Tempest on other occasions. She is aware that many people feel she is overbearing and too involved with her daughter's life, but she is unapologetic. Gillian and Kim appear to support one another in dealings with people outside the home. Tempest's father comes round a few times and is asked if he wants to be involved and also make some financial contribution, but as Gillian comments: "he wouldn't do anything with her. He wouldn't play with her or nothing. And then it just fizzled out."

The overarching theme of the Thompsons' family story is one of downward social mobility, declining social capital and the lack of cultural capital. In less than a decade, Gillian and her family have moved from occupying a position of affluence in Zimbabwe to living on a sink estate in a new town in the UK, a loss of status that signals a troubled reintegration into working-class life on the borders of social exclusion. Gillian recalls leaving Zimbabwe with "three children and four suitcases", an emblematic memory of who they were and what was left. Downward mobility, for this family, appears congruent with growing health problems and increasing reliance upon state support, social services and medical services. Considering the family over time highlights the unfolding of social experience across generations and how specific events have an impact upon family members as agentic beings and gendered subjects. The story of this family points to the ways in which families shape-shift through changing socioeconomic circumstances, and in this case adapting to a new social and material environment. Kim's unplanned pregnancy provides a focus for the trauma of displacement and a reorientation of family resources and strategy. Gillian remains the mother, allowing Kim to continue to be a child.

It is possible to see families as always bound on class journeys, intensified by moments of generational change. The Thompsons' troubled re-integration into the English working class is marked by conflict, contradiction and the constant need to differentiate themselves from those around them. While Kim appears at first glance to conform to the stereotype of teenage pregnancy being predominantly a working-class phenomenon, the family's recently affluent past makes their present status difficult to live with. Marion West's family, by contrast, is travelling in the opposite direction and can be placed on an upwardly mobile trajectory. As members of the labour aristocracy in a northern mill town, the family narrate a version of themselves as the archetypal, aspiring working-class-made-good.

The Wests can be seen as a post-war, welfare-state success story. Reaping the benefits of universal healthcare, improved schooling and grants for higher education, both daughters went to university, achieving professional careers and positions that were out of reach for their parents. A rich vein of working-class respectability runs through the family narrative, making hard work and moral integrity essential features of the quest to live a good life. In separate interviews, Marion and her sister Christine conjure up a loving family and a caring, well-ordered childhood. Being a child was a rule-bound affair – there were places they were allowed to play and places that were prohibited. The boundaries changed over time, as they got older; incrementally they could do more and go further. There were set routines for everything – play, homework, television, mealtimes, bedtime. Offering a glimpse into the seemingly random sediments of memory, Christine recalls that they were "all together as a family" and that she and Marion were dressed in the same clothes on special occasions – she remembers identical blue party dresses.

At 49 years old, Marion regarded this pregnancy as her last chance for a longed-for baby. She and her husband, Richard, have become more closed and isolated since the birth of their daughter. Both have been married in the past, but for each, this is their first child. Working as public sector professionals, Marion and Richard met on a social trip organised by people at work. Spending a day together they found that they had a lot in common, thought the same way about things and finished off each other's sentences. The relationship developed rapidly from that point. Marion had always wanted children, and at the age of 48, after two earlier miscarriages, she was overjoyed to be pregnant. In contrast, Richard had always felt ambivalent about fatherhood; in his words: "I didn't ever think that I would miss not having children ...", although he was very happy when it happens. In contrast to Kim's situation, everyone was thrilled by Marion's pregnancy. Sadly, Marion's mother died some years before and Marion expresses intense regret that she isn't there to share the joy with her. She takes solace in the thought that her mother knew that they were continuing to try for a baby. Her father is delighted at the news, and becomes very emotional, he always felt that Marion should be a mother. Friends are also pleased, although

Marion reports that many of them don't seem do have adjusted to what this may mean for them, and they may not be able to expect the same level of involvement from her in the future.

For Marion, the couple–marriage–children is very much the appropriate order. It had worked for her family:

> "I have this very clear idea that um, having a baby is something about being in a couple and being close together, it's not about you doing it individually. And in a way I could have had children a lot earlier if I'd had a different viewpoint. But to me it was absolutely essential that it was part of a loving relationship, not – not anything else …"

Marion often refers to her "core values", seen as a legacy of the previous generation, particularly those that her own mother had imbued in her: integrity, trust and doing the right thing. For Marion, the couple is paramount, the guiding framework that takes you through life and from which all other things emanate. The couple relationship is so important that it has to be right – and that means emotionally right rather than anything else – "an equally balanced strong relationship". Marion's ideal bears a strong similarity to the 'pure relationship' as conceptualised by Giddens (1991), suggesting that this ideal theoretical category may have its origins in the modernism of a post-war working-class childhood. Marion's preferred version of intimacy suggests that the reflexive project of self may be linked to ideas of coupledom and respectability within particular class-cultural contexts and with a longer biography than late or high modernity.

After having their daughter Bethan, Marion and Richard decide that they don't want anyone else to look after her before she goes to school. Working freelance, Marion occasionally takes on a training job, then Richard arranges leave of absence from work to take over the childcare. Kim and Marion illustrate the contrasting nature of coupledom in this early period of family life. For Kim, the couple that counts is herself and her mother, Gillian, who provides emotional and practical support and makes joint decisions about Tempest.

For Marion, because of the closeness of the family unit and the preciousness of a longed-for baby, the couple is extended into a tight threesome that includes Bethan. The situation of motherhood is shaped profoundly by age and the existing duration of the couple relationship. While Marion is not representative of all the older mothers in our study, her case communicates the logic of her situation, where motherhood involves a folding inwards and a connection to memory and the past. There are literally fewer relatives, and those around have less capacity to help. Yet friends are not invited in and childcare is considered with some suspicion; the couple appear to have the capacity to absorb the project of the child in its entirety. The mapping of social class onto age is not straightforward, however. Marion and Kim illustrate to the possibilities that motherhood opens up in relation to each. As financially stable mature parents, Marion and Richard have a relationship that is consolidated by the birth of Bethan and they have the resources to support their choice to be sole carers of their daughter. Young motherhood, by contrast, throws Kim into an expanding network of relationships as Tempest becomes part of the extended family of parents, grandparents and siblings, with Gillian as the co-parent. Social services and healthcare professionals are also involved in the care of Kim's daughter. For Kim herself, intimacy and the possibility of coupledom are mediated by the presence of her family and her daughter. Having a child has not put her off relationships, but it may involve some delicate manoeuvring that family members are likely to have something to say about. The contrasting experience of Marion and Kim illustrates the very different challenge that can be posed by new motherhood, generating very different ways of 'doing' family; a personally financed retreat into the privacy of the couple and the home or a more public set of connections to extended family and local service providers.

Compulsory parenthood?

One of the most profound markers of social change in personal life has been the gradual disaggregation of sexual activity from reproduction and the institution of marriage. The availability of reliable birth control in the UK from the late 1960s weakened the link between sex and reproduction, facilitating over time a decline in the authority of marriage – characterised by scholars as the shift in marriage from an institution to a relationship (Clarke and Haldane, 1990). Divorce was made more widely accessible from the 1970s and was taken up predominantly by women, encouraged by improving opportunities for economic independence and a growing sense that unhappy marriages no longer had to be endured (Lewis, 1992). Jeffrey Weeks (2007) describes these elements of the 'permissive moment' as contributing to a welcome 'democratisation of everyday life' in which both marriage and remarriage flourished alongside cohabitation, serial monogamy and premarital sex, and 'illegitimacy' gradually lost its power to shame.[1] Some late-modern commentators have argued that, with the demise of the traditionally gendered biography, the key life commitment has shifted from that of marriage to that of childbearing – the relationship between the parent and the child understood to be permanent and irrevocable, unlike the relationship with a romantic partner (Beck and Beck-Gernsheim, 1995).

In this context, marriage continues to play an important cultural role, although the meanings that it articulates are increasingly symbolic.[2] The securing of civil partnership status for same-sex couples represents an important moment of social inclusion and citizenship, both relying on and subverting the imagined coherence of heterosexual marriage as a national and global institution (Kiernan, 2004; Shipman and Smart, 2007; Ryan-Flood, 2009). The increasing take-up of reproductive technologies such as assisted conception, donor insemination and *in vitro* fertilisation further unpick the 'heterosexual imaginary' that underpins understandings of conception, paternity and legitimacy (Nordqvist, 2008). For Jensen, 'reproduction without sex, sex without reproduction – does not solidify the normal; rather, this "queering" pushes into and pulls away from normativity, recasting the terms of reproduction itself' (Jensen, 2009, p 143). One consequence of this is a shift away from a compulsory heterosexuality that circumscribes the conditions of legitimate parenthood and towards a sense that parenthood is available to everyone. In policy terms, this continues to be associated with the formalisation of the couple relationship (through marriage or civil partnership), yet increasingly the couple is legitimised by the well-being of the child, a motif relied on by both sides within debates as to whether the government should or could formally act to encourage marriage and its equivalents through the tax and benefits system.

For the women in our study, questions of marriage and legitimacy were private matters shaped by choice and the negotiation of family sensibilities, which in turn express tensions born of intergenerational changes in values. When we plotted women's situation and relationship status we found some clear patterns. Most of those who did not report being in a couple were in the 15–25 age category, who were, in turn, mostly working class.[3] The one exception to this was Orla (described in Chapter Two), who at 40 had decided to go it alone while she still had a chance. The 12 cohabitees were spread across each age category. For some but not all of these couples, the arrival of the child prompted discussion of marriage, although the outcome of these discussions varied. Hannah (32) had initially hoped that her pregnancy would convince her partner to agree to marriage, yet as the pregnancy developed she reported becoming increasingly relaxed about this as the commitment of shared parenting began to make an impression. Tina Wagland described how the pregnancy had "tested" her commitment to her long-term fiancé but had not convinced her to marry. However, Anna was keen to explain that she and her partner would be married before the baby was born, something she presented as a response to parental pressure. The married/civil-partnered category was the largest group of respondents, and again was spread across the age categories (n=36). In the 15–25 age group the married were all women of minority ethnic backgrounds and working class, and included women for whom marriage was understood as the precondition for motherhood as well as those for whom marriage was very much a personal preference.

The meaning of marriage for women was complicated, shaped in part by whether they had experienced divorce in their own families, the degree of religiosity of their upbringing and decisions about parenting. Marriage could act as a gateway or barrier to further ceremony (such as christenings[4]) as well as a pathway into faith schools, and some of the talk about marriage in the interviews related to this. Marriage continues to be associated with economic security for women and children, yet in a nuanced way that does not simply assume a male breadwinner. Several of the married mothers were the primary breadwinners in their families (for example Sofia Sezgum, Lorraine Hales, Monica Fortune), and marriage could be an element within a broader process of biographical planning shaped, in part, by economic considerations. Elaine, for example, was keen to secure financial security for herself before taking on parenthood, having grown up with a single mother who struggled financially. At 39 she was "finally pregnant", having been in her couple relationship for eight years and married for five. In the interview she tells the story of terminating an earlier pregnancy when she was 26, in her view the "perfect age" for becoming a mother, but not with "the perfect guy" – even though she was with him for 12 years. At this point in time she was getting her "foot on the ladder", taking on a joint mortgage for a flat with her sister, with the support of her mother. She explains: "it sounds really materialistic, but I just knew I'd end up with nothing, and all the responsibility". In Elaine's account, marriage coincides with deferred motherhood and a commitment to economic security.

Sometimes couples did not live together, a category that reflects a wide range of situations which were themselves changeable. As a disabled woman, Clarissa had managed to live independently through the support of a personal assistant. Impending motherhood had led her and her partner to consider cohabitation for the first time in their relationship. As we suggested in Chapter Two (Conception), issues of paternity tend to continue to be in play, even where individual men are absent or unwanted. In several cases male partners were physically absent, yet imaginatively central. This included cases involving migration, such as that of Lorraine Hales, whose family was shaped by a pattern of chain migration in which mothers tended to leave both children and partners in pursuit of work (Phoenix, 2008). For Lorraine, the physical presence of men in the family is important but not essential, as it is accepted that if there is a migratory movement between England and "home" in the Caribbean, her husband may be here or there. Her family originated in the Caribbean and continues to see the Caribbean as "home" and wishes to eventually return there for a better climate and less stressful way of life. Lorraine grew up with her siblings in the Caribbean, under the care of her stepfather, while her mother worked in the UK. She and her siblings joined her mother in the UK in their early teens. Lorraine met her husband when she was back there on holiday, returned here, married and became pregnant at the age of 20. Believing that things happen for a reason, she was happy to be having a baby, and her husband was overjoyed when they found that she was going to have a son. However, because of visa problems, he was in the Caribbean for most of her pregnancy and the birth and Lorraine relied heavily on the support of her mother and her younger sisters. Our initial impression of the Hales family was of an independent group of women who were prepared for and capable of managing life largely without men. Yet, over time we gained a sense of the family dynamic and understood that the men played a central role in connecting the family over time and space. When her son was nine months old Lorraine took him to the Caribbean and left him to "bond" with his father, returning to the UK to work day and night to earn enough money so that her husband could obtain a visa to come to, stay and work in England. This she achieved, and at this point they became, for Lorraine, a "proper family", albeit with the acceptance that her husband can always return to his house in the Caribbean if he does not find work in the UK.

Another way in which fathers may be 'absent' is pregnancy through donor insemination. There were two mothers in our research for whom this was the case. One was Orla, who entered motherhood self-consciously as a single woman (see Chapter Two Conception). The other is Nadia Woolf, aged 36, who was in a long-term lesbian couple. Nadia had met her 44-year-old partner, Kay, some eight years earlier. She had always assumed she'd be a mother one day, and by her mid-30s she had decided it was time to act. Kay was an only and adopted child, her father is dead, and her mother is elderly. She had never particularly wanted a family but she had always known Nadia was committed to having children. Nadia explains: "she's much less – I mean she's – she's not broody, and she's not – she doesn't have a sort of immediately maternal instinct in terms of giving birth to her own child. So though she always said she would support me, and bring it up, and be a parent, she didn't have the same sort of maternal urge or anything." So they discussed it and decided to give it a try using donor insemination.

It was always clear that Nadia would have the baby, and she commented, "the fact that (Kay's) adopted I think makes it much (.) easier for her to not be biologically connected to this child.... And the fact that she didn't want to (.) carry the child herself, so there was never any kind of dispute or discussion or anything." They managed to find an appropriate donor for insemination, someone that they knew, as Nadia was very against having an anonymous donor, but they went through the formal procedure with a clinic to ensure all the legal processes for parental responsibility were in place and to ensure that Kay was the legal parent. The grandparents were delighted.

Initially the couple kept their distance from the donor/father, who visited very occasionally, understanding their need for space. After a second pregnancy and birth, again with his sperm through the same clinic, his visits became more regular and he was beginning to form a relationship with their son. Nadia said they have explained to Gabriel that it takes a man and a woman to have a baby and he has two mummies and a man who helped his mummy to have a baby, but he won't be called his father, and that's what Gabriel will have to say if he's asked at school. Both Nadia and Kay see themselves as 'mothers'. Both now have part-time work and they have adopted a system of each spending an allotted time with the boys, so they both have quality time with them. They see Nadia's parents, and occasionally Kay's mother, and often see friends. Kay explains how their couple relationship shifted into a joint parenting project:

> "I mean obviously we're now responsible for him so the first call on anybody's time will be his, but I think probably because we've always had a sort of responsibility with other people, different people and whatever, you know over our lives, certainly since we've been together that we've never gone in for that really exclusive very insular relationships that some people go in, and I think when a child comes along it's a real shock because it sort of feels like it's kind of pulling, it has a danger of pulling it apart. It's changed in that we probably, obviously we see a lot more of each other because we tend less to be out."

Lorraine, Nadia and Kay point to some of the ways in which motherhood may be reconfigured and differently lived in response to personal situations. Lorraine's approach to motherhood and parenting draws upon cultural traditions shaped by colonial and post-colonial experience. Patterns of migration and separation characterise relations of intimacy for many Caribbean families sharing a historical specific legacy of western expansionism in the early industrial period (Bauer and Thompson, 2006). Emerging initially as an enforced aspect of colonial structures and plantation economies and continuing subsequently as a strategy to financially support the family, leaving, working and reuniting remain recognisable and recurrent patterns of family life for Lorraine and her mother. Leaving her husband and son in the Caribbean while Lorraine returns to London to work can be seen as a traditional and familiar way of generating funds to keep the family together. Nadia, by contrast, can be seen as eschewing tradition by forging a new path to motherhood that is not a recognisable part of her particular family script, yet in doing so strengthens and extends the family tradition. In a lesbian relationship, Nadia and Kay evolve an approach to conception, coupledom and parenting to suit their personal circumstances. Faced with 'new' decisions concerning biological, medical and legal procedures, the everyday presence of two mothers and the role of the donor father, the maternal project is renegotiated and rewritten. Or rather, the potential exists for such a reconceptualisation. In practice, however, Nadia and Kay dedicate themselves to an intensive style of child-centred parenting in keeping with their middle-class peers, suggesting that sexuality may not be the category that distinguishes them from other couples in their class-cultural cohort nor from their family of origin (Gabb, 2005; Taylor, 2009; Nordqvist, in press). By drawing on her own experience of adoption, Kay is able to reproduce a key family narrative promoting elective over blood ties, thus maintaining a family dialogue between generations.

Partners, whether of the opposite or the same sex, and assuming they are present, have an important although sometimes understated role to play, especially in the domestic division of labour, which has changed significantly over the last few generations. Although most of the 62 expectant mothers that we spoke to were in relationships, we talked to partners in only 6 of the 12 family case studies. The data that we have appears to concur with Tina Miller's (2010) findings that men see themselves as becoming more mature, which is often related to work and their role as economic providers. She also notes the importance of men's own experiences of being fathered as influencing their own fathering intentions (see also Shirani and Henwood, 2010). And also as with mothers, this influence is there, whether their fathers are present, inconsistent or absent. But men's opportunities for choosing to be more involved may depend on age and class. While parenthood was generally seen as a joint endeavour, the extent to which couples embraced a division of labour varied. For some, the project was shared, associated with a commitment for the father to be at the birth and to share in subsequent feeding and childcare. These men tended to attend antenatal classes and helped to prepare for the baby's arrival in terms of such activities as researching, reading, shopping, constructing and decorating nurseries – activities that could expose differences in values that may have been insignificant at earlier stages of the couple relationship, as Hannah, described below, exemplifies. Others embraced a more traditional division of labour, ceding authority over domestic and parenting matters to mothers. But as Tina Miller also found (Miller, 2010), fathers' intentions of 'being there' for their child have ultimately be translated into reality against a backdrop of societal expectations whereby men's lives are generally defined by their involvement in paid work, and the onset of fatherhood can crystallise a gendered division of labour and significantly change what couples do.

Richie Arben (46) would ideally have spent more time being a father and house-husband, but instead he had to work long hours to provide the family income when his son was very small. Lately he has been able to alter his work time so that he now works longer shifts but has several days off. The importance of paternity leave has been recognised and extended by successive governments, and some fathers, like Jamie Fortune (41), have been able to choose to stay at home to care for their child while their partner works. Others split the care, both working part time, as we saw above with Marion and Richard West. For Richard (42), work has become less important and less of a priority now that he has a baby, and he appreciates home life, although he observes how his relationship has changed and they have no time as a couple any more. While less apparent during pregnancy, once the baby is born restrictions on a joint social life become noticeable. In our case studies, there were several fathers who had not been out with their partners as a couple since the birth of their baby, which varied in age from a few months to a year, mainly because of distrusting anyone with the baby other than themselves.

Obviously the role of men as fathers is integral, if not apparent, in women's narratives. New mothers-to-be have expectations of their partners as fathers that may reveal themselves after, or even before, the baby is born. For Hannah, mentioned earlier, a 32-year-old practice nurse, who was pregnant with her partner, a web designer, becoming pregnant was the trigger for discovering that she and her partner had some critically different views and values, even though they came together around shared interests. Although Hannah says that pregnancy has made her and her partner closer and "I feel that it's just me and Gavin against everyone now, to be honest ... I feel much closer to him", parenthood may prove quite a shock for them, as the prospect of becoming a family has raised some real differences associated with the baby that reflect the very different ways in which they were parented. For example, they disagree about the sort of schooling to choose: she'd prefer a Catholic school, her partner is an atheist; they have opposing views about the MMR immunisation, whether to christen the baby, and the sort of discipline to impose. They may have to work hard at meshing two rather incompatible biographies and deciding whose values will ultimately guide the parenting practice.

Intergenerational dynamics: accounts of progress and decline

Running in parallel with the transition to motherhood, becoming a grandparent for the first time is a significant event similarly shaped by age, biographical stage and historical and geographical context (Brannen et al, 2004; O'Connor, 2011). New grandmothers, like Gillian Thompson, struggled to see their children as adults or themselves as no longer the parent, while the oldest of our grandmothers worried that she was "past it", unable to engage in physical play. We interviewed the mothers of all the 12 first-time mothers in our case studies. These grandmothers were diverse in their origins and experiences, and in their relationships with their daughters. Their ages ranged from 38 with a pregnant teenage daughter, to the oldest grandmother, in her late 70s and a great-grandmother in her 80s. The roles they took varied between complete involvement and occasional visits. For some, the desire to have grandchildren was strongly anticipated and long standing, occasionally creating a point of friction between generations, while others were surprised and unprepared for their new role. Grandmothers reported playing a pivotal role in the family as arbiters and guardians of justice and fair play. Recognising that sibling rivalries can be rekindled at times of generational change, several grandmothers expressed concerns to be even handed when dealing with their children and grandchildren, being careful not to show favouritism.

It is hard to talk about change and continuity within intimate and family life without also invoking optimism and pessimism and the motifs of progress and decline (Weeks, 2007). These are not simply alternative political stances but can be understood as complementary 'perspectives' formed through different kinds of identifications. The anthropologist Jenny Hockey (2008) has suggested that we are more likely to characterise the world in terms of change when in conversation with our peers, and in terms of continuity when in conversation with those who are younger or older. Whether and how feelings of loss and gain are voiced in these conversations is also circumscribed by the context of the telling. In our conversations with grandmothers we not only asked them about their changing relationships with their daughters but also invited them to comment more generally on changes between generations in the social context for mothering. We sensed that the women were careful in their replies, uncertain as to their audience and aware of a changing balance of power between themselves and their daughters. The resulting accounts were marked by ambivalence and complexity. On first appearances they told a story of social progress, the components of which included the increased involvement of men in birth and sometimes parenting, and an increasingly sociable, public and material enactment of mothering, captured in practices of baby massage, support groups and the availability of labour-saving products. One grandmother commented wryly that now there seemed to be "a wipe for everything". On the whole, these changes were seen as good, although a tendency to conceptualise motherhood as 'easier' also reveals some complicated feelings about the losses associated with the commercialisation of the domestic, as well as an underlying sense that today's mothers lack the resilience and stoicism of the past. Great-grandmother Rose Wagland (82) was very direct about this:

> "It's much easier to be a good mother now, because you've got so many things to help you in the house. I mean they've got dishwashers and washing machines, and things that just need washing. You don't have to iron, and disposable nappies, things we never had, you see. I mean it's EASY to be a good mother now."

Jean Woolfe (65) employs a language of 'need' to characterise changing practices of mothering in a way that both betrays ambiguity as to whose needs are in fact being met by the commercialisation of mothering, and also maintains solidarity over generation. For Jean the 'me-me' time of indulgence and availability presented by the commercial world can be double edged:

> "This incredible choice, and stuff that is apparently essential these days. And no doubt my own mother thought exactly the same thing about us, because we had far more things than the previous generation. She goes to huge numbers of classes – baby massage, baby sing-song, none of which existed … When things become available, then you become used to them and you feel you need them. It's definitely more social, the need to go out of the house to meet people just wasn't there before."

Suspicion over the rewards of commercialisation extended to ambivalence about the psychologised understandings of babies and maternal attachment that are implicit in the activities aimed at mothers and their babies. Although contemporary mothering was presented as being less isolated and lonely than in the past, there was also a sense in which the increasing sociality of motherhood somehow diminished the freedom of the mother from the demands of the baby. This sentiment was evident in concerns expressed by several grandmothers that their daughters might be carrying and holding their babies more than was sensible – hinting that they may regret this intensive attachment in the longer run. Barbara (65), who had the help of nannies and boarding schools in bringing up her children, is acerbic about her daughter's use of her maternity leave:

> "Bonding … that's a new word, the bonding with the baby. She makes me laugh, she knows I laugh, but when you have 'bonding massage', I mean it's getting a bit far isn't it? … Anyway she was making quite a social life for herself."

Grandmothers were also acutely aware of an intensification of the rhythms of daily life. So as well as being "easy" contemporary mothers' lives were also described as "frenetic", "pressured" and "unbearable". Erica Fortune (67) brings the two motifs together in her account of how the time liberated by domestic technologies has been eaten up by female employment:

> "I think on the one hand today's mothers have a lot more time to spend with their children – automatic washing machines and stuff like that. Unfortunately of course the other side of the coin is, now that they have this time most of them have to spend it working away from their children. So they've kind of gained something and yet they haven't. And I find that rather sad. You see I really, I wanted to be there. I always said I wasn't going to have children and have somebody else bring them up."

The perspective of younger working-class grandmothers was also ambivalent, narrating the same changes but from a different position and scanning a shorter time period. This brings into view specific observations, such as rising housing costs, the consequences of female employment and a perceived decline in parental authority.

> "The house prices are so high now and people are forced to work. There's not so much involvement with grandmothers I think. In some cases there is but I think in the old days everyone lived with their mums anyway and got helped. So I suppose sometimes people do nowadays they do rely on grandmothers but that's if they're lucky if the grandmother is not working. Most grandmothers work as well and people are having babies still very young so the grandmothers are younger." (Selma Sezgum, 47)

> "It's not parenting today, the kids do what they want, it's reversed. The kids today are the parents, and the parents are the kids." (Jackie Shaw, 55)

Where families had the experience of migration, the resulting perspective is further complicated by a proliferation of contexts (Hummel, 2008). As grandmother Beverley Hales explains:

> "I have two life-styles to compare with. I have the life-style of a mother in the Caribbean, and also life-styles for a mother in England. And I think on both sides of the ocean it's changed. And for me, it's all become more – I can see it's become more materialistic." (Beverley Hales, 42)

If Beverley is able to compare two life-styles divided by space, 58-year-old Matty reports her experience of two versions of parenting divided by time. For Matty, the key marker of generational change is the involvement of men and a shift towards a less isolated maternal experience:

> "Of course fathers are playing much more of a part of the whole business, which is wonderful. I think now that is an enormous improvement. Because we were twixt and

between really, I mean my mother – I don't think the husbands played a part at all. You would ask the father if you were desperate to change a nappy and he would really … not do it." (Matty Chapman, 58)

Matty presents her own biography as spanning this divide. Her first marriage, at 24, was miserable, and living at a distance from her family she experienced isolation and loneliness in motherhood, subsequently struggling to survive as a single mother after divorce. A second, much happier "companionate" relationship enabled her to revisit parenthood:

> *Matty:* I had a beautiful husband and I had – I had such support, such incredible support. I had Mum and Dad, and I had everything. It was just the complete, complete opposite.…
>
> *Interviewer:* So you did two different versions really of motherhood then?
>
> *Matty:* Hmm, hmm totally, totally. The first two was, you know, um a rotten situation, a rotten marriage, um very draining.

Evidently, social change is apprehended differently from different social and biographical locations. The stories that individuals tell about change reflect their personal investments and experiences. Yet certain markers of change appear to transcend the diversity of biography, forming broader cultural (or canonical) narratives that are shared and which take on a life of their own. Our research with mothers and grandmothers resonates with other studies with fathers, suggesting that 'doing parenthood differently' from their own fathers has become is a key narrative that connects men across differences of social class and ethnicity (Dermott, 2008; Miller, 2010; Shirani and Henwood, 2010). The idea of the involved and intimate father is increasingly the norm, despite evidence that the gendered division of labour around childcare is deeply entrenched, with UK fathers much less likely to share in the everyday work of parenting than those in other northern European countries. Again, this suggests that there is no neat relationship between identities (the kinds of men and women we would like to be), subjectivities (our feelings and desires) and our practices (Bjerrum Nielsen and Rudberg, 1994). The stories that we tell about social change and continuity are not simply reflections of historical fact, but rather can be understood as active work, undertaken in the present, in the context of specific audiences, which seeks to manage the reconfiguration of situations and relationships over time. These stories may be contradictory, get stuck or change, yet together they constitute a 'dialog' (Rosenthal, 1998) which is not simply made up of words but rather can be understood as an arena of ongoing communication and exchange that involves bodies, emotions, habits, images and objects.

Mother–daughter dialogues

While the shift from being the mother within a family to becoming a grandmother is characterised by a heightened awareness of change, loss and gain, the shift from being a daughter to a mother can be associated with a revitalised connection to the past. When we met women at the end of their pregnancies we gained a sense of them as located along a kind of continuum, positioned in terms of being more or less open to the involvement, both practical and otherwise, of their mothers. Where they stood was, in a sense, the culmination of their journey as a daughter. Some anticipated motherhood with the benefit of a positive and close relationship with their own mother, but most expressed some complicated feelings, and for some the relationship was remote or rejecting. Other studies exploring the relationships between generations of women confirm the complexities involved. Social reproduction is far from simple, given the changing material circumstances of successive generations, and may be deeply unattractive to many. Brannen and colleagues (2004) distinguish between solidarity, incorporation, differentiation and reparation as characteristics of intergenerational relations, terms that are echoed by O'Connor's (2011) typology of mimicry, resistance and coincidence in approaches to motherhood between generations of mothers.

The case-study approach allowed us to follow women and their significant others over the first year of new motherhood, and we gained insight into the ways in which this transition could enhance the mother–daughter relationship, with a daughter beginning to understand aspects of her mother and experiences in her mother's life that she had not been able to before, or had never asked about. It seemed that, as their pregnancies progressed, women became increasingly curious about their own mothers' experiences and began to demand and share knowledge that had not seemed very relevant before. Erica Fortune characterises her daughter Monica as undergoing a transformation from sulky daughter to dutiful and empathic mother, recognising and interested in the sorts of experiences her mother had been through. Erica is careful not to be an interfering mother, commenting that "I don't like people telling me, so I don't tell them." She describes Monica as "opening up more" as she "realises what it means to be a mother", and considers that they share a "common-sense approach" to parenting. She is quietly pleased to find that her views on the delegation of childcare are echoed by Erica and Jamie, who eschew nursery and child-minding options, planning for Jamie to be a stay-at-home father when Monica's maternity leave is over. After her son is born Monica explains that she just "can't see enough" of her mother, and is revisiting her memories of childhood through a new identification with her mother:

> "I just think, God and she had all that to go through and
> you know getting us off to school in the mornings, and
> just coping with three small children and also her mum
> wasn't here, her mum was in Germany, she had no close
> relatives, she was out in like a village you know, you just
> think, blimey that's pretty well done really."

Hannah is another who has a close relationship with her mother, but she and her partner have differing views on how far she can be involved in the birth of their baby. Her mother is desperate to be at the birth, "but I've had to say no, because 'Gavin feels that he wants it just to be us', you know, and um, you know, a kind of special moment." Hannah is disappointed, commenting: "But I don't think he quite sees that a mother and a daughter – that relationship is just so (.) um special ... Because she just doesn't want to miss anything ... Because it's like their child ... I am her baby, and my baby will also become like her baby as well." Hannah hopes her mother won't be too upset or offended, sensing the need to balance the intergenerational connection with the creation of a new bonded unit in the present.

For some women, pregnancy and motherhood could raise difficult family dynamics. For example, Heather explains that until recently she thought that she had "the most uncomplicated, easy-going family, no dramas". But since her sister had her baby five years previously, she has discovered that "it's so twisted and there's so many dynamics and there's so many different angles that you could come up, that make you wonder why our family is the way it is, you know". While not rejecting the relationship, a significant number of mothers considered the experience of their own mothers around pregnancy and motherhood as irrelevant and out of date, and even if they loved and respected them, they would not go to them for advice and information. For example, Deborah, aged 33, dismisses her mother's experience as being "too long ago" and "too medicalised". Although this rejection is licensed by perceptions of a constantly changing body of technical knowledge about birth and babycare, we sensed that the source of women's ambivalence towards the their mothers' advice was more complicated, involving distancing strategies that may result from the experience of upward social mobility, as well as fears of reproducing problematic patterns of attachments (see also Lawler, 2000; Brannen et al, 2004; O'Connor, 2011).

Women whose relationships with their own mothers had not been good in childhood or beyond might not want their mothers involved now they were pregnant, nor after the birth, and some described how they wanted to be different kinds of parents from their own mothers. Kate (31), for instance, has a sense of disconnection from her mother, who had a breakdown after she was born and never really recovered. Faye, aged 35, felt that her mother neglected her and her sister, so was rejecting her as her role model now that she was pregnant, focusing instead on her child minder and a woman for whom she nannied when she was at college. Anastasia reviled the Eastern European model of socialised childcare that had shaped her mother's experience and was alienated by her mother's racist views towards her Guyanese husband. She had developed a close relationship with Jill, her next-door neighbour, a woman in her 50s with grown-up children, who was very supportive, so much so that she elected for us to interview her as her "substitute mother".

Where women did not have a positive relationship with their own mother we sensed that they tended to invest more heavily in peer maternal cultures, with alternative figures outside the family and/or in their couple relationship. They might also assert connection with members of their partner's family, taking the opportunity to become part of a different family lineage and dialogue. Certainly, the arrival of a new generation constitutes a moment when family can be reconfigured and displayed in new ways (Mason and Tipper, 2008; Dermott and Seymour, 2011). In this context invitations to be connected can be made and responded to in a range of ways, including gift giving, naming practices and offers of care (Kehily and Thomson, 2011). The objects that women shared with us in pre-natal interviews as part of their preparations for birth can be understood as mapping the affective world into which the child would emerge, including 'hand me downs' from trusted friends who had already made the transition, hand-made clothes from the family, fashionable baby clothes from colleagues and girlfriends and treasured heirlooms representing absent loved ones and places. Anastasia was relatively unusual in the definitive way that she distanced herself from her mother. More common were a range of partial identifications, where women claimed a particular kind of connection with their mothers. Given that so many women saw their lives as following a different sequence than their mothers' (with a greater investment in education and career), the idea of a biographical inheritance over generations could be difficult. Although some women explicitly cited their mothers as role models for both working and 'stay-at-home' mothering, more commonly their accounts emphasised a kind of cultural inheritance – expressed through shared values concerning parenting style and personal appearance.

A theme of intergenerational recuperation also emerged, where women understood their biographies as an extension of those of their mothers – realising thwarted ambitions for education or career, or repairing the isolation or hardship that their mothers endured. An important and reassuring intergenerational claim was that of bodily inheritance, where women assumed affinities between their own embodiment and that of their mothers in areas such as infertility, ease or difficulty with birth and breastfeeding (see Chapters 3, Body and 8, Birth). Overall, women variously (and in combination) reproduced, recuperated and rejected the practices of their own mothers, revealing the extent to which this intergenerational work is central to the project of new motherhood. But whatever their strategy, it was constituted in conversation with their own experience of being parented, and circumscribed by their socioeconomic circumstances.

Father–daughter relationships

Grandfathers, like brothers, appeared much less in women's narratives, although they remain important in the general landscape. Mainly they were included in remarks about the general delight and happiness expressed by most grandparents-to-be on receiving news of the pregnancy. While some mothers may be present at the birth of their grandchildren, grandfathers almost never are. They come much more into focus when mothers are absent through death or remarriage. In 28-year-old Gail's case, her mother had died of cancer some years before she became pregnant. She gets on well with her father, who lives locally, but because he has strongly traditional attitudes about being married before you have children, she and her partner have let him think that their planned baby was accidental, to preserve their good relationship and avoid his disapproval. Cody, aged 20, was living with her father because her mother had remarried and her older sisters lived elsewhere. She had an on-off relationship with the father of her baby, who lived with his aunt. Although her father was not the most communicative of people, he was quietly helping to look after her, got things for her, and had organised and painted a nursery for his impending granddaughter, "my dad is like *her* dad really, he's stepped up a lot more than [my boyfriend] has". In many cases, grandfathers were simply quietly but supportively in the background.

But this was not always the case. Father–daughter relationships can severely break down, especially if the father intensely disapproves of his daughter's choice of partner. The problems that some men as fathers can have in accepting that their daughter has a relationship with 'another man', who might take her away, have been described (for example, Sharpe, 1994). Fathers may consider that 'no one is good enough for my daughter', a disapproval that may be overcome with time and effort, but for others it may be unchangeable. One of these was Sofia Sezgun, who was 20 when she married her 18-year-old husband, Rifaat, and had a planned pregnancy three years later. The family originally came from Cyprus and her father strongly disapproved of this marriage, viewing Rifaat as a ne'er do well, and Sofia as marrying against his wishes. To this day he will have absolutely nothing to do with Sofia, her husband or their daughter. They cannot be in the same place together, which means Sofia has missed various family gatherings, such as her older brother's wedding. For her mother, it is a tragedy, as she longs to be supportive but cannot care for her granddaughter because of her husband's total rejection of his daughter and son-in-law. She is devastated that she cannot be a "proper granny", and it saddens her that it is her son-in-law's mother who looks after her grandchild every day instead of her. Fortunately, Sofia's is an extreme case, and the majority of grandfathers appeared positive and happy, but operated more as two-dimensional figures in the wider family landscape.

Conclusion

First-time motherhood is an event that can reconstitute and re-energise the shape and appearance of a social and familial network: like a kaleidoscope, the picture changes with every turn in time. But while all the women in our research were sharing the same event – the birth of their first child – the varied sequencing of this in their lives demonstrates the diversification of women's biographies. Becoming a parent in the locality where you grew up and went to school is very different to encountering motherhood as a socially and/or geographically mobile migrant. Patterns of friendship, sociality and social networks are profoundly marked by social class, and patterns of mobility are shaped by education and employment. Mothers rely more on friends if they don't have relatives around. Where a couple is not embedded in a network of family support it may be more likely to 'bond', sharing and planning things together, and independent in its approach. We can then think about how, with the advent of motherhood, family relationships become more or less contained or open, isolated or connected.

This chapter considered the ways in which families change and regroup in the face of new motherhood. Reflecting on developments in family studies, the chapter has been concerned to explore matters of practice and display that highlight what families do, as well as what they are. Drawing upon empirical examples, the chapter, and indeed the book, underlines the significance of age in shaping the situation of new motherhood. The biographies and parental practices of Kim and Marion provide illustrative examples of how the timing of motherhood defines possibilities and limitations that have consequential effects for the maternal landscape of both women. Financial resources and the status of the couple relationship make particular parenting practices available, producing a privatised experience for Marion and a more publicly accountable, state-supported childcare arrangement for Kim. Both women remain in touch with intergenerational dynamics that exist as a legacy for Marion in memories of her mother, but as everyday lived relations for Kim, whose mother and grandmother play an important role in supporting her and her daughter. The social mobility of the family as a whole plays an important part in framing the context for the arrival of a new generation.

Grandmothers in our study reflected upon changes in the experience of becoming a mother in ways that enabled us to trace intergenerational ruptures and points of continuity. Significant in grandmothers' accounts of social change were the increased participation of fathers, the expansion of consumerism and material goods and the enhanced choices available to mothers in contemporary times. Grandmothers also noted that choice may be mitigated by the need to work, often in demanding and pressured environments. Grandmothers and new mothers reflected upon their positions in the intergenerational female chain in ways that brought each other into focus. Mothers and daughters looked to each other to bridge the transition to motherhood, to personalise the experience and make it real. The connection could produce intense moments of identification and the recognition of a shared inheritance, as well as moments of disconnection marked by a felt need to break with the past. Both positions call upon new mothers to engage with their own mothers in order to fashion their own maternal identities. The chapter also touched elliptically on the role of men in motherhood and the ways in which maternal projects may take non-normative routes shaped by needs, desires and personal circumstances that may be well travelled or uncharted. In each case we suggest that the event of new motherhood demands creative responses of those most closely involved, including a drawing together of imaginative, affective and material resources in ways that connect and reconfigure past roles in new circumstances and in relation to a changed horizon.

Notes

[1] Ferri and Smith (2003) provide an overview of relevant demographic changes using the successive birth cohorts.

[2] Although we have been sensitised by policy and popular commentary to think of teenage pregnancy as a new demographic trend, fertility rates among low-income young women have been remarkably consistent historically; it is rates of marriage that have declined dramatically for this group (Arai, 2009).

[3] Six of the teenage group lived with their families, several other teenagers were in a mother-and-baby home and a few lived alone.

[4] Case-study families held a range of ceremonies to mark the entry of children into the family, including christenings and naming ceremonies. In one case a christening took place when parents were not married.

FIVE

Expert advice

> A vast industry of childcare advice has arisen. Bookshops groan under the weight of warring theories about the best way to bring up baby ... The feminist-driven 'Women' sections of magazines have largely been replaced by pages given over to 'parenting' issues. Mere mothering is out. Specialist magazines have never been more numerous. Innumerable self-appointed experts have established websites ... Information overload is turning parenthood into a nightmare of anxiety and stress. (Hardyment, 2007, p 283)

Questions of how to be a mother and what I need to do/know surface in late pregnancy as women prepare for and think themselves into their new role. We sought to find out about the ways in which expectant mothers engaged with expert advice via a range of methods, including a questionnaire, interviews and by exploring texts in their own right. Our initial enquiries as to where women turn for advice suggested that pregnant first-time mothers rely on people (doctors, family members and friends) rather than texts (magazines, books, websites or leaflets).[1] Yet when we met women in their own homes for interviews and asked them to share with us their preparations for the baby they often showed us piles of books and magazines that they had gathered in order to help themselves imagine their way into motherhood. In considering the status of expert advice in this context, we analyse the material that women signposted as significant for them, attempting to think about what this material represents as part of a wider picture of contemporary mothering, but without overemphasising its significance in shaping expectations and practices.

This chapter considers the expert advice available to new mothers-to-be and the ways in which they relate to this body of knowledge.

The chapter begins by locating the contemporary landscape of expert advice in some historical context before going on to consider the key genres through which women reported accessing expertise: pregnancy magazines, childcare manuals, other mothers and evolving sources of advice such as websites. The final section considers how women may be differently positioned in relation to expert discourses, drawing on contrasting examples of a young mother's parenting course and an older mother's collection of books. In keeping with the expanding material culture of motherhood, expertise and advice is plentiful, having grown exponentially over the last 20 years (Hardyment, 2007). In this chapter we show that engaging with experts, taking advice and building a personal knowledge base can be seen as part of the *work* of motherhood that, as Miller (2004) and Clarke (2004) point out, has material effects. Their study of mothers in north London demonstrates the ways in which resources, products and local networks create a particular version of middle-class mothering. The selection and blending of advice literature may appear as an accessorising activity at the fringes of mothering practices. Our study, however, suggests that a competing body of expert advice is much more central to the maternal experience as a resource in the construction of types of mothering that have currency at the level of the local.

The expert and the mother

> "It's very hard in pregnancy to get reasonable advice. It's either the obvious, drink moderately, eat sensibly, don't bounce yourself down the stairs or you MUSTN'T do this, that and the other, you MUSTN'T take any medicines AT ALL or immediate death ... The diets they recommend are ludicrous. I can't help thinking that there must be a lot of women out there who just beat themselves up constantly for failing at these impossible tasks." (Eleanor, 26)

In contemporary times becoming well informed about your pregnancy can be a contradictory and unrewarding experience.

There is a sense that mothers-to-be must encounter and navigate the accumulation of specialist knowledge about maternal and child well-being, including the layers of moral injunction and pathology created by successive waves of expertise. In seeking this advice, contemporary mothers join a continuous chain of mothers and experts that stretches back to the industrial revolution, with different models of babycare coming to represent competing forms of personhood – for both the woman and the child. In a comprehensive history of advice to women, Barbara Ehrenreich and Deirdre English show how the manuals of the early 20th century constructed the expectant mother as a 'domestic engineer' – the representative of the expert in the home, applying the rationality of the factory and the office to the project of producing the family: to time and on budget. In the second half of the 20th century the gaze turns inwards, with advice increasingly psychological in its focus. The expert now identifies with the 'permissive child', whose needs are assumed to guide the 'libidinal mother', 'the two happily matched consumers, consuming each other' (Ehrenreich and English, 1979, p 199).

Writing in 1979, Ehrenreich and English argued that as the end of the 20th century approached the 'romance between the expert and the mother' was effectively over, the former having lost much of their authority as advice proliferated, becoming more a matter of choice and taste rather than diagnosis or science. Their prediction that wisdom would no longer be hoarded by experts has in many ways been realised. In the new millennium there is no cultural consensus about the right way to give birth or to care for babies. Different perspectives coexist, sometimes uncomfortably and often to comic effect. Standard texts are updated to incorporate new values and perspectives (Hardyment, 2007) and readers can gain relief from retro-advice when overwhelmed by the demands of attachment parenting (Cusk, 2001). What 'counts' as expert advice is also fluid. Christina Hardyment's historical analysis of childcare guidance, *Dream Babies*, can be found on a shelf alongside traditional parenting manuals and a proliferation of 'mumoirs' which range from the literary (Cusk, Enright) to the celebrity (for example, Mel Giedroyc's *From Here to Maternity*, Jules Oliver's *Minus Nine to One* and Myleene Klass's *My Bump and Me*) and the comic (such as the 'laugh out loud' *Best*

Friend guides to pregnancy and childbirth). In a review article of yet more, 'hen lit' critic Jenny Turner reveals her own omnivorous maternal reading habits as taking in the poetry of Sylvia Plath, the radical feminist classics of Dorothy Dinnerstein and Adrienne Rich, the child development theory of Donald Winnicott, plus a full range of 'manically comic memoirs' that she 'binges on' in her local library (Turner, 2009).

Engaging with advice is not simply a matter of discovery or fact finding (although this plays an important part); it is also about finding a position for oneself within 'maternal culture'. This positioning goes beyond reading. Increasingly, it is the medium of display rather than the advice itself that is the site of innovation and significance. Initially a new breed of pregnancy and mothering magazines intervened in order to both mediate and package the plethora of technical and consumer discourses. Internet-based social networking sites such as Mumsnet and Netmum are now the premier forums in which motherhood is displayed and consumed, and reality TV shows such as *Supernanny*, *Wife Swap* and *House of Tiny Tearaways* provide public texts around which intense moral feelings about mothering circulate (Skeggs and Woods, 2009; Jensen, 2010).

Focusing firstly on pregnancy magazines as social texts, the following section explores the ways in which advice is encoded for pregnant women within recognisable cultures of femininity that structure women's magazines as a genre.[2] Through magazine scholarship, it is possible to trace key themes at the interface between normative femininity and feminism: a concern with issues of power and subordination; a consideration of the pleasures of femininities; and, more recently, a recognition of the 'failure' of identity and the impossibility of coherence at the level of the Subject (McRobbie, 1978a; 1978b, 1981, 1991; 1996; Tinkler, 1995; Blackman, 2004). Further work considers the reading practices in which pleasure and fantasy can become strategies for the organisation and verification of domestic routines and lived experience and the creation of 'communities of interpretation' (Radway, 1984; Hermes, 1995; Kehily, 1999, 2002). Blackman (2004) suggests that late-modern accounts of subjectivity largely evade the ways in which the injunction to make sense of one's life is culturally translated in popular discourse.

She notes the increased volume of advice and self-help literature in women's magazines, where the need for transformation and self-improvement remains key to successful personal relationships – the psychopathology of contemporary femininities is culturally produced in women's magazines by presenting women's experiences as dilemmas that can be resolved through personal development. Pregnancy magazines can be placed in the slipstream of this development, aimed at women who, having successfully resolved the relationship dilemma, now must focus on maintaining a sense of self while looking after others.

Pregnancy magazines as purveyors of knowledge

Pregnancy magazines present themselves as sources of information and as conduits for other sources of information. Key information on pregnancy, labour and new motherhood is rehearsed in different ways in every issue. Most magazines include 'baby basics' features, introducing women to the rudiments of childcare such as bottle feeding, weaning and sleep routines. Additionally, books, cable TV channels and websites on pregnancy, birth and childcare are frequently reviewed and profiled. Generally the approach to advice and information is instructional without being overly didactic. The emphasis is upon common sense, relying upon a post-Spock settlement that suggests to women – *if it feels right for you, then it is right.*

Given that most pregnant women in our study reported that their family, friends and, particularly, mothers provide the richest source of information and guidance during pregnancy, it is perhaps surprising that the magazines do not comment more freely upon family communication and intergenerational conversations. While some features allude to pregnancy as a time to 'rediscover your mum' (*Prima Baby*, October 2005), there is little acknowledgement that new mothers form part of an extended family undergoing change and exchanging experientially based knowledge. Mothers of new mothers are particularly noticeable by their absence, indicating that the magazines may be implicitly addressing the mobile couple of late modernity, living a version of the 'pure relationship' and geographically distant from the extended family. Additionally, there is little discussion of mother–daughter relationships, despite their increased significance during this time. A rare feature entitled 'Blast from the Past' (*Mother and Baby*, October 2005) takes a light-hearted look at advice for new mothers in previous eras. Compared with instructions to swaddle infants, breastfeed every four hours and keep babies outside as much as possible, women today have a lot to be thankful for. The article concludes with 'five reasons to be glad we live in 2005': family planning; lower infant mortality; pain relief during labour; disposable nappies; and washing machines. The lack of intergenerational conversation across the magazines as a whole suggests that a simple yet significant message may be at play – it's different for new mothers today, the experienced voice of grandmothers may no longer be relevant.

All pregnancy magazines have a stable panel of experts that commonly includes a GP, health visitor, midwife, couples therapist, consumer expert, childcare specialist, psychologist and obstetrician. Experts are often profiled in the opening pages of the magazine, suggesting that their presence offers readers comfort, reassurance and authority. Experts feature heavily within the problem page sections of the magazine, where readers are invited to request help for particular difficulties they are experiencing. Many queries straightforwardly ask for the opinion of a specialist – 'What can I do about morning sickness?' or 'Why isn't my baby gaining weight?'. In keeping with women's concerns over work (Chapter Six), it is in the interactive features of the magazines that women's difficulties with childrearing emerge. Running counter to the generally uplifting tone of the magazines, a question-and-answer item invites a panel of experts to respond to the 'confessions' of 'brave mums' who admit to the otherwise contemporary taboo subjects of modern mothering such as 'I think my baby's ugly', 'I smack my child' and 'I don't like being a mum':

> I had my daughter at 17 and have found it tough. When she was small and woke up in the night, I'd pretend to be asleep so that my partner would get up. If I'm honest I did it because I didn't like being around her ... If I have

a bad day I find myself thinking how much easier life was before she came along. (*Mother and Baby*, October 2005)

In this case a health visitor responds, suggesting that this mother may have been suffering from post-natal depression and should seek advice and support from her GP, her partner and close family and friends, indicating that, with the right help, she will get over these feelings in time. The hard-to-voice response represses the unspeakable idea that some women may not like their children and may not enjoy having them around. Rather, this thought – that the experience of motherhood itself may be undesirable – is regarded as a temporary aberration, the regrettable effect of a depressive illness that can be overcome.

The extent to which other mothers drew upon pregnancy magazines for expert advice reflected patterns of magazine readership prior to pregnancy. Women who enjoyed magazines related to pregnancy magazines in a similar way as a pleasurable leisure activity that blended positive thinking with humour. Fashion, gossip, celebrity news, problem pages could be enjoyed in what was usually a fleeting engagement with the form. Other first-time mothers were drawn to the idea of a magazine that was especially *for them*. Initially at least, pregnancy magazines contain valuable information; however, the format of the magazines follows a formula in which key features such as the step-by-step guide to pregnancy are repeated, making it less useful as time goes by. Many women found magazines helpful as an initial guide to products, informing them of what was on the market. Some women, concerned with matters such as the provenance of advice, the status of expertise and the reliability of recommendations, expressed a preference for books, websites or research-based accounts for more detailed information.

A significant feature of much advice literature on pregnancy and birth is the paradoxical treatment of men as central yet marginal to the maternal project. Our study of pregnancy magazines over a period of 18 months showed that for the most part they do not explore the father–child relationship or conjure it up as a potential relationship to be developed. Rather, the focus is upon the couple relationship and the possible displacement of the father by the new baby. Men, for their part, when they do appear, put forward the perspective that pregnancy and birth is a bewildering, if not scary, time for them in which their partners are not quite themselves. The text tends to draw heavily on laddish language and the idea of men as fish out of water in the pregnancy and birth arena, and suggests that while men may be motivated by the best of intentions, they can't quite be trusted to do or say the right thing. Fatherhood is inextricably linked with masculinity, and an infantile masculinity for some men has to be transformed into adult responsibility – some magazine features suggest that fatherhood profoundly changes men, transforming them from unreconstructed lads in the men-behaving-badly mould to sensitive and caring fathers with a newly found sense of responsibility. It calls on them to re-evaluate their lives and finally grow up. While this can be somewhat exaggerated, it is often based on real change, as illustrated by 30-year-old Andy Chapman, who explains:

> "I've always wanted to be a father, I've always, my end goal was to be a good father and now it's happening, well okay, this is it so I'm trying to do my best by Heather and do my best by Ben. So I think it's brought a lot more maturity and a lot more purpose to my life."

Gathering expert advice

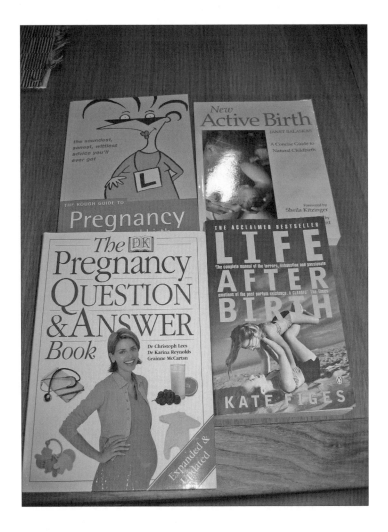

He describes how much closer he thinks he and his wife have become through having their son, and how they've bonded. Richard West also describes the birth of his daughter as an emotional awakening. Having Bethan has debunked all his earlier thoughts about not wanting children. Richard spoke of how having children is actually "nice, rewarding and makes you realise what life is all about". He describes the relationship with his wife as equal and balanced, there are no great issues about roles and responsibilities, they both do everything equally. He is very aware of the responsibilities parenthood brings, saying that whatever he does will shape Bethan's personality and the way she is in the world. It's a big responsibility, to be taken seriously, but it does mean that he and Marion don't have so much time for each other, as Bethan is the focus for both of them. They both see it as the price they pay for the reward of bringing up Bethan.

Tina Miller's research on fatherhood (Miller, 2010) notes how fathers-to-be are inevitably cast as onlookers to some extent, as less involved in the pregnancy, even if encouraged by their partners. They cannot experience the changes, bodily and otherwise, experienced by their partners, and find their role more in undertaking physically harder activities, like assembling and decorating a nursery for the baby. They may accompany their partner to antenatal classes, but tend not to read the literature. They look forward to making an attachment with the baby, but not the messy bits. Miller says that pregnancy for men can be 'an "inbetween time" when nothing physical is actually happening to them but they feel a sense of change or that they should change and/or impending significant change in their lives'. It doesn't change their lives, nor is it a frequent topic of conversation when they get together with male friends. They look at the growing 'bump from outside, they can touch it, feel the baby kick, or even try and distinguish a heartbeat'. Miller's account resonates with the perspective of Jamie Fortune, who describes his partner's pregnancy as a "strange process" characterised by alternating nervousness and excitement. While Monica got bigger and bigger – luxuriating in her pregnancy bloom – he "just stayed the same". It was not until Monica and the baby returned home and he was holding his son that "Boom – you first feel love for him". Jamie is aware that a nostalgic reconnection with his early childhood and his own father are part of his identification with his son. He comments wryly that "it helps when they look like you", observing that "it's a revelation really. This is me, a bit younger and unsoiled."

Books

The contradictory nature of advice available to new mothers is most evident in the best-selling guide books. That babies don't come with a manual remains a cliché of everyday discourse. Advice on how to be a mother is big business and an enduring site of struggle. Fashions, authors and practices ebb and flow. Indeed, in some cases it may be possible to guess the year a woman became a mother by asking her what books she read while pregnant. Whether it is *Breast is Best* or *The Fabulous Mum's Handbook*, the unfolding story is one of proliferating and diffuse voices of authority. The abundance of books aimed at pregnant women suggests an increasing diversity, fragmentation and the absence of consensus on the whole maternal project. Late-modern perspectives may point to the struggle for meaning across texts as indicative of choice, reflecting the pluralism of new times. The incitement to discourse, in Foucaultian terms, however, can be seen as regulatory, productive of new and creative forms of surveillance and control. Some women like Eleanor were particularly attuned to the disciplinary effects of advice literature, though at other moments they may invoke a knowing and agentic choice narrative:

> "You look for the sort of advice you feel comfortable with … I mean everyone that I know who has babies about the same age as me lies to their health visitor about something (laughs), sleeping in bed with them, weaning, you know, something." (Eleanor, 26)

The most popular books among the women we surveyed were the information-heavy *What to Expect When You're Expecting* and a series of guides written by Miriam Stoppard (*Conception, Pregnancy and Birth*, 2005 and *The New Pregnancy and Birth*, 2004). Yet women had relatively little to say about these texts, other than that they were useful and comprehensive. The two books that most featured in women's accounts were *The Baby Whisperer* and *The Contented Little Baby Book*. As polar opposites of different child development traditions, they acquired symbolic significance for women who read them. Gina Ford's *The Contented Little Baby Book*, first published in 1999, reinstates the importance of routine for babies. Following Truby King, Ford recommends that mothers settle babies into a sleeping and feeding schedule within weeks of birth. The aim is to establish a pattern of three-to-four-hourly feeds, ending at 10pm and beginning again at 6am the next day. As Ford explains:

> Routines teach you to recognise the difference between hunger and tiredness and how to listen to what your baby is really saying. They are all about providing your baby with security and comfort, giving him what he wants before he needs to cry and demand it, and the result is a contented little baby who is likely to sleep the longest spell at night at around six to ten weeks. You'll also be able to claim a little time back for yourself, which will help you enjoy the experience of parenthood much, much more. It has worked for hundreds of thousands of parents all over the world and it can work for you too – I promise. (www.contentedbaby.com, accessed 17 August 2010)

In a move that runs counter to baby-centred, feed-on-demand practices embraced by feminists in the post-Spock era, Ford advocates structure that is determined by real time and instigated by mothers. The idea that mothers can 'claim a little time back' suggests a baby–me tug-of-war for individual space that challenges the selfless devotion of other methods, echoing the grandmotherly warning about the dangers of holding babies too much. Ford also advocates leaving babies to cry for up to an hour to train them out of expecting to be picked up. The contented baby idea outlined in Ford's first book has grown into a babycare empire. There are more books, products, a website and an online community of followers. Critics of Ford are quick to point out that her babycare credentials are slight; she has no formal qualifications and no children. Consolidating her status as 'easily the most popular baby care guru of the new century' (Hardyment, 2007, p 292), Ford's approach inevitably generates controversy, notably from members of the internet website Mumsnet and, more recently from deputy Prime Minister Nick Clegg, who described her routine as 'absolute nonsense'. After many critiques, parodies and a posting on Mumsnet amusingly suggesting that Ford 'strapped babies to rockets and fired them into south Lebanon', she took legal action to ban the site from discussing her methods.

Women we spoke to also expressed strong feelings about the contented baby approach, one respondent describing Ford as a "baby Nazi" whose methods appear to invite pastiche:

> "It's all timetabled [Ford's methods]. Oh it's horrible, horrible, like 6.51am you should get dressed in your heels and make up ready to feed your baby at 6.52 and make sure your baby is awake at 6.52. It's just not me." (Deborah, 33)

The other book frequently referred to, *The Baby Whisperer*, appears to occupy less controversial territory. Written by midwife Tracey Hogg and first published in 1988, *The Baby Whisperer* encourages mothers to approach babycare from the perspective of babies themselves. How to read your baby's signals becomes a starting point for the development of routines that respond to the needs of babies rather than seeking to impose a regime on them. Like Ford, Hogg describes her approach as simple and even brands it as the EASY routine, based on a common-sense pattern of eating, activity, sleep and your time. Having read both books, Clara (40) comments:

> "*The Baby Whisperer* is just interesting about how you can get different personalities of babies into some sort of semi-structure and be flexible given their type. But because it would help my partner because he LOVES routine, it would help him if he knew there was some sort of pattern to things. I would never be able to follow a '6.15 is when you the feed' sort of thing … But it would be nice to know that maybe over time there's some sort of pattern of sleep or feeding or whatever … to ensure that he [partner] doesn't feel like the whole, everything about us, has been taken over by the baby."

Clara's reflections raise the question, 'Who are routines for?'. Apart from the obvious need to make sense of postpartum chaos, mother–baby routines may be established to serve people and practices beyond the dyad. In this example, the desires and expectations of her partner become an important reference point; for other women, work schedules, childcare arrangements and financial resources may play a part in decisions relating to the early care of babies. Christina Hardyment observes that Ford and Hogg, the two best-selling experts of the age, were both trained as maternity nurses. She suggests mischievously 'that women have fallen in droves for the seductive idea of being in themselves the maternity nurses they can't afford. Their methods also envisage baby adapting to a mother's absence easily because his or her routine can remain unaltered under a carer' (Hardyment, 2007, p 325). There is a sense in which these two texts exist in conversation for contemporary mothers – revealing the strains of working motherhood and contributing to a form of intensification that combines the lingering spectres of the rejecting and the over-protective mother. What is currently being called 'intensive mothering' (Hays, 1998) is a charge generally laid against absent (that is, working) mothers who are acutely conscious of what their children may be missing – and thus seek to replace or compensate for this through professional input. It is a model that fits with Arlie Hochschild's understanding of the commercialisation of the domestic that has followed women's transitions into the workforce, and which set new standards that are beyond what any stay-at-home mother could achieve. Within this logic, then, it makes sense for women to imagine themselves as the maternity nurses that they cannot afford, consuming contradictory advice which echoes powerfully with their own experiences of being parented, as well as fantasies of social mobility.

Mothers as 'organic experts'

Judy recognises how advice can change over time. Her own mother advised her to swaddle Debbie on her side to make her more comfortable. Yet six years later by the time she had her second daughter there was a greater fear of cot death which made her "paranoid", so she refrained from swaddling and put her on her tummy to sleep which she now recognises is not seen as good for the baby. She has "held back" from giving Debbie advice because "things have altered so much" and "there is nothing worse than giving old fashioned advice". Judy feels that she was influenced by the "fashions" when she was a mother and regrets not breastfeeding Debbie because at the time it was not the done thing. Judy's main source of advice was a booklet given to her by the hospital She did also have a book which gave advice on the timetabling of feeding, sleeping etc. and feels she has less of an "enquiring mind" than her daughter although she has learnt so much from Debbie's research (Rickards – case history extract).

Grandmother Judy reflects on her maternal practice as formed in the confluence of time and place. Responding to intergenerational advice, changing medical opinion and current fashion, Judy recognises that motherhood is reconfigured by successive generations of new mothers. Alongside dalliances with professional childcare experts, we found women building up their own local networks for advice and support. Invoking the idea of mothers as 'organic experts' gestures towards the everyday meaning-making of 'organic intellectuals' (Gramsci, 1971) whose experience is grounded in an understanding of local conditions that make change possible. Many women consumed the commercially available advice literature while establishing parental practices in relationships close to home. Making sense of neighbourhood networks and local knowledge in the development of a closely observed account of what works, new mothers generate a personally blended and contextually specific form of expertise that is suited to their experience and personal circumstances. For some women, this involved a search for new contours of community, establishing connections with groups in the neighbourhood such as the National Childbirth Trust and yoga classes for mothers-to-be, in the hope of extending their network of fellow travellers. Crucially, women valued the advice of family and friends who had children and commonly gathered together a coterie of those they trusted emotionally.

Many women cited their own mothers as important in the development of their maternal identity, even when the relationship was troubled, distant or absent. For some women, their mother became an example of how not to do it, seeing her as representing the residual trace of an older generation whose advice was no longer relevant. Pregnancy could produce powerful feelings of dis-identification with their own mother, though they usually conceded that successfully reaching adulthood was testament to their mother's good-enough parenting. A more benign version of this acknowledges the fragility and impermanence of human experience:

> "I was talking to my mum, although it's quite interesting, you realise people forget pregnancy so quickly. It's a long time since my mum was pregnant and she's forgotten loads of things. I mentioned Braxton Hicks the other day and she said 'Oh are you supposed to be getting those so early?' so I had to explain and she said, 'Oh yes I remember that now but I don't think we called them that'." (Orla)

Seemingly in parallel with the acts of memory and forgetting that shape the evolution of the conception story, the experience of pregnancy and birth is also selectively remembered. The temporary nature of pregnancy exists in harmony with the temporary space it occupies in the memory as details and feelings fade over time. Other women became closer to their mother during pregnancy, identifying with her more closely as a source of knowledge that was entirely dependable as an intergenerational legacy of biology and experience. For some of the younger mothers, their mother was an important and ever-present source of support and someone who provided a template for their own mothering. While still living in the parental home, their mothers often made pregnancy and birth possible through the provision of financial and emotional resources. In these cases, new grandmothers became the uber-mummy of an expanding family that absorbed the arrival of a new baby.

Impending motherhood invited women to evaluate their experience of being mothered and to position themselves in relation to their own mothers. Eleanor's (26) experience, for example, was closely connected to her mother's style of mothering and she felt that this shaped her approach to advice and expertise:

> "Looking for this [advice] is definitely down to my mother … We had conversations but I knew, I think I must have picked it up from a thousand comments and just her general attitude. And then she gave me this Penelope Leach book and she says, 'This is what I brought you up on' and she wanted me to have it. And it's a lovely book, it's very nice, she's very much 'follow your instincts, don't let anybody tell you you're failing at something' … I would say that my mother is a far stronger influence than anything I've read. I mean, I've developed the ideas further by reading … but certainly the catalyst, the starting point was definitely the way I was mothered."

As someone who blends learning with experience to produce a unique form of praxis, Eleanor's mother achieves the status of organic childcare expert. Eleanor continues the tradition of generating organic knowledge by adding insights from her own reading. The Penelope Leach book passed on by her mother is likely to be *Your Baby and Child: From Birth to Age 5*, first published in 1977. Leach's academic background as a psychologist enabled her to interpret the Piagetian-style stages of child development for a broad audience of parents and non-academics. Her approach suggests that understanding the emotional and physical development of young children increases the confidence of parents and, in turn, the happiness of babies. Leach continues to contribute to debates on childcare, her comments acting as an anchor for child-centred, respectful and humanitarian practice. Leach is critical of the spread of contented baby-type methods, and particularly of controlled crying, saying that babies are too young to be 'naughty' and do not act with the intent that routines ascribe to them. In a new twist in the development of her ideas, Leach draws upon neuroscience to support her comments, claiming that unresponsive carers increase baby's levels of cortisol, the hormone responsible for stress. The touchstone of Leach's comments rests on her disapproval of the me-me-ness of contemporary motherhood, hitting out against women who want a baby but do not want their lives to be disrupted. Leach bluntly points out that having a baby *will* change your life (www.independent.co.uk/life-style, accessed 17 August 2010).

Eleanor extends her mother's child-centred approach by adding attachment parenting methods to a framework shaped by Penelope Leach. Bill and Martha Sears popularised the idea of attachment parenting in the *Baby Book*, first published in 1993. Their philosophy drew inspiration from the work of anthropologist Jean Liedloff (1986), who documented the mothering practices of an Amazonian community of Yequana Indians who keep their babies strapped to them continuously during infancy, until the child struggles to move away. The other reference point for attachment parenting lies in psychological studies of the 1950s. John Bowlby's attachment theory explored the emotional bond between parent and child and its impact upon the child. Emphasising the importance of the caregiver's physical presence and closeness to the baby, attachment theory was concerned with matters of secure attachment, and particularly the relationship between maternal deprivation and childhood depression. The Sears adapted these ideas in an approach that advocated the constant use of a sling to promote mother–child bonding through close physical contact. Attachment parenting involves total commitment to your baby, breastfeeding and sleeping together to enable mothers to become attuned to the needs of the child. Eleanor responds to the charge that attachment parenting is too demanding of mothers by describing how it worked for her in-home-based family business:

> "The important thing is to make sure your child is happy and cared for and knows you're there for them ... This whole baby-wearing thing, it sounds very labour-intensive but in fact your baby doesn't need your attention if he's got your physical comfort, so you can put your baby on and do whatever you were going to do ... I would work at the computer, I would do everything. Keeping to some kind of schedule seems

more labour-intensive to me than being able to bring him into the centre of your life and then carry on with it."

Attachment parenting has increased appeal for some new mothers as the idea of 'slow parenting' gains currency among a substratum of middle-class parents. As a riposte to the accelerated speed of urban life and work-based practices, slow parenting advocates country living, home cooking, de-schooling, green everything and an unhurried approach to family life that values spending time together. Although Eleanor was the only mother in our study who put herself into this category, many others identified with aspects of slow parenting as a desirable ideal to be aspired to, and possibly realised in a re-evaluation of priorities.

Sociable mothering – groups, self-help and social networking

In the UK, women's first encounter with experts during pregnancy is likely to be through the NHS professionals in their locality. Beginning with the GP, antenatal care is likely to be offered by nursing staff at the GP practice, a local centre or the local hospital. Antenatal classes in particular provide an opportunity to meet peers. Literature given to all women at this stage includes *Emma's Diary*, a maternal primer documenting 'the highs and lows of being a mum', available in hard copy and online and involving weekly e-mails to the mother-to-be. Resembling pregnancy magazines in its presentation and mode of address, *Emma's Diary* covers much of the same ground in documenting every aspect of pregnancy and birth in ways that make biological processes and medical procedures accessible. Looking beyond universal provision, women seeking a more specialised experience, and possibly a less medicalised one, may be drawn to the National Childbirth Trust (NCT). With its roots in 1950s and 1960s activism as an organisation campaigning for natural childbirth, the NCT pioneered an alternative to NHS provision by training women in natural methods to prepare for home births, breastfeeding and less medical intervention during birth. The NCT can be seen as an exemplar of successful lobbying, influencing politicians, the medical profession and changing public opinion on the experience of birth. With the exception of home birth, the original aims of the NCT, published in 1956, read as a good birth guide for contemporary times. Advocating the humane treatment of women, more 'homely and unfrightening' maternity units and the presence of husbands, the NCT established a model of good practice that disrupted the regulatory medical practice of the time and ultimately changed government policy. The NCT is now a key provider of maternity and postnatal services in the UK and a significant voice in the formulation of government policy in this field. The growing influence of the NCT can be seen as a success story for women-centred approaches to pregnancy, birth and childcare. It can also be seen as an organisation subject to hegemonic incorporation in forming a working alliance with dominant forces of policy makers and implementers. At the local level the NCT has struggled to shake off its reputation for being middle class and judgemental. From the perspective of new mothers unsure of their place in the maternal project, the NCT can appear as another disciplinary voice telling women what to do. A rich source of anxiety for women in the study was breastfeeding (see Chapter Three, Body). The NCT's proselytising approach created ripples of self-doubt and inadequacy as women in late pregnancy wondered if their bodies could live up to the ideal of 'breast is best'.

A participant who had worked for the NCT in the mid-1990s gave us a privileged insider perspective on the workings of the organisation during this period:

> "Around the time the Winterton Report and Changing Childbirth came out it was VERY much about women having choice and control in labour and delivery … Seeing the sort of dilemmas the NCT was going through – were they a NATURAL childbirth organisation whose job was to advocate home birth and normal birth rather than Caesareans? Or was their role to be telling women about the whole range of options, allowing them to be informed? The central CORE of the NCT was heading in a much more modernising way. But they had a huge volunteer base who actually ran the programmes and

they weren't necessarily taking them with them. And it was perceived to be – and actually was – a middle-class organisation. And trying to move it into a more generalist organisation and available and accessible to all was proving harder than they thought … There was a great schism about breastfeeding and whether or not they should take sponsorship from Sainsbury's because they have their own brand of formula milk … It really helped me to see that things are complicated, that people care deeply, deeply about them." (Clara)

Going back to the NCT as a client rather than a worker, Clara reflects on the evolution of the organisation from a pressure group to a mainstream provider of maternity care. She concludes that there may be a need for a radical voice on childbirth but it is more important for the NCT to occupy the central ground which changes the message but reaches more people. Her experience of antenatal care at the NCT has been overwhelmingly positive. She notes that her teacher gave a balanced account of childbirth options and "didn't make ANYONE in the class feel bad if they chose to have an epidural or chose not to breastfeed".

Outside of antenatal settings, decision making and information gathering for most women drew upon the self-help practices they developed through the internet. Many women commented on their habit of searching websites for *everything* when further information was needed – a practice that was often well established before pregnancy. Women used the internet to follow up information offered by health professionals, but they also consulted websites routinely to satisfy a curiosity or check the progress of their pregnancy. One respondent referred to this as her own instinctive brand of research, "If something happens to me, the first thing I do is go to Google (laughs)". Other women felt that the onus was on them as individuals to find out more, as health professionals were cautious and rarely provided full accounts:

"You've got to go and look for the information yourself … I suppose it's the way they've been trained, maybe they don't need to tell the patient too much … I'd rather know than not know. People say don't hear too many scary birth stories and I say at least I'm prepared, I'd rather expect the worst than go in and come out the next day and think, 'oh brilliant', I don't want that." (Lyn, 31)

Seasoned website users commented on the prevalence of commercially sponsored sites, notably Pampers, Huggies and Babycentre, sponsored by Johnson's. "They all seem to peddle the same rather bland material about how it's the most natural thing in the world," Eleanor jadedly remarks. Yet more week-by-week guides and reheated pregnancy magazine fare; however, many women found the message boards and other interactive features more exciting, as joining in or being a lurker held more immediate appeal as a fun-time activity.

A distinct genre of self-help literature can be found in the peer-generated and collectively written handbooks of the by-women-for-women tradition. Commonly a riposte to the conservatism of mainstream manuals and emerging from second-wave feminism, this style of advice literature seizes upon the potential to tell previously untold stories of women's experience. Aiming to educate and support women by raising awareness of women's health issues, the most celebrated example remains *Our Bodies, Ourselves* by the Boston Women's Health Book Collective. First published in 1973 and now in its 12th edition, the book has become a global success story of feminist endeavour, marked by the publication of a book about the making of *Our Bodies, Ourselves* (Davis, 2007). Judy Norsigian, Executive Director of the Boston Women's Health Book Collective reflects on the 'knowledge gap' filled by the book:

> About 40 years ago there was very little information in lay language and we had to turn to healthcare providers and mostly our doctors to get information and there was terrible sexism, paternalism and condescension within medicine … [asking questions] was always considered inappropriate. You were always speaking out of turn. So we had to educate ourselves. (http@//bigthink.com. ideas/20147, accessed 23 August 2010)

Putting into action the radical premise that women are the best experts on their own bodies, the Collective ran community courses to increase self-knowledge in all matters of health and well-being. The Collective explicitly set out to change women's relationship to healthcare professionals from demure subjects to assertive and informed actors. Its writing on pregnancy and birth has much in common with NCT approaches; however, its agenda has always been broader. The Boston Women's Health Book Collective remains committed to the politics of promoting women's health across the life course. A recent initiative to address the inappropriate influence of the pharmaceutical industry over doctors' prescribing practices suggests that it has not run of ideas or energy.

'Our Bodies, Ourselves': a landmark in sociable mothering

In contrast to the activist model pursued by The Boston Women's Health Book Collective but branded in a similar way, a recent addition to the self-help stable is Mumsnet. Created 10 years ago by Justine Roberts and Carrie Longton, the London-based website has an extensive online presence and 850,000 members. With its groovy logo and the strap-line *by parents for parents*, Mumsnet, at first glance, appears to be a support group for that less-than-radical of social categories – families. The home page is full of campaigning issues to draw parents in: Labour Party leadership hustings; the sexualisation of girls; doctors should be more involved in pregnancy care (www.mumsnet.com, accessed 20 August 2010). A closer look suggests the site may be more concerned with products and protection issues: DryNite nappies; camp sites and tents; Ford Galaxy summer cinema tickets; recipes; BHS back-to-school vouchers; online safety. Parents-to-be find an ovulation calendar and a baby name finder. A final feature offers parents guidance on choosing schools. Signalling its growing influence, Mumsnet has been courted by politicians as a vote-catching site, while its creators enjoy the metropolitan lifestyle of networking in high circles. First-time Mumsnetters will need plenty of time to navigate the pages of news, politics, travel and holiday information, campaign features, detailed *Which?* magazine-style product reviews and the expansive, woefully serious and wildly ironic Mumsnet Talk discussion board. Under headings such as 'Am I being unreasonable?' members post messages scorched by the flammable content of their lives. The posts and their responses leave a trail of combustible commentary:

> My ex-husband [we aren't divorced] has fallen for the oldest trick in the book and is now a father-to-be – not entirely from choice and not entirely willingly. She told him she had a special machine that stopped her becoming pregnant ... words fail me. How do I deal with this gracefully? We did not have children as he categorically didn't want any; he's middle-aged and is desperate with anxiety about the future as he barely knew the girl when she announced her pregnancy. He is doing all the right things; what can I do to support him? His happiness is

of paramount importance to me and watching him deal with a situation he did not choose is very difficult. Help.

Special machine lol. I am sorry but how did he fall for that and how did she have the brass neck to suggest something so stupid.

Doesn't sound gullible to me – sounds quite manipulative actually. Wants the freedom to come and go and have sex when and with whom he chooses while he knows that you're still sitting there waiting to accommodate him – no strings attached.

I'd like one of those special machines.

Don't you think it's more likely that he has cooked up the machine story to avoid Mummy being Cross? And still you place his happiness as paramount.

Have a thought for the baby which deserves a father who is an adult, not one who has all his decisions excused for him on the basis that he is a diddums.

You sound like a right twat, tbh. He *chose* to stick his dick in, unprotected, and the pregnancy that resulted is 50% his responsibility.

I don't get why you even *care*.

Dunno about your ex falling for the oldest trick in the book.... you seem to have fallen for the oldest line in the book ... (www.mumsnet.com, accessed 20 August 2010)

Browsing Mumsnet feels like a pornographic experience, generating a scopophilic rush that is dirty and compelling at the same time. Journalists are to be found rekindling the vicarious high in reprints of discussion threads in the national press, the most visible being the *Daily Mail* column 'This Week on Mumsnet'. As a resource born of new times, the Mumsnet blend of politics, relationships and parenting presents a hyper-real display of the obscenity of middle-class sensibilities. Unsurprisingly, it provides a rich source of parody for its critics. At times, however, the critiques appear to take on the quality of pastiche, as in the following example of one disappointed Mumsnetter speaking out about the bullying on the site:

What dismays me is how cliquey and spiteful some users of the website have become – and the relentless finger-wagging by a cabal of sanctimonious bossy boots on the discussion boards who consider it their duty to comb messages for evidence of heterodoxy … Mumsnet has played a huge part in my life since I became a mother three years ago … When, a few days before I was due to give birth, my doula (birthing assistant) baled out on me, leaving me facing the prospect of giving birth alone, Mumsnetters on the pregnancy discussion board rallied, finding me a wonderful replacement in a matter of hours. (Oakeshott, 2010)

The extended responsibilities parents now have for the education of their children is another area where development in the range of advice literature for parents can be seen. A range of educational games and accessories are available to support the idea that parents should begin in infancy to boost their baby's IQ. Inevitably these products involve creating a regular time commitment and developing a disciplined approach to learning within what may be an already overloaded pre-school childcare schedule. Evidence provided by brain scans lends further support to early learning, suggesting that babies' grey cells need stimulating and that parents can play a key role in making their children brighter, smarter and more advanced. The quest for self-improvement rests with parents and begins in week one, or, as Baby Einstein suggests, 'It's never too early to start discovering'. The Baby Einstein company draws upon an assemblage of science, education and parental aspiration to promote its products:

Baby Einstein offers a wide range of developmentally appropriate products for babies and toddlers. What makes Baby Einstein products unlike any other is that they are created from a baby's point-of-view and incorporate a unique combination of real world objects, music, art, language, poetry and nature – providing you an opportunity to introduce your baby to the world around them in playful and enriching ways. This simple principle is the foundation for The Baby Einstein Company and its products.

Parents become charged with the technologies of the self that will launch their child into the world. Women in our study who worked as professionals in medicine or education appeared aware of their responsibility in this respect, adding to the range of expert discourses that shaped their parental practice:

> "Working as a medical professional, I think everyone would expect me to turn my child into some sort of neurological experiment or something (laughs). And I do try to be realistic, although I do find myself succumbing to the commercial things that one has to have, like the developmental mobile and Baby Einstein this, that and the other thing.... I think children will survive but there's no doubt that you can give them a good start. I try to take a moderate line really. I've ordered 125 Baby Brain Games to play with your baby but that's as far as I would go." (Alex, 34)

The situation

Throughout the book we have attempted to understand new motherhood as a situation that is constituted in different ways yet which also constitutes solidarities and commonalities. We have argued that age has become an organising category through which normative notions of mothering are constituted, with a powerful discourse of efficient biographical planning incorporating social class and mediating differences of sexuality, ethnicity and disability. Yet age is rarely spoken about explicitly within the texts of new motherhood. Instead, a more subtle message is communicated in which becoming a mother is posed as the centre of a female-choice biography, associated with the challenge of synchronising the couple and career, and the capacity to enact parenthood through consumption. Those women in our study who constructed motherhood as part of an explicit project of self tended to have highly developed narratives about the kind of mother that they wanted to be, which included drawing (often ironically) on popular cultural resources. The 'choices' that women presented themselves as having appeared to focus on a series of binary divides between: natural and medical births (often associated with a commitment to either the NCT or NHS antenatal classes); either child- or adult-centred parenting (exemplified by the choice between *The Baby Whisperer* and Gina Ford's 'Contented Baby'). Although women of all ages and backgrounds drew strategically on the 'common culture' of mothering, it was women in the 26–35 age group who tended to position themselves in relation to these distinctions. In this final section we reflect on how women are positioned differently towards the common culture of motherhood.

Kate, who is expecting her first baby at 31, can be understood as typical in many ways of the middle age group of mothers, in the way that she orients to expert advice. Part of the process is to connect to new social networks, given that until her maternity leave she has worked full time and she and her husband have no family living in the vicinity. She explains:

> "I've signed up for all these like Pampers websites, they keep sending me stuff now, you know. And Mumsnet, that's quite good, sort of – I don't really sort of contribute to it, but it makes me feel quite secure that there's lots of people going through the same thing. And then um – and then I've got – I've bought loads of books as well, nice little baby books. (laughs)"

As an early years teacher, Kate has significant 'expert knowledge' herself, which she must accommodate alongside her inexperience. The interviewer observes a whole shelf of books on child development:

> *Interviewer:* Hmm I was just looking up there, you've got … (interrupted)

> *Kate:* I mean some of that's work stuff as well but um (.) yeah I bought a few. They were like the kind of most useful ones I found.

Kate has selected several books that reflect her preparations for motherhood. The way that she talks about these texts with the interviewer suggests the ways in which expectant mothers operate as readers, using books as a means to create an imaginative space for the changes that are coming and as experimental forays into the ways in which social class is encoded into distinctive mothering cultures.

Expectant mothers as creative readers

Interviewer: Are these the ones that you've found useful?

Kate: They're the ones that I've read the most, yeah.

Interviewer: What do you think of this one, *What Mothers Do?*

Kate: I think that's my favourite one. I mean I haven't read it all yet, but um – and I've signed up to join the mothers' talking group at the Active Birth Centre, that's brilliant that place.

Interviewer: Yeah, have you been there for classes?

Kate: I just went there once for a breastfeeding talk. And I just thought it was absolutely wonderful. I mean it was a fair few quid but, you know, I sort of got there, and it was when I was still working, and there was all these beanbags and cushions, and I thought, 'This is fantastic'. And we were just lolling around talking about breastfeeding, and it was really nice. I keep meaning to go back there. And that's when I came back with this ball as well, you know, and the cushion, the breastfeeding cushion.

Interviewer: They have nice things in the shops there.

Kate: Yeah I spent about 100 quid or something. (laughs) And I was just like, 'This is great, I love it,' you know. But um yeah I put my name down, I think it's Friday morning or something, and you just sit and talk.

Interviewer: Is that once you've had the baby?

Kate: Yeah about sort of six to eight weeks after you've had it they'll contact you. So it's good because you can just dip into it. And um (.) I mean obviously I think it's quite middle-classy, in a way, you can tell, you know, 'My husband had an important barrister case,' or something, that sort of thing. (laughs) But um it's – it's very human, and very kind of – and I often read that when I wake up in the night, and I come in here and just have a read, you know, try not to wake up my husband, (laughs) you know. Um so that's been great. It's quite comforting and reassuring. And this has – this has been quite good.

Interviewer: What to Expect When You're Expecting.

Kate: Although it's a little bit – it's a bit American in that it's very, very health conscious and – and they say slightly different things to the Miriam Stoppard.

Interviewer: What do you use this one for?

Kate: Um it just had loads of questions, it's got all these questions. You know, and just um it's got like a monthly thing – roughly you should be feeling like this. So it's been more sort of practical things really.

Interviewer: Yeah. And *Birth to Work*?

Kate: And that was really good, that was for work more. But um that was just really – it's just really interesting, really a lot of um – it was more about um babies in day care settings and stuff. But it's made me think a lot about sort of childcare and – for later (laughs) you know – scary.

Interviewer: Yeah (?) *Why Love Matters.*

Kate: Hmm, hmm that's a fantastic one. Yeah I've seen her, she did a talk at one of the courses I was on, and that was really good, I found that quite um emotional to read actually (laughs) as well. But um (.)

In this fragment of conversation we can see the complexity of Kate's relationship with what we might call 'expert advice', including the ways in which texts can link to communities, spaces, both intimate and public. In reading, reflecting and rejecting Kate is working through the complexity of her biographical position – seeing herself in comparison to other kinds of mothers and rethinking herself through her own expert gaze. To see oneself and one's dilemmas reflected back through cultural representations may be both anxiety provoking and affirming, and not all mothers look to expert advice for guidance or recognition. Young mothers tended not to read pregnancy magazines or books, citing soap operas, family and friends as helping them make sense of their situation. For some of the youngest mothers in our study alternative learning environments offered a rich source of advice, and these sites in turn mediated more traditional expert discourses, making them accessible and attractive – for example, using pregnancy magazines as a kind of pedagogic practice.

Some young mothers in the study were accessed through a project that provides programmes to support young women (age 15–18) who are pregnant or have a young child. The project has been running for 20 years, offering a range of courses and community initiatives to support young people. Its principles include 'a focus on groups in the margins' and 'a commitment to deliver the highest possible standards, so as to challenge low self esteem, raise expectations and enable our trainees to take significant steps forward in their lives'. Funded by the Learning and Skills Council and the European Social Fund at the time of the research, its emphasis is not on formal educational qualifications. Rather, the course offers a range of activities and training sessions such as parenting classes, relaxation classes, literacy and numeracy classes and support with CVs and job applications. The focus is upon practical learning and skills development that prepares young people for parenthood in direct ways. Young people attending the course reported feeling supported in an environment that sought to meet their needs. Sophie, 17 and expecting her first child, looks to the project as a source of support and an alternative site of learning. When her parents found out she was pregnant they asked Sophie to leave home. At the same time her boyfriend broke up with her. Sophie described this period as a "rubbish" time in her life. She moved into a mother-and-baby unit run by the council, and through staff at the unit she found out about and began attending the project. She speaks of the course in the following way:

> "All different ones [professionals] come to project. Baby massaging people came in and we've had Indian head massage and Bollywood dancing, art and craft where you can make your first baby's picture frame … It's given me so much more confidence … I think all the girls there feel that kind of confidence … And it makes you feel much more knowledgeable … Going to the project is

the best thing I think I could have done. And I think
that's easily – that's better than my GCSE grades, going
there and learning absolutely everything that you can
learn about – everything from labour to breastfeeding
to child development."

Sophie's comments indicate that, far from signalling the end of
education usually associated with young motherhood, pregnancy
has heralded the start of a whole new learning process that she has
eagerly embraced (Rudoe, 2011). The education of young mothers
is a sensitive and controversial subject that commonly touches upon
a moral agenda shaped by ideas about teenage sex, single parenthood
and public resources. Intertwined with this moral agenda is a clearly
discernible class dynamic. As Walkerdine et al (2001) point out,
teenage pregnancy is largely a working-class affair. Of the 20,000
under-18-year-olds who become mothers every year, the majority
are more likely to be working class and disaffected from school.
For middle-class girls, however, pregnancy is usually regarded as
a disruption in the education process and a barrier to educational
success. Indeed, the goal of a professional career 'acts as a contraceptive
for middle-class girls' (Walkerdine et al, 2001, p 194).

Viewing expert advice as part of the common culture of
motherhood illustrates the significance of age and the fragmentation
of generational cohorts based on shared life experiences. The
abundance of advice across different media, available in a range of
formats, speaks most clearly to the 26–35 age group as experienced
consumers, well rehearsed in the ways of the market and the
significance of choice and taste. Keen to integrate motherhood into a
biographical project of self, this group of women assimilated features
of the common culture, creating a convergence between practices of
consumption and maternal identities. By contrast, other age groups
demonstrated less fluency in the common culture of motherhood,
either having less access to the fruits of it as younger mothers, or
feeling dislocated from it as older mothers.

Conclusion

The post-war period has been marked by the proliferation of expert discourses on motherhood and childcare and the changing status of the expert in women's lives. Early 20th-century manuals spoke with authority and prioritised efficiency, telling women to run their homes like a small company. By the end of the century, advice manuals for women were more concerned with the psychological domain, paying attention to the unconscious world of desire and affect that assumes importance in mother–child relations. The shift in focus to matters of interiority runs parallel with other key developments – the declining authority of the expert and the breakdown of a cultural consensus on motherhood and childcare generally. The early care of children continues to be a publicly contested issue in which different models of babycare come to represent competing forms of personhood for both mothers and babies.

Our study illustrates the many ways in which women use expert advice to imagine their way into motherhood. Drawing on a diverse range of expertise, from best-selling books to local and virtual resources, new mothers negotiated a pathway through the common culture of motherhood in a quest to find their own place in the maternal project. The increased availability of advice through digital technology offers women more 'choice', but also potentially more pressure as domestic space is commercialised in ways that re-evaluate what mothers can achieve. Engaging with advice literature and different forms of expertise may entail encounters with class-coded and value-laden approaches, requiring some affective manoeuvring. Blending and personalising advice become ways of managing information, containing contradiction and ascribing authority to the self as organic expert at the centre of a unique female choice biography. Intergenerational perspectives reveal the contingent nature of advice literature and maternal practice as subject to fashion in the constantly reconfiguring politics of motherhood. Finally, it is important to bear in mind the age-specific relationship to expertise as a cultural phenomenon that speaks to and resonates with the concerns of 26- to 35-year-old women as receptive late-modern subjects in whom motherhood is central to a female choice biography constituted through the synchronisation of coupledom, career and consumption.

Notes

[1] In the total questionnaire sample of 144 the most popular source of advice was the doctor, with 87.8% (115) of respondents seeking advice from their doctor; 74.8% (98) took advice from their mother or family members; 52.7 % (69) took advice from friends; 39.7% (52) took advice from pregnancy magazines; 42% (55) took advice from internet websites. The least popular source of advice is advice leaflets: 38.9% (51). In the interview sample of 62 the most popular source of advice was the doctor, with 51 respondents seeking advice from their doctor; 36 took advice from their mother or family members; 35 took advice from friends; 23 took advice from their partner; 26 took advice from pregnancy magazines; 27 took advice from internet websites. The least popular source of advice was advice leaflets (26).

[2] This sector of the magazine market is well developed in the UK, supporting a range of titles, produced monthly and with circulation figures of over 50,000 for the more popular magazines. This chapter draws upon the popular and commonly available magazines in this sector over an 18-month period from September 2004 to April 2006. A total of 28 magazines and 8 titles were surveyed: *Prima Baby and Pregnancy, Pregnancy, It's the Time of Your Life, Pregnancy and Birth, Junior Pregnancy and Baby, Mother and Baby, I'm Pregnant, Baby and You, Practical Parenting.* Magazines were bought and analysed in parallel with the 18 months' fieldwork period.

[3] www.independent.co.uk/life-style, accessed 17 August 2010.

SIX

Work

Unless you're a celeb A-lister, it's likely you'll spend most of your pregnancy working. (*Pregnancy and Birth*, September 2004)

While reading and watching representations of motherhood in the popular media during this study, we noticed what a careful path the pregnancy and mothering magazines steer through the perilous waters of employment. As the words of *Pregnancy and Birth* above suggest, work is a landscape against which motherhood gains meaning. Yet, despite the centrality of work to most women's biographies, and the proliferation of debate over working mothers in the broadsheet and tabloid press and blogosphere (Hadfield et al, 2007; Franklin, 2008), it is not the subject of extensive discussion in the magazine. Poised on the cusp of new parenthood, welcoming successive waves of women into the fold, the magazines do not dwell on the complications of childcare and the emotional and financial practicalities of sharing and delegating care. Typically, articles avoid a direct focus on work status, emphasising values and styles of parenting. Over a two-year period we found just four articles explicitly addressing work: *Junior's* analysis of Generation Z's search for 'pure hybrid equal parenting'; *Mother and Baby's* debate on 'Working mums – for or against'; *I'm Pregnant's* investigation of 'Who will look after your baby?' when you go back to work; and *Prima Baby's* 'Work/life balance – dealing with guilt'. It is as though the wage-slave working mother is too tired and torn for the upbeat tone that infuses the magazines. In contrast, the home-based 'Mumtrepreneur' is a favourite. Showcased in regular slots such as 'Business mum of the month' (*Mother and Baby*, April 2006) and 'Big women in business' (*Pregnancy, Baby and You*, August 2005), she reassures the reader that she too could make a business out of her mothering – generally by marketing or making a new 'must have' item for women like her – and still 'be there' for her children.[1]

The real angst about work emerges in the letters pages and special Q&A opportunities for working mothers. Here we encounter the voices of women scared to take time off for antenatal appointments, unclear as to their eligibility for sick and holiday leave, worried about the health of their unborn child and uncertain as to whether they have the right to withhold knowledge of a pregnancy to existing or prospective employers.[2] This is the real yet hidden politics of pregnancy at work.

Motherhood can be a critical moment in the making of gendered biographies and in the negotiation of a gendered division of labour within a couple and a household. In this chapter we use 'work' as a lens through which to encounter new motherhood. We begin by contextualising our discussion of working motherhood in relation to the academic literature before moving on to showcase the findings of our empirical study. Initially, we draw on interviews conducted with women at the end of their pregnancies which capture something of the emergent collision of working and maternal identities. Like the 'letters pages' of the magazines, we reveal women's experiences of being pregnant at work, including the kinds of deliberations they were going through in anticipating and managing maternity leave. In the second part of the chapter we present four contrasting case studies which animate the personal dramas involved in reconciling working and maternal commitments. Here we trace how women's feelings about work change over time and how they negotiated a division of labour with partners, family and the market. The case studies are akin to the 'features' section of the magazine, and we have borrowed titles to reinforce this connection – real-life stories of how women manage to be both 'good enough' mothers and workers. As Sue Sharpe observed in her 1984 book on working mothers, 'full-time mothering has never been accessible to all women in the same way at the same time' (Sharpe, 1984, p 22). Social class, locality and migration shape a range of cultures of mothering within which work features very differently. Divisions exist between women who share a generational location as well as between women of different generations. In this chapter we attempt to capture something of this complexity by juxtaposing the voices of mothers and grandmothers, suggesting that, paradoxically, work may serve to both divide and unite women in the project of motherhood.

Work and social change

Ever increasing levels of female employment, including of mothers with dependent children, have been a distinctive feature of post-war British society, paralleled by an overall improvement in living standards, and yet a rise in inequality. The 'family wage' that was consolidated during the second half of the 19th century began to unravel in the later decades of the 20th, giving way to dual-earner households and a slow and incomplete convergence in male and female pay (Ferri and Smith, 2003). Much of the continuing disparity between the earnings of men and women can be explained by the 'motherhood penalty', which has been estimated to diminish women's average earning capacity by one-fifth (Davies et al, 2000). In comparison to other developed economies, the UK has high levels of female employment but low levels of subsidised childcare; a survey of seven industrialised countries found that the UK had the highest motherhood pay penalty[3] (Harkness and Waldfogel, 1999). Mothers are far more likely than fathers to take time out from paid work or to work part time in order to care for their children, with more highly skilled women much more likely to return to work after the birth of a child and lower-skilled women being more likely to stay at home (Crompton, 2006, p 46). The campaign organisation the Fawcett Society sums this up as follows: 'becoming a parent marks the start of the great divide between women's and men's pay. Motherhood has a direct and dramatic influence on women's pay and employment prospects, and typically this penalty lasts a lifetime' (Woodroffe, 2009).

The cultural significance of these social changes has been characterised in terms of labour having become *feminised* (increasingly precarious and communication based) and women having become *labourised* (considered as workers first and as mothers second) (Power, 2009). Education and work are now ubiquitous features of the individualised female biography, with the acquisition of qualifications creating new gender divisions between women and men. Young women are outperforming boys at school and university and taking up many of the new places created by the expansion of higher education. Consequently, the social divisions that matter for the young are increasingly those constituted around poverty and qualifications rather than around gender, sexuality or race. Angela McRobbie captures this change through the idea of a post-feminist sexual contract, which celebrates educationally successful young women as the active and aspirational subjects of social change. Extended periods of education and work on an apparently level playing field delay motherhood for the majority. By the time they encounter the motherhood penalty, they may find themselves without the political and cultural resources of feminism. McRobbie argues that 'How successful the individual heterosexual woman might be in achieving equality in relation to domestic labour and childcare then becomes a private affair, or rather evidence that she has chosen well from the range of possible partners, her life-plan in this regard has worked to her advantage' (McRobbie, 2007, p 18).

It is little surprise, then, that the contemporary politics of motherhood are fragmented and privatised, played out through a splitting of destinies on the grounds of consumption, age and choice. Academic debates over working parenthood are also caught up in this maelstrom, with attempts to guide policy according to women's 'preferences' for home or work (Hakim, 2000) criticised for failing to capture the political, economic and cultural contexts in which 'choices' are made (Gatrell, 2005; Crompton, 2006; Armstrong, 2010). For those such as Adkins, mass female employment and the socialisation and commodification of childcare are a sign of the end of the patriarchal order as we knew it (Adkins, 2009), associated with a gendered division of labour within a private sphere. The divisions that should most matter now for feminists are between women.

Work in biographical perspective

The women in our research approached motherhood at very different stages in their biographies. The youngest were still in secondary education, and experienced pregnancy either as a disruption to that education and associated career plans or as a different pathway to maturity and responsibility than that promised by the extended forms of youth associated with further and higher education. For some, the experience of being pregnant had given them insight into new possibilities, encouraging an interest in midwifery and childcare as potential areas of training and work. Others, like Kim, significantly downscaled their ambitions in the face of new motherhood, drawing on the support provided by a young mothers' project to rework a dream of being a lawyer into a pragmatic plan to train as a florist. The oldest of our new mothers tended to be well established in their careers and in a position to privilege motherhood over work, or at least to control their work in such a way that they could exercise a high level of choice in regard to how they managed the relationship between parenting and career. For 40-year-old Pauline it meant having the confidence to ignore the disapproval of her sister and leave a job as a nursery manager, embarking on motherhood without work and supported by benefits. Older mothers were more able than most to make their work fit around their mothering rather than vice versa. In the middle age group, women's attitudes towards combining work and motherhood were shaped in large part by the nature of their work, including how well they were paid, whether or not they understood themselves as being in a career and the extent to which it was possible to disrupt this career path.

Of the 62 women whom we interviewed in late pregnancy, 47 were in work, 8 were students[4] and 7 were unemployed. Overall, we classified 36 women as falling within a lower middle-class category, 21 as working class and just 5 as upper middle class. The kinds of work that women were involved in were diverse, spanning public and private sectors as well as salaried and self-employment. Occupation did not map neatly onto our judgement of social class positions, being complicated by factors including migration and the occupation and resources of partners and families. However, it is our contention that the kind of paid work that women were involved in shaped their experience of motherhood significantly.

It doesn't have to hurt your business

Our interviews were generally conducted during the later stages of pregnancy, once women had begun their maternity leave from work.

Pregnant in the workplace

Relax, this doesn't have to hurt your business one bit.

In April 2003, working laws changed to benefit employers as well as their employees. Mothers can take 6 months paid maternity leave and up to 6 months more unpaid leave if they want it, and fathers get weeks paid paternity leave." To help with cash flow, employers can now claim statutory maternity and

Conversations about work were prompted by an image taken from a national newspaper and gave rise to a range of reactions. Here we contrast four responses that illustrate something of the diversity of women's work situations as they approach motherhood.

Emily, a 33-year-old nursery teacher, had no intention of returning to teaching for several years, and she read the image as follows:

"Poor woman, she should be sitting down having a cup of tea, or at home at that stage, not commuting in to work and putting the extra stress ... she's sat on a train, or stood up on a train cos no one will give her a seat, she's gone through pregnancy absolutely knackered and then she's feeling a bit guilty as well that the business is having to give her money and she's having to take time off work and ... well no, we need the next generation!"

Alice, a 32-year-old fundraiser, interpreted the image as representing "the business woman, being pregnant and still being at work". In her view, "there should be more advertisements about it. I mean the magazines are fantastic, BUT ... you don't read much about it in sort of recruitment papers or anything like that. And I still think it's a concern now, that if somebody is pregnant and they're walking into an interview, that there's 99% of them thinking, 'I'm not gonna get the job because I'm pregnant'."

A quite different response came from 32-year-old teacher Jessica, who had struggled with the decision to give up her work and to dedicate herself to home making. She responded defensively to the image:

"So she's actually at work is she? Yeah I mean, you know, I agree with that. I think, you know, again each to their own. I mean I – you know, I was working until three weeks ago ... And um so yeah, I mean I – I suppose I'm still, like I said earlier, a bit old fashioned. I suppose once you've had the baby I think you should – I think you owe it – I think you – you owe it to yourself and to the baby to just at least give it some time."

The response of unemployed 27-year-old Anastasia captured the way in which working motherhood also signifies high-status work and an imaginative alternative to motherhood:

"I would say this would have been me if I was working, for DEFINITE. But I don't work, (laughs) but the style is actually what I would wear definitely ... How can I put it? – if I was working at the same company where I was working before, I wouldn't be here today pregnant."

The ways in which these four women responded to this image provides a sense of how women can be differently positioned in relation to work at the point of motherhood, and thus how difficult it can be to articulate a coherent politics of motherhood. Although paid work is a common experience among women, it is also something that divides them, locating some within a self-actualising trajectory of career and others in much more precarious and exploitative relations of employment. Pregnancy and motherhood change women's relationship to work, but in a way that is particular to their circumstances and which is often experienced in isolation.

Pregnant at work

Social policies around pregnancy and the workplace have been shaped by two competing impulses – a gender-neutral discourse that seeks to minimise the impact of pregnancy on performance, and a discourse of gender difference that recognises the vulnerability of pregnant women and their need for protection, with pregnant employees 'struggling with the expectation of equality and fearing the consequences of difference' (Fredriksen et al, 2010, p 179). The image discussed above asserts that pregnant bodies can be a normal part of the workplace, displaying yet underplaying the embodiment of pregnancy and lactation.[5] The workplace is not neutral, and the accounts that women gave us of being pregnant at work suggested a wide range of experiences, depending on the character of the workplace. Carly (26) worked in a car showroom which she describes as "a very male environment", demanding "a certain persona" of employees in order to survive. Being pregnant disrupted this, making her feel vulnerable, as colleagues and clients felt free to comment on her changing body size. Nadire, who worked as a manager, shared these sentiments, explaining how difficult it was to be read as female in her work environment:

"I've had to go into meetings, I've had to be smart with suits and stuff, um and my team are all like, 'Oh my God, you can really see your stomach.' And it's sort of like, you know, I'm sort of like – a little – I'm a LITTLE bit embarrassed at times. Cos I'm sort of thinking, you know, this is me being a woman, and this is me having a baby."

The physical impact of pregnancy varied for the women in the study, and changed over time. Many experienced exhaustion and nausea during the early pregnancy, which could be very difficult to manage at work. In such circumstances the flexibility and safety of the working environment became incredibly important. Clara, a 40-year-old researcher, describes how overwhelming nausea caused her "ability to just juggle everything and do everything kind of start […] to fall apart at the seams". She recalls one especially bad day when she had to sleep on the office floor, noting that "sleeping on the floor of my office was not something that I'd been known to do before". Louisa (35) commented on how "lucky" she had been to have the option of working at home during her pregnancy in her husband's business, once she was faced with debilitating nausea. She felt that in another environment she would have been forced to begin her maternity leave early, something she described as "every parent's nightmare".

Whether or not women felt comfortable taking time off work 'sick' during pregnancy depended largely on the culture of their workplace (see also Cunningham-Burghley et al, 2005, 2006; Fredriksen et al, 2010). Women distinguished between business-oriented working environments and those which were "supportive". These did not simply map onto private and public sectors respectively. For example, 32-year-old nurse Hannah observed of the GP surgery in which she worked: "pregnant or not, get in here and work as hard as anyone else really, you know. I don't get any special treatment." Women working in educational settings reported a mixed picture. For example, Faye (35) commented on the welcoming atmosphere of her primary school, where "everyone likes children and, you know, so it's really, really positive … I feel quite spoilt". However, 31-year-old Kate, who worked as a nursery teacher, experienced the physical demands of working with small children extremely challenging in the late stages of her pregnancy and sought the support of her union when required to accompany children on trips at the height of summer. Some of the specific challenges experienced by teachers are explored later in more detail.

Yet, in general terms, those working in the public sector had a sense of some entitlement regarding their right to maternity leave. They were confident about drawing on the advice of unions to clarify their rights, and frequently did so, sometimes complaining as to the lack of clear and accurate information provided by employers. Women working in the private sector and in small companies communicated a much greater sense of personal responsibility for the disruption that their pregnancy caused their employer and colleagues. For example, 32-year-old events manager Charlotte described work as being "horrible", quoting her boss as saying "How could you let this happen?", communicating the message that she was "letting the side down". He also complained about having to pay for her maternity leave, even though he "gets to claim it back, I think, my maternity pay and stuff … it's a really tiny company, there's only nine of us, and the rest".

Even where they worked in ostensibly supportive environments, women felt that pregnancy rendered them as "bad colleagues" or "unreliable workers". For some women, like Charlotte, the realisation "that my job's not going to be the only thing in my life" was associated with a new assertiveness, which gave at least one woman the courage to walk away from punishing or unrewarding work environments. The power of an informal and unspoken organisational culture is communicated by 39-year-old Elaine, who has worked her way up slowly to the position of sales executive in a legal company where hardly any of the "high fliers" have children. She describes her boss as "40, the MD, so he's quite young, and they've decided, him and his wife, she's a lawyer, that they're not having children". He reacted to her pregnancy with shock, having "just assumed we were on that same sort of thing". For Elaine, it was important that she did not take "loads of time off" during the pregnancy, as "it would have just sort of re-emphasised that". Her company is providing her with the "basic minimum" maternity deal, and although she is aware of her rights to return to a job at the same level of pay and on a part-time basis, she is under no illusions as to how difficult this might be to pull off. She explains that she is looking into "more flexible options" in the meantime, such as work as a teaching assistant in the locality. Although she believes that she deserves her rights in her existing workplace after 17 years' service, securing them in a company with neither senior women nor part-time workers is a daunting prospect that she cannot face alone.

A sense of choice?

At the time of our initial fieldwork the statutory entitlement for maternity leave was still only six months, although the policy change of extending this to a year was in discussion. Most women were eligible for maternity leave, although a couple had recently changed jobs, and so lost out on their full entitlements. Many of the women whom we interviewed were uncertain about their return to work, and several felt pressured by the need to let their employers know how much time they would be taking off. How much maternity leave women were able to take was generally dictated by their financial situation and the generosity of their maternity package. Several were clear that their return to work after the six months was motivated purely by "financial reasons". Sofia, for example, who was the main breadwinner in her family, felt that she had no choice but to go back to her work as a beauty therapist after just four months of maternity leave. Others explained their choice as involving a desire to work, associating employment with independence and good mothering. For example, 23-year-old supermarket worker Farah looked to work as a source of independence. She could not countenance giving up her job and remaining at home with her unemployed husband and mother, asserting that "no one can stop me working" and that she would "work for myself and for my child". A similar account came from 21-year-old chef Lorraine, whose son lived for a period with his father in the Caribbean, enabling her to work long hours, a pattern of parenting that had shaped her early life also (Reynolds, 2006; Phoenix, 2008). Some of the youngest mothers in our study, who had often been disaffected from school in advance of the pregnancy, drew on their experiences to imagine a working future in areas such as midwifery, childcare or floristry (a course often provided in young mothers' support projects). For these young women, a commitment to work is an integral element of a narrative of self-improvement and economic independence that is promoted by service providers working with teenage mothers (Rudoe, 2011; Ponsford, forthcoming, 2011).

Others welcomed the prospect of escaping from work for a period of time. Again, this might be for a range of reasons – because they were dissatisfied with their work, wanted to change their priorities, or felt that they were sufficiently secure in their working lives to be able to "afford to take some time out". A significant group of women had decided to take an extended period out of work, choosing to be stay-at-home mothers. In general, these women were in couples where it was financially viable to survive on a single wage and where the calculation had been made that the financial and personal costs of childcare were greater than the loss of a salary. For 29-year-old administrator Sharon, "it all depends on money really, child-minding fees don't appear to be cheap and I think if I look into it, it's got to be a case of well it's worth it, because I would hate to pay to go to work just to pay child-minding fees and just walk out with a couple of hundred pounds in my pocket". For others, the choice to stay at home was presented as part of a moral project of self and a self-conscious embrace of a child-centred model of parenting. Women's deliberations depended largely on the overall economy of the household. For some, the demand to pool resources was very challenging. Journalist Vickie (33) talks about her panic on stopping work, having been financially independent since her teens: it was hard to re-conceptualise herself and her money as part of a "family" or a "team". However, others, such as Anastasia (who sells second-hand clothes on eBay to make some money), considered themselves to be unemployed rather than stay-at-home mothers, finding it impossible to afford the childcare that would allow them to return to work and having no alternative but to stay at home..

Women's accounts of being pregnant at work and planning around maternity leave do not simply reflect their different biographical situations. They also communicate something important about variability between and within workplaces in terms of how pregnant workers are treated. The most difficult experiences appear to be associated with small-scale organisations and businesses and those dominated by gender-neutral discourses of the good worker. In these contexts, the pregnant body may be unwelcome and disruptive and the pregnant worker may be constructed as demanding and disloyal. Women working in these kinds of organisations may see it as easier to withdraw rather than fight for their rights. Larger organisations with established traditions of human resource management, health and safety standards and negotiations with unions appear to provide a more promising environment for the negotiation of flexible working and quality part-time work (Lyonette et al, 2010). Whether women see motherhood and paid work as compatible or not depends in part on their circumstances, the extent to which they are invested in work and the kind of workplace, if any, that they would return to.

Goodbye, and welcome to maternal work

Making motherhood work

"I was talking to somebody at work and I said, 'Oh I have got to decide about what I want to do about going back to work and all this, that and the other', and she said, 'Can I say something and I hope you will take this in the way it is intended. At least you have a choice. I didn't have a choice when I was your age, when I had my kids

I had to resign and that was it, I stayed at home.' And I thought, Oh is it better to have choice or no choice? Now, if somebody said right you have got to resign now and go and have a baby, would I be like, 'This isn't fair!', or would I be, 'Oh, okay then'? (laughs). You know it is funny." (Deborah, 33)

The combination of work and motherhood is nothing new for many groups of working-class, migrant and minority women, who, far from perceiving tensions between motherhood and work, may assume work as an arena through which competence as a mother and a provider is demonstrated (Duncan et al, 2003; Gillies, 2006; Reynolds, 2006; Armstrong, 2010). Yet for much of the white middle class, working motherhood constitutes an intergenerational rupture, especially where daughters are better educated than their mothers and becoming parents much later (Sharpe, 1984). These patterns were reflected in our study, with middle-class mothers and grandmothers having much more to say about work and about how work and education complicate their relationships. Where their own mothers had tended to marry early (compressing childbearing and rearing into their 20s, and returning to employment in their 30s), this generation of young women spent their 20s establishing themselves in careers and relationships (Crompton, 2006). The way in which the grandmothers responded to this generational change varied.[6] Most were delighted that their daughters had access to educational and professional opportunities that they had perhaps missed. Yet they also expressed concern about the double burden of working and mothering that their daughters faced, feeling that the tempo of mothering had become much more intensive. Jean Woolfe (65) acknowledged that she was relatively unusual to have been "born in the generation that enabled me to be a stay-at-home mother when my children were young, and at the same time to have the experience of being a professional person. That's ideal." It is not something that is available to the young mothers that she works with in a university context and for whom "there's almost intolerable pressures on them to do both, it's impossible".

Grandmothers in our study tended to be very careful about how they described their daughters' situations and choices, distinguishing between the imperatives to fulfil one's own potential and to prioritise the needs and well-being of children. Avril, who had a long and successful career in teaching, explains that "years ago teachers were not allowed to work when they were married. It had to stop. I suppose we've come a long way in that respect. But I think it's good if you can work and still feel that you can give your child what they deserve, then that's fine. I wouldn't have liked to have had a job that I couldn't do that." Tension between self-actualisation and the realisation of children's potential forms a vital dynamic in intergenerational relationships which is amplified when children face the prospect of becoming mothers themselves. Mercedes (43), who works as a self-employed language teacher, eloquently characterises the feelings involved in her family as follows:

> "I see lots of positive things about my mother but not everything. For instance, I wouldn't sacrifice so much, being so careless about myself. What I see about my mother is that she gave everything; she didn't need anything because it was all for us. I think this is not a good education for your children because you have to put them limits, saying, 'You are important but I am important too. You have your space but I have my space too.' In that sense I think my mother was more *us* than *her*."

Each new mother faces the challenge of negotiating work and care from the position of having been mothered herself, which means that she must engage in an intergenerational conversation about the shape of the female biography (Lawler, 2000). Women respond differently: some daughters of working mothers are keen to reproduce something like the model provided by their mother, while others embrace the possibility of being at home full time. Those whose mothers felt frustrated by their own lack of opportunities may find themselves involved in a kind of recuperation of thwarted ambition, while others are distraught by a sense that they are not providing their children with the 'hands on' parenting that they had enjoyed themselves.

The practical, moral and interpersonal complexities involved in this terrain are inadequately served by concepts such as work/life balance that dominate policy discussions and much of the academic literature (Everingham et al, 2007). A more promising approach is offered by those promoting a 'new sociology of work', who call for attention to be paid to the 'matrix' through which household labour and the market economy interact, including the interplay of processes of consumption and production, paid and unpaid 'work' (Pettinger et al, 2005). Others have adopted the metaphor of a 'caringscape' as a way of thinking about the interaction of work and care over time and space (McKie et al, 2002). Yet what still seems to be missing most from this debate is a sense of the kinds of emotional, psychic and creative work involved in being good enough as a parent and a worker. We would concur with feminist commentators such as Rosemary Crompton that it is worth looking closely at the divisions of labour that are struck within families and the kinds of gender relations that these make possible and available (Crompton, 2006). In her view, certain responses to the challenge of parenthood (such as dividing work and care, or simply delegating care to the market) can create or confirm traditional gender roles, while other strategies (such as fully sharing the tasks of breadwinning and care) may unpick them.[7] It is in the small but growing body of qualitative research on mothering that we find evidence of how individuals and families work through the limits and opportunities of their situations, demonstrating the local and contingent factors that shape ideas of good mothering (Duncan et al, 2003) and the everyday practices through which mothers combine, breach and separate the worlds of home and work (Cunningham-Burley et al, 2005).

In the following section we counterpose four examples of women who all might be characterised as middle class, yet whose accounts reveal the diversity of this category and the particularity of these women's situations. Middle-class women with careers had a great deal to say about combining work and motherhood, experiencing the two as competing projects. As illustrated earlier, working-class working mothers were more likely to understand motherhood and paid work as complementary projects and consequently had less elaborate accounts. Here we focus on this particular hotspot within the class politics of motherhood. Informed by the spirit of the new sociology of work, we seek to bring together an analysis of paid and unpaid work, tracing the consequences of private deliberation over childcare and the division of labour for the kinds of gender relations that arise. The case studies benefit from a longitudinal perspective, including at least two interviews with the mother, before and a year after the birth, and in two cases interviews with the partner, as well as in each case interviews with the grandmother.[8]

Working mums – for or against?

We met Deborah Rickard at the beginning of her maternity leave from a full-time post as information specialist in a public sector organisation. At this time Deborah was moving between "plan A" (returning to work full time after six months' maternity leave and placing her child in nursery) and "plans B–F" that involved longer maternity leave and part-time return. This was a fraught time for her relationship as she and her partner communicated previously unspoken feelings about their perceptions of each other and their attitudes to work and parenting. Deborah was upset when her partner expressed his view that she should return full time after 18 weeks, using his own work colleagues as an example of the "norm". They argued over whether there was a financial need for her to return so quickly to work, with Deborah asserting that they were relatively well off and could afford to cut down on their expenses. She also reports his concern that women in his workplace "go back part time and they seemed very frustrated because they were stuck at the level they were left at and are not able to progress in their careers". She reports his words as follows: "You have worked so hard and you have got to where you want to be and I don't want to see you throw it away." While she appreciates his sentiment she expresses exasperation that he cannot understand that she might want to take a break from work.

Deborah's initial strategy is to suspend decisions about work until the baby is born, predicting that her partner "WILL want me to stay home when the baby arrives, I don't think he will like the idea of me going back to work. He is quite a sensitive soul. It will upset him putting the baby in the nursery." She has also had to fight with him over paternity leave, recalling a recent episode while at a meal with friends when he had announced that he would only take a week's paternity leave. In Deborah's words, she "went ballistic", upset that he had not first discussed it with her. At this stage she is deeply uncertain as to her priorities. In an ideal world she would like "to work part time, still get promoted and still have a fantastic salary", yet feels that this is unrealistic. Yet, working full time feels like an overwhelming prospect: "40 hours a week and have someone else look after your child and then come home and you spend 10 minutes with it before it goes to bed so you miss it crawling you miss it talking all those kind of things". As she faces the birth of her first child, Deborah has no clear sense of how she will deal with this challenge, explaining that she "will cross that bridge when I get over it. I may want to go back to work full time in January or I may want to stay home, bake cakes and keep chickens."

We interviewed Deborah's mother, Judy, eight months after Debbie's daughter, Ruby, was born. Judy explained that when Deborah shared the news of her pregnancy she had burst into tears, having "made up my mind that she wasn't going to have any, when she reached that age, I thought, oh she's decided not to bother you know, she's going to go for the career". Education and work loom large in the relationship between mother and daughter. Judy expresses regrets that she had given up paid employment when she had had children. Not only does she worry that she does not have a pension (unlike many of her friends), but she also asserts that she might have been a more "interesting person" if she had had a career. Nevertheless, she is confident that she did a good job bringing up her children and illustrates her priorities by telling a vivid story of going for a job interview as a school secretary but realising that she had miscalculated the hours and deciding that she could not leave her daughter for that long.

There is a sense throughout the interview that Deborah's university education and career success created a gulf between mother and daughter. The arrival of her granddaughter has made this a little easier. Judy feels that Deborah is "different" now she is a mother: they have more to talk about and she doesn't feel "bozeyed" like she was when Deborah talked to her about her job. Her sense of connection with her granddaughter is also strong. Yet Judy struggles to align her own experience of motherhood with Deborah's situation. She asserts that her daughter has shown her an alternative way of doing motherhood which allows women to have more "independence", while also recounting conversations where Deborah has questioned whether it is possible to "have it all". Judy's assertion of hope that Deborah will "make the most of her education" by returning to work after her maternity leave followed by the admission that she herself would have liked to go to university but feels she is "not clever enough", and her concerns that that her second daughter, who did not go to university, will miss out on the "modern experience".

When we meet Deborah again over a year after the birth of her daughter she is much less ambivalent about work, explaining that she found she was "really glad to go back, and I didn't have any qualms about leaving her either". Deborah started off working three days a week, which she claims was long enough to feel "organised at home but disorganised at work", and then started working four days a week, which she claims "makes me feel disorganised everywhere". When she is at work she reverts to being "pre-pregnancy Debbie", but as soon as the nursery calls her she becomes "mummy Debbie": "I'll just be, not torn, but I'll be completely mummy Debbie, there is no middle way." She attributes her ease with returning to work partly to her daughter's "confidence" and her ability to "settle" into nursery, although she acknowledges that a second child could disrupt this delicate balance.

Deborah describes her work environment as having been supportive and attributes this to the fact that it is dominated by women and many of her colleagues have children. She has found that her four-day week is actually a full-time job but feels that any fewer days wouldn't make her feel the same sense of "value" that she gets from working four days a week, attending important meetings and so on. She reports experiencing a form of prejudice from a colleague who expressed the view that part-time staff with children only work their hours and want to return home to their children. She felt offended that this suggested that she had less "commitment" than non-mothers. Outside of work, she has noted differences with her peers from the antenatal groups, some of whom have commented on her "fancy job title". She also feels different from her peers who just see work as "something they do", unlike Deborah. She also reports feeling a "bit out of it" where mothers arrange to meet, not being part of either "the stay-at-home set or the full-time set".

Deborah is in a relatively privileged situation compared to other women in the study: she and her partner could afford for her to stay at home and her wages are sufficiently high to pay for childcare. She had achieved a position of some status at work before she became pregnant and was able to maintain that on her return from maternity leave. Having some 'choice' over how they would manage the division of labour within the family gave rise to intensive negotiations within the couple relationship, involving ideas about appropriate masculinity and femininity as well as what constitutes good parenting. However, it is Deborah who appears to be shouldering the burden of the identity work involved, attempting to square the circle of 'having it all'. This contrasts with the following case study of Monica Fortune and her partner, Jamie, who were the only couple in our study who seriously attempted to reverse the traditional gender roles of breadwinning and care.

Pure hybrid equal parenting?

Monica Fortune was interviewed towards the end of her pregnancy, after she had begun her maternity leave from her post as a civil servant. At 39 and 42 respectively, Monica and her partner, Jamie, recognise themselves as being older parents. Where many of the other women in their NCT class talk about not being able to wait until they can 'get back to normal and work', Monica and Jamie don't want to get back to normal, looking upon parenthood as an opportunity for their lives to change. Although Monica had a childhood image of herself as a mother, it is only very recently that she has begun to imagine a life with children. She describes university as enabling her to forge a trajectory away from young parenthood, in which having fun and personal fulfilment were a priority. There are few children in her friendship networks, although her brothers have both had children. She speaks warily of the dangers of becoming a "baby bore" and recounts several stories of the dangers of spoiling children or becoming a "competitive mother". It is only very recently that she has felt ready to take the step to motherhood, and she frames it in terms of having financial security and an appropriate home environment. Monica describes herself as having been a "late starter" in terms of intimate personal relationships, and characterises herself and Jamie as not being risk takers. It is ironic, then, that she also conceptualises parenthood as an opportunity to transform their lives in radical ways.

Monica is keeping her options open as to what the future holds. In the short term she is planning to return to work as soon as possible so as to build up her entitlement for a second maternity leave if they decide to try for a second child. They are planning that Jamie will stay at home with the baby, taking advantage of their ability as civil servants to share their entitlements for parental leave and career breaks. Conscious of the possibility of birth complications, they are unwilling to make firm plans at this point but are open to the possibility of a flexible and shared pattern of childcare and work. Monica has researched local childcare options and is concerned about the cost involved and her lack of local networks. She has recognised that the hour-and-a-half that it takes her and Jamie to get to work means that the standard nursery hours of 8am to 4.30pm will pose a difficulty. She is wary of having "strangers" take care of her children.

Joining the local NCT group is one strategy Monica has used to meet other mothers. She acknowledges the selection process involved in choosing which group to join (the "Stapleton hippies or the Fieldview professionals") and that in joining a "private" scheme such as the NCT they are electing to make contact with, and position themselves in relationship to, other middle-class couples. So far she has been disappointed with how little social contact has arisen from the group and she fears that her honest declaration that she was taking part "to meet people" made her appear to be "desperate". Being in a group also exposes Monica to the way in which the practices of mothering are marked by social class. She is particularly anxious about breastfeeding, which she fears that she will not be able or willing to do. Her description suggests her awareness of her own class journey and the ways in which the practices of motherhood in themselves are a form of cultural display.

When interviewed six months later, Monica's partner, Jamie, explains that they decided that he would stay home and care for their son after the end of Monica's maternity leave. It was a circular deliberation. Their initial fancy, based on their different orientations to work (she likes it and he hates it, and she earns more than he does) were initially dismissed by the impossibility of surviving on a single salary. Once they realised the expense of childcare and "read the research" (on the impact of nursery education on child development) they returned to their initial impulse – "what's the point of going to work to pay for childcare?". Jamie describes himself as "old-fashioned at heart" and explains that he has had to overcome his underlying feeling that Monica should stay home with the baby, as her whole antenatal class have done. Full-time fatherhood provides him with the opportunity to escape an unsatisfying job and to earn "pin money" through an internet-based business. After the birth of their son, Jamie took two weeks' paternity leave, which was important as Monica was not at all well. After this he returned to work, sleeping through the night while Monica breastfed. Now that Monica is returning to full-time work he is preparing to be a full-time father, something that he suspects he will do mostly alone.

We met Monica again just over a year after the birth of her son Lucien. She went back to work full time at the end of her year-long maternity leave and negotiated a flexible working pattern that enables her to work from home two days a week. She talks about how challenging she and Jamie are finding her transition to work and how they found themselves "competing over the mothering". Lucien was born at the beginning of a long, cold winter and the first months of motherhood were lonely for Monica. Contact with other mothers resulted in her comparing and finding herself wanting. She became increasingly aware that she and Jamie were "at the bottom of the economic ladder", as mothers employed nannies and cleaners to manage the labour of childcare. Most of the mothers in her NCT class had chosen to stay home with their babies, while Monica felt that she had no choice but to return to work full time. She comments that it was probably best that she did – hinting that Jamie is better able to handle the tempo and the pressures. He does not get drawn into competitive comparison and has a more relaxed and laid-back approach in general.

Monica had dreaded going back to work. She describes herself as becoming "totally immersed" in her baby, such that she could no longer "comprehend" herself at work. She continues to be torn between a desire to have Lucien all to herself and to share him with others. In practice, her return to work has not been as bad as she had imagined. She has negotiated a flexible working pattern and has managed to maintain breastfeeding through her return to work, giving Lucien a feed in the early morning, on her return to the house and before bed. She is pleased that she does not have to deliver Lucien daily to a child minder but can leave father and son sleeping peacefully when she leaves early in the morning for the office. In her view, she and Jamie are the "happiest" they "have ever been", and although returning to work has been hard, parenthood is an "enjoyable struggle". She talks how they are "fascinated" by their son and enjoy watching the emergence of his character and the "subtle cleverness" of his changing modes of communication. Monica has been broody for some time and she and Jamie are keen to have another child, although she first has to build up her maternity leave entitlement. Parenthood has made them more adventurous as a couple. Their plans for the future include having their own business and moving abroad, involving a life-style where neither works full time and where they can enjoy time together. Their dreams of self-employment and mobility echo the working lives of their own parents.

Again, Monica and Jamie are in a relatively privileged position, both having secure jobs and access to what, for the UK, are generous and flexible parental leave packages. Although their approach to the division of labour is unconventional in relation to the wider sample, it is also highly conventional in its own terms, allowing them to embrace and create 'traditional' gender roles and ideas of parenting. Although Monica and Jamie benefit from secure jobs, they have ambivalent feelings about their work and see parenthood as providing a welcome interruption that might reveal new possibilities for them as individuals and as a couple. This contrasts starkly with the next case study, of Alex Calder, for whom motherhood has to be squeezed around the exacting demands of a medical training.

Who will look after your baby when you go back to work?

We met 32-year-old Alex Calder at the beginning of her maternity leave from a demanding job as a junior surgeon. As the daughter of a pilot and a "socialite", Alex claims both the desire to be a surgeon and the "courage, drive and organisational skill" necessary to realise the ambition as all her own work. She is married to another high flier and describes their social location in terms of being "professional people", for whom money is relatively plentiful but for whom time is in very short supply. From the outset, she anticipated a short maternity leave and an efficient return to work, causing as little disruption as possible to her professional duties and to the progress of her training and ultimate goal of securing a position as a consultant.

Alex's strategy for survival in the highly competitive and intensive field of surgery (becoming "one of the boys") had been profoundly disrupted by pregnancy. She struggles to maintain her reputation with colleagues, going out of her way to ensure that she is not seen to get special treatment just because she is pregnant, even where such dispensations are part of official workplace policy. Although she acknowledged that some areas of medicine are sympathetic and supportive to mothers, she fears that in her own field of emergency surgery any attempts to reform the punishing timetable of on-calls, rotations and training merely results in senior members of the profession making "mental notes not to employ women in the future". Yet Alex is also determined to change the norms of her chosen profession, whatever the personal costs. She questions the received wisdom that you cannot be a mother and a surgeon, presenting a life plan that involves at least two children and a consultant position before the age of 35. She is adamant that if faced with the death-bed choice of being "a happy grandmother or a professor of surgery" she would choose the former.

Childcare is a major cause for concern for Alex and her husband, and they are frustrated by how difficult it is to find an option that fits with their long working hours. Alex is aware that her version of working motherhood stands in tension with the values of those women in her neighbourhood and NCT class, and she deliberately avoids having conversations that expose this gulf. For Alex, the mother-bond will be mediated by a deferred form of gratification, where the child is "proud of what their parents *do*". Although her parents have encouraged her to "throw money at the situation", she struggles to find a local and affordable option that satisfies all of her requirements. Meanwhile, she saves for private school fees and spends money preparing for the baby, which, because of the long hours she works, mostly involves internet shopping.

We met her mother, Barbara, a few months after Alex's daughter was born, bringing her tally of grandchildren to five. Barbara's first experience of grandmotherhood came with her eldest daughter's children (now in their early teens), with whom she was and continues to be very involved. She describes her eldest daughter as being very like herself, and "the children were dragged up rather like I dragged up my children", alternating between "any old child minder", boarding school and a rambling home in the country with dogs and horses. In contrast, she likens Alex to her own father, "being very capable, strong mentally and physically". Barbara admits to uncertainty as to how Alex will cope, balancing motherhood with "a real career".

As an upper middle-class girl growing up after the war, Barbara describes her own choices as "marriage or university". Her sister did the latter and Barbara was more than happy to follow her parents' advice to get married to a pilot. Although she presents her own experience of early motherhood as a period of pleasure and routine, she also comments on how she became increasingly bored and frustrated as the children got older. When her youngest child was 5 years old Barbara went to college and completed the secretarial training that she had started before her first marriage. She then began a 30-year pattern of working part time, and explains that "I rather liked earning, as they used to call it in those days, pin money", noting that it was "lovely to get out and meeting people and do something for yourself". The interview with Barbara coincided with the period during which Alex was returning to full-time work, and her mother recognised that "this little hump" would be very difficult.

She described Alex's maternity leave as "highly sociable", involving "masses of classes, a full-time job as far as I could see".

When we meet again 16 months after our first interview, Alex is in the eighth month of another pregnancy and the first week of her second maternity leave. She encapsulates her birth experience ironically as "just another day at work kind of thing, that's done now let's get on with the next job". Yet she also expresses contradictory feelings concerning her need to balance the demands of motherhood and career. On the one hand, she tells a story of an efficient return to work after a happy and sociable six months' maternity leave which itself maintained the busy tempo of her working life. Although she had loved breastfeeding, she had weaned her daughter from breast to bottle quickly and completely, considering more gradual or partial solutions impossible – despite support from her Sure Start breastfeeding group and an awareness of NHS guidance that protects her rights in this area. The necessity of returning to her work and training regime is presented as a bold choice, with Alex explaining that "I didn't enjoy looking after Sian as much as I actually enjoyed a really good day at work". Yet on the other hand there is evidence within Alex's account of a more ambivalent position. The experience of moving quickly from breast to formula was traumatic for both and something that, with hindsight, she says she regretted. She presents the process of weaning in terms of a curtailment of her own desires as much as of those of her daughter. Returning to work after maternity leave is likened to the return to boarding school after a vacation, "painful but necessary", and something that she is proud of herself for managing to do. The decision to avoid "the mess" of being a nursing mother is presented as the price of "not messing" around her colleagues.

Alex's resolve to erase her maternity from the workplace is further complicated by her next pregnancy, itself planned in order to fit around training timetables. She explains that in the last few months before her maternity leave she had been "profoundly tired" and that concerns about the health of her unborn child as well as her ability to work safely had forced her to request her right to be exempted from on-calls. She illustrates the male-dominated culture of her particular specialism with the resentment expressed by colleagues who went so far as to challenge her right to full pay, while also admitting that they would "not want their wives to work at all during the final stages of pregnancy". Even during her maternity leave she was preparing to travel for an interview, despite her fear that she might go into labour during the journey. If the interview was not successful, she planned to take up an unpaid training position abroad later that year, which she hoped would improve her chances of securing a permanent position at home. She and her partner had accepted that they faced "a difficult few years" during which they had to prioritise her career in order to realise the investment in her training. That this period coincided with the arrival of their children and the expense of childcare was a challenge that they just had to absorb. At this stage Alex did not feel that she could afford to jeopardise her prospects, and she was struggling to compensate for the toll of the two pregnancies on her personal appearance – itself a vital professional asset.

Alex's return to full-time work had been made possible by Cheryl, her child minder. Living close by and with a young child of her own, Cheryl offers 7am to 7pm childcare and has been a vital support to the family. Mother and child minder communicate primarily through a written diary in which activities and requests are recorded. Alex describes Cheryl as honest and open, and she is reassured by her interest in organic and whole foods. Sian is a fussy eater, and more willing to eat at Cheryl's house in the company of other children than at home. Alex movingly describes the Sunday-night sessions in which she prepares and freezes three meals a day for Sian to take with her to the child minder's for the whole week. In her words, "the cooking kills me", particularly when Sian refuses to eat it. Alex has decided to keep Sian with the child minder while she takes maternity leave, being loath to disrupt her routine, even though she could save a significant amount of money.

The strong boundaries that Alex must maintain between her working and maternal identities and spaces exact a high price and are possible only with the support of paid childcare. Alex draws on her family history in making sense of and surviving her situation, a childhood shaped by boarding schools and paid 'help'. Her primary project at this stage is to complete her training and to secure a position that will enable her to pay for high-quality education and care for her children. She does not feel a moral obligation to provide this herself, and reasons that investment in a career will ultimately secure her children's well-being. This is a pragmatic calculation concerning the relationship between income, standard of living and life chances.

The final case study draws on what appears to be a child-friendly field of work – teaching – and explores the potential for the mixing up of working and maternal identities, as well as how this can incite troubling forms of insight that need to be defended against through the reassertion of boundaries between home and work.

Work/life balance – dealing with the guilt

Heather Chapman (26) and her partner, Andy, were both teaching in inner-city primary schools when they discovered that she was 19 weeks pregnant. The pregnancy was unplanned and disrupted their well-laid plans to work for three years in their current jobs in order to pay off their mortgage on a house "back home" before returning to Australia to settle down and start a family. Despite her initial fears that the head teacher and senior-management team would punish her for the pregnancy, the school had been extremely supportive, reassuring Heather that she was eligible for maternity leave and that it would support her return to work. She describes her colleagues as "a family of people", which she valued enormously, having no family of her own in the country. Heather recognised that financial necessity meant that she would have to return to work after her maternity leave but that this was "a shame", having always envisaged herself as a stay-at-home mum. She had no sense of how she would manage this return to work and was struggling to imagine how to balance the school timetable with childcare, while fantasising about the potential of creating a school-based crèche that could support the seven babies under 3 that were currently "on staff".

We interviewed Heather again just over a year after the birth of her son, Ben. At this time she was "back home", living in a suburb of an Australian city – and missing the networks and sociability that had characterised their former life in the inner city. When asked to recall the story of Ben's birth, Heather presents it, ironically, as fitting into her working timetable: "he was out at three thirty, so it was a school day, nine to three thirty, the bell rang and he was there". Her account of returning to work after her maternity leave suggests how integrated and entwined her working and parenting were at this stage. She explains that she would go to work at 6am with Ben in her arms. She had all the security codes and could let herself in and chat with the cleaners. After having his bottle, Ben would sleep until 7am while she caught up with work. When he woke, she would take him to the staff room, where he was occupied until the start of school. At the classroom door she would pass Ben over to her child minder, Karen, until the end of the school day. If she had things to do in the afternoon she "could give him to someone to have a bottle down in the staff room and then I'd come down".

However, this integrated life did not last, and after two months Heather gave her notice and the family returned to Australia, where it became financially possible for her to stay home with Ben. She explains that she may feel more at ease about day care when he is 2 or 3 and has sufficient language to "talk back to me", noting that her teaching experience has prepared her well for the moment of separation when, as a teacher, you "have to hang on to them and have them sob hysterically as mum walks away". At the moment he is "still too baby-baby and I want … him to be the age where he understands why I'm walking away".

In this second interview Heather also explains that her previous passion for teaching is slipping. She is "nowhere near as motivated or driven", and while being a teacher had been a huge part of her life, "it doesn't matter anywhere near as much" now. In fact, she draws on her teaching identity as a way of explaining that "I'm really happy to go and do painting in the backyard and I'm really happy to sit in the sandpit for an hour, because that's what my teaching was – to do activities". Heather also reveals some more difficult ways in which her professional training and expertise intrude on her mothering practice, as well as some of the ways in which her maternal experience encourages her to rethink familiar classroom scenarios. Knowledge of both home and classroom incites her to translate experiences of learning and mothering across this boundary. She explains that Andy, her husband, "often says he hears my teacher voice coming out with Ben". And although she feels happy about using her "teaching strategies on Ben", she is much more circumspect with the children of family and friends, whom she does not want to judge, but "I'm like … oh I wouldn't have allowed that in my classroom". In particular, she struggles with her and her sister's very different parenting styles. Again, she draws on her professional identity to remind herself: "these are my little nieces and they're beautiful, and they're at home in their environment and its okay".

We asked Heather whether studying child development has had an impact on how she thinks about what Ben should be doing and what's normal for him. She replies that this knowledge is a source of anxiety for her and that she almost wishes that she "didn't know – I think it would be so much better, maybe I wouldn't care so much", because "it's all well and good to have the knowledge and the background but the actually doing and putting into practice of your own child" is a different matter. Seeing your own child through teacher's eyes can be challenging, exposing the contradictions between a disciplinary educational gaze and an unconditional maternal perspective. During the interview, Heather shares a number of concerns about Ben's social development, describing her frustrated attempts to find friends for him of the same age and sex within a highly privatised suburban neighbourhood. The following extract shows how anxiety-provoking professional knowledge can be, and also the partial and destructive impact of its mundane classifications:

> "It had never occurred to me that Ben could be a child that could be isolated. I've taught in so many classes, and you walk into the room and you can immediately pick the child that is the isolated, ostracised one in the room.… I'd never considered, it wasn't until that night seeing Ben isolated, that oh my goodness he could be the one.… Andy said 'Don't be silly, it takes all-rounded parents to produce an all-rounded child, he'll be fine.' And I said 'But if I was to go back to teaching now I would view it so differently, because somewhere there's a mother who every night might be feeling the way I am tonight, every night when she lays down in bed.' I've only got one night of this feeling sad about Ben,

being ... isolated, just devastated me, I've never ... and I always work hard with those kids and try and make them special and get them involved in a group, you know. I make them, I give them a nickname, a cool name in the class, and try and get them involved. But I just thought, if I think back over those kids that were the isolated ones, and it just devastates me that there's a mother and a father seeing their child come home upset or knowing ... and that would change my teaching for ever, which I didn't understand before. Without a child I didn't get it. I felt for those kids and I worked hard for those kids, but I didn't have an emotional ... oh ..."

Heather's decision to step back from teaching during her children's early years needs to be understood in relation to the intensive reflexivity produced by the permeable boundary between working and maternal identities and practices. Moving between social fields can give rise to heightened awareness which, if unrecognised and unrewarded, may turn inwards (Lovell, 2000). She narrates her pre-mothering self as able to give unconditionally to her pupils, "spending weekends planning and programming and putting effort in, above and beyond". With motherhood, this generosity can no longer be afforded. Although she "still cared about the education of those children, it still mattered extremely to me but I did, I did what was required of me, I didn't go beyond the call".

As a profession, teaching has a particular and complicated relationship with parenthood, a kind of 'mothering made conscious' centred on the professionalising of a particular middle-class cultural form (Steedman, 1985; Ailwood, 2008). Mothers inevitably draw on their working techniques in their parenting practices. US commentators have argued that the middle classes draw on a range of professional techniques to access and organise activities for their children and to secure and defend privilege (Lareau, 2003) – findings that have been supported by UK studies of parenting (Vincent and Ball, 2007). Yet occupational groups may produce specific cultures around parenting (Kohn, 1963; Weininger and Lareau, 2009), and we found that the teachers who became mothers while involved in our study certainly struggled to create boundaries between their own mothering and their working identities, despite drawing on aspects of their professional expertise in their mothering (Thomson and Kehily, 2010). The juxtaposition of working and maternal identities can be productive of insight and reflexivity, yet it can also produce troubling feelings, defensive responses and the desire to flee from other people's children.

An interview with Heather's mother, Matty, further enriched our perspective on the ways in which work and mothering are negotiated over the generations. Matty had also trained as a teacher, a job that had enabled her to escape a hard life of farming in rural Australia, that had ruined her own mother's health. Her first marriage was unhappy, and ended in divorce soon after the birth of her first daughter. Matty had relied on her teaching to support herself and her daughter, and had strong regrets about some of the childcare that she had had to use during this period of survival. A second, much happier marriage provided her with the financial security to give up work and to become a full-time mother to her second and final child – Heather. So can we understand Heather's example as revealing something of the particularity of working-mothering projects for an occupational group such as teachers, as well as showing how these projects exist in conversation across and between generations within families. That the two sisters, who experienced very different kinds of parenting from the same teacher/mother, are in turn adopting very different approaches to mothering is no coincidence, expressing the contradictions, possibilities and limits of the female biography in differently constituted situations.

Conclusion

These four case studies provide a taste of four distinctive professional cultures, showing how workplaces contribute to the definition of women's *situations* at the point of pregnancy. Not only do we find a proliferation of local work-based cultures, but we find that within the same organisation women workers may experience very different working conditions and norms. The evidence in this chapter suggests not only that motherhood has an impact on the kinds of workers that women are, but that work influences the ways in which women mother, not simply in terms of their presence or absence, but through the transposition of skills and values between the fields of work and home. The extent to which motherhood influences the workplace *itself* is much more limited, although the example of Heather Chapman suggests that it might be possible to imagine ways in which such interpenetrations might be possible.[9] For most middle-class women at least, work and mothering continue to be constituted as conflicting projects that must be 'balanced' – most often with work being fitted around children, or less often with children being fitted around work (Everingham et al, 2007). Moving beyond this involves a radicalising of the couple relationship and inspecting the centrality of work to ideas of success and well-being – perhaps both features of a working-class habitus (Stacey, 1998). The position that a woman strikes in relation to work appears to be highly consequential in the kind of mothering project on which she subsequently embarks, including how she orients to expert advice, consumption and childcare.

In this chapter we have explored motherhood through the lens of work. This has involved looking at the ways in which work comes between mothers as well as providing a source of common interest and solidarity. From our review of women's experiences of pregnancy at work it is evident that many women are ill informed and unprepared in terms of understanding their rights and entitlements as pregnant workers, and subsequently as parents. For many, the 'motherhood penalty' comes as a shock that is faced in relative isolation. Although the rights of pregnant workers could and should be a site of solidarity in the politics of motherhood, too often they are something that women negotiate when feeling vulnerable and exposed. Informal working cultures play an important part in shaping norms of what appears to be reasonable and fair behaviour, even when this departs from statutory obligations. The examples explored in this chapter point to the ways in which different kinds of workplaces vary in terms of the kinds of maternity packages on offer to employees and the flexible working patterns available. Women tend to meet other mothers outside of the world of work, through antenatal groups and in neighbourhood settings. Although these provide social connections they can also expose differences and insecurities. Women's initial attempts to seek out work-based support for pregnancy and childcare generally turn into local and individual solutions involving family, partners and the market.

One of the shocks associated with pregnancy is being made to feel female at work. The dominance of a gender-neutral discourse within workplaces, typified by the advertisement 'It doesn't have to hurt your business', creates a bifurcated world where questions of embodiment, care and reproduction are constituted as private matters that do not belong in the workplace, yet are implicitly assumed through reliance on an increasingly female workforce. This is the post-feminist contract conceptualised by McRobbie, where the right to assert sexual difference is traded for the right to be treated as the genderless worker. Yet sexual difference continues to exist in workplaces, and our case studies illustrate the kind of work that can go into making this invisible, or at least untroubling, for colleagues and employers. Despite appearances, working and mothering are entangled and entwined, creating insights that are both exciting and intolerable. Our findings support the thesis that women are increasingly labourised, constituted first and foremost as workers rather than mothers, and expected to make things fit into their own time and space. If labour is increasingly feminised, it is feminised in a particular way that does not include or involve the fertile female body, nor the lactating nursing subject. Understood in terms of the new sociology of work, we can say that there are asymmetries in the matrix that brings together the forms of work involved in mothering. Traffic moves in certain directions and not in others. While it is possible for women to transpose working skills into mothering projects, to take their work home and to turn their mothering into a business or to consume the products created by others, it is much less possible to bring mothering into the workplace and into the versions of publicness constituted through paid work.

One reason for this may be the divisions that motherhood asserts between women and between genderless workers. In forging private solutions to public problems, women provide solutions to each other as child minders, as formal and informal carers. Again, women are drawn into holding tensions between exploitation and solidarity and between instrumental and intrinsic forms of care (Maher et al, 2010). We would support Rosemary Crompton's view that there is no inevitable correlation between female employment and the evaporation of traditional gender relations. The micro-politics through which domestic labour and childcare are shared, delegated and entrusted to others is important moral terrain in the contemporary politics of motherhood. Thinking about mothers as workers forces us to recognise the politics of class and qualifications and chains of care that may connect families (Ehrenreich and Hochschild, 2003; Chavkin and Maher, 2010). By capturing women at the same biographical moment (maternity) we also capture the fragmentation of women's biographies along class lines and the difficulties for forging solidaristic relations between women. Unfortunately, in motherhood women are isolated from each other, even from those who are most like them.

Notes

[1] The mounting evidence that suggests that women running their own small businesses take less maternity leave than any other group of workers (Rouse, 2010) appears not to find its way into the world of the magazines, for whom the Mumtrepreneur is, first and foremost, a pin-up for the new mother-to-be, living proof that you can have it all.
[2] Internet-based resources such as Mumsnet dispense with expert advice, facilitating peer support and contact between mothers. This less-mediated space reveals more conflictual landscapes around working motherhood, including tensions between mothers as employers and those that they employ. The largest single category within the childcare and work discussion area on Mumsnet is 'childminders, nannies, aupairs etc' and includes discussion between mothers about the legal and moral obligations of being an employer, as well as discussions between those providing care.
[3] This was primarily because more mothers work part time, and because of the relatively low national wage levels for part-time work.
[4] Six of these were enrolled in a full-time preparation for parenthood course.

[5] Similar arguments have been made about campaigns promoting breastfeeding among working mothers (Gatrell, 2011).

[6] Not all of the mothers of the middle-class women were middle class themselves, reflecting some social mobility over the generations. Moreover, there was considerable diversity within the category 'middle class', as is evident in the case studies reported here.

[7] Rosemary Crompton (2006) has argued that the kinds of substitute care provided can 'perpetuate traditionalism in gender relations as well as increase class inequality' (p 193). She distinguishes between state services, profit-making services and directly employed household workers (living in and out), arguing that where dual-earner households access marketised reproductive work via hiring domestic servants then it 'can easily co-exist with enduring traditionalism in domestic relations' (p 196).

[8] These case studies are drawn from the case-history analyses that bring together and synthesise the data for a whole family. These case studies draw on the words of the participants without quoting at length, but placing key verbatim phrases in quotation marks.

[9] In trying to imagine the possible, it is worth remembering that in the early 1980s small tailoring factories in Yorkshire which relied heavily on female labour allowed children to be present in the workplace after school and during holidays in order to 'stop the production going down' (Sharpe, 1984, p 124).

SEVEN

Commodities

First-time pregnancy beckons women into an ever-expanding consumer world of specialist goods and niche marketing, providing products for every stage of the maternal experience. This chapter considers the domain of consumer culture, materiality and the commodification of motherhood. The increased commercialisation of motherhood can be seen as a key change in the way motherhood is lived and experienced in contemporary times. The commercial world is omnipresent in the lives of new mothers, inviting them to buy their way into this new identity and simultaneously position themselves in relation to the universally available offerings of consumer culture. While consumer culture appears to be ubiquitous, the open-to-all invitation is deceptive. Access to the commercial world is constrained by the availability of capital resources and the ability to use them in rule-bound consumer contexts. Working-class and marginal groups commonly carry the stigma of exclusion from consumer culture and of excessive, inappropriate spending during periods of participation.

From the routine consumption of everyday maternity wear and baby products to decorating nurseries and collecting exclusive artefacts, this chapter examines the work of commodities as preparatory, expressive and identity producing. As we have argued throughout the book, new motherhood can be mapped as a dynamic stretch of the commodity frontier. The chapter discusses the expansion of the commercial sphere into areas once considered the preserve of the medical or the family. The commodification of antenatal ultrasound scanning and stem-cell storage, for example, present parents with new frontiers for spending, caring and creativity. Drawing upon the experiences of a diverse group of first-time mothers, we discuss the many ways in which new motherhood is imbued in consumer culture. We argue that becoming a mother is potentially a *total consumer experience*, involving full immersion in the market and active engagement with diverse practices of consumption. Maternal subjects can be seen as desiring subjects, wanting things to furnish and make sense of the maternal project. As the chapter illustrates, non-participation in the market, including anti-consumerism, still entails modes of engagement with the tropes of consumer culture. Central to our argument is the idea that the materiality of motherhood matters. Through material culture and consumer 'choice', mother and baby are brought into being as socially connected and emotionally realised actors in the drama of having a family. Additionally, it may be productive to ask where the extent and limits of the market lie in relation to new motherhood. Is it boundaried by the needs of the new-born, or does it extend to housing, childcare and education for example? If this is the case, then new motherhood can be understood as a politically important moment in which relations with the market and the state are reconfigured.

The chapter is divided into seven sections. The first two consider theoretical approaches to consumer culture and the ways in which material culture is profiled and packaged for mothers in popular cultural forms such as pregnancy magazines. Section three, on maternal economies, documents the impact of age and socioeconomic circumstances on impending motherhood and approaches to consumption. The remaining sections draw upon our data to explore specific practices of consumption and consumer 'choice'. An analysis of women's relationship to the commercial world and their unfolding maternal identity is discussed in sections considering: baby things; new/second hand; buggies and nappies; decorating the nursery.

Considering consumer culture

Early sociological work on consumer culture, pioneered by the Frankfurt School, viewed the expansion of mass production as a *bad thing in itself*. Developing a Marxian-inspired analysis of cultural practices, these studies suggested that the commercial world creates commodities which lack authenticity and meet 'false' needs (Adorno, 1991). A common theme in this body of work is the emphasis on the power of production, placing consumers in a passive position as the manipulated dupes of omnipotent and highly persuasive commercial and ideological forces. The tendency to cast consumerism as a deceptively destructive power has residual traces in contemporary times that can be seen in the work that individuals do to justify their consumption practices as distinct and necessary. What is clear is that the market increasingly acts as a form of governance, penetrating further into the 'lifeworld' of the private in ways that can be associated with freedoms and loss. The negative impact of consumerism is a theme reworked by Bauman (1988), who argues that consumer freedom has become a major medium of social control in late capitalism. Arguing that consumerism has replaced work as the main instrument of social cohesion, 'the hub around which the life-world rotates' (Bauman, 1988, p 76), Bauman concludes that consumer culture offers individuals freedom at a high price. Presenting individuals with a smorgasbord of choice, pleasure and seemingly endless 'model identities', the consumer market provides 'a substitute for permanently frustrated power ambitions, as the sole recompense for oppression at work, the only outlet for freedom and autonomy' (Bauman, 1988, p 73).

In contrast to the negative impact of consumer culture on individuals, Bourdieu (1977; 1984) develops a theory of consumer culture that illustrates the relationship between social structures and individual agency. In developing the concepts of 'habitus' and 'field theory', Bourdieu illustrates the ways in which consumer taste may appear to be a matter of personal choice but can be seen more broadly as an expression of the structuring principles that emerge in relation to unevenly distributed levels of economic and cultural capital. Linking two versions of capital, the cultural with the economic, allows for the development of a more expansive and delineated account of privilege that considers levels of education and cultural accomplishments as well as social class and wealth. Bourdieu uses the concept of 'habitus' to capture a sense of a cultural environment organised in terms of taste and distinction, learnt in childhood and applied in later life. Habitus works to define and classify consumer taste, often through everyday practices such as eating, dress, bodily comportment and television viewing. Occupying a particular habitus provides individuals and groups with a comfortable and familiar place to be, while simultaneously positioning them within structures indicative of their ability to access economic and cultural resources. Keen to hold on to notions of agency in the confluence between lived lives and capital-based structures, Bourdieu considers the identity work made possible through acts of consumption. He suggests that identities are produced through practices of 'distinction', allowing individuals to identify with or differentiate themselves from others. Through practices of consumption, individuals and groups exercise cultural capital, express taste and articulate a sense of identity. Such practices point to the potential for consumption to become a 'moral project' (Miller, 1998, p 47), a vehicle for the expression of priorities, judgement and choice. Bourdieu has been critiqued for his tendency to formalise and overstate consumer practices (de Certeau, 1984). In recognising limitations, the social relations at work in the creation of habitus have eerie points of resonance with market-research strategies that seek to generate capital by mapping purchasing practices onto ever more detailed socioeconomic classificatory systems documenting occupational status, home ownership, level of education, age and postcode. Creating a habitus for the brand or incorporating the product into already existing spheres of habitus can be seen as a descriptive interpretation of what marketers do.

Consumer culture provides a medium within which representations of family life can be projected and embellished, informed by fantasy, fiction and desire. These are the families we 'live by' (Gillis, 1996), expressing aspiration and comfort, and rarely conforming to the mundane and messy practices of the families we 'live with'. Considering practices of consumption alongside the emergent social practices of late modernity has many implications for motherhood. Beck comments on the privileged status of the child in the context of individualisation and new practices of intimacy:

> The child is the last remaining irrevocable, unexchangeable primary relationship. Parents come and go. The child stays. Everything that is not realisable in the relationship is directed towards the child. (Beck, 1992, p 18)

The idea of the child as a treasured emotional investment can be seen to suit the contingent nature of the 'pure relationship' in which coupledom is based on the meeting of mutual needs, unfettered by other forms of obligation and extended family ties. In this context the child becomes the emotional anchor for the couple, the thing that turns choice into permanency and commitment. While late-modern approaches to intimate relationships appear to reconfigure a romantic ideal, children may also exist symbolically as an enhanced fantasy of late-modern coupledom. Consumption can be seen as one of the spheres in which coupledom is actively imagined and played out. Practices of consumption offer the potential for forging a couple identity that complements the developing individualised version of self that each party brings to a relationship. Through mutually articulated desires and a joint venture into the commercial world, the couple produce a unique identity for themselves as 'the kind of people who ...'. The barcode-validated consumer couple can be seen as one of the ways in which intimacy is created (Wilson-Kovacs, 2007) and new parenthood is approached. Before pregnancy and birth, the idea of having a baby may, from a postmodern perspective, invoke the baby as the first commodity, especially in the light of new reproductive technologies that explicitly commodify conception and the scientific production of embryos. While maternal consumption is more conventionally seen as the things women buy for pregnancy and new motherhood, lesbian parenthood, single motherhood and the experience of infertility open up routes to motherhood that position the baby as the product of itemised and costed medical procedures, what Mamo (2007) characterises at 'Fertility Inc'.

The material culture of motherhood

Popular culture aimed at pregnant women is awash with the stuff of motherhood. Commodities are everywhere, especially in pregnancy magazines, saturating every feature, only to drench further in advertisements, promotions, inserts and consumer guides that take a shamelessly direct marketing approach. As observed in Chapter Four (Relationships), grandmothers in our study commented upon the proliferation of stuff both as a material advance, marking progress in the domestic sphere, and, less generously, as making motherhood "too easy". Additionally, most magazines offer 'free gifts' to attract a wider readership.[1] As with other women's magazines, the advertising potential of the title is a 'value-added' attribute promoted by the publisher to generate further commercial interest. The idea of pregnancy as 'me-me time' encourages women to indulge. In commercial terms, this indulgence can range from a Body Shop toiletry to a four-bedroom house or a 4 x 4 vehicle. Interestingly, the invitation to indulge stands in tension with the idea of motherhood as provoking a loss of self and the need to prioritise the needs of another. As Stephanie Lawler (2000) persuasively argues, the notion of mothers having 'needs' is effectively eclipsed in a discursive pincer movement in which her needs are either equated with those of the child itself (as in the child-centred attachment parenting literature) or reconstituted as potentially destructive and selfish 'desires'. Lawler offers the example of childcare advice and tabloid and broadsheet coverage of bad/desiring mothers to illustrate her argument. Yet, in the pages of these pregnancy magazines we can identify another mode of address that brazenly works the terrain between unspoken need and uncomfortable desire.

Pursuing the idea of treating yourself, one magazine promotes the latest products for pregnant women in a regular feature entitled, 'It's all me, me, me' (*Pregnancy and Birth*). Body essentials include everyday items such as maternity jeans, nursing bras and moisturising creams, profiled as 'must-have' items for expectant mothers. In keeping with other women's magazines, common strategies for showcasing products include information on the best and latest 'labour bag luxuries', for example, or the 'beginners guide to toys for newborns', as well as features that put items on trial – 'the best changing bags/pushchairs/baby monitors/stairgates/mobiles', or 'infant carriers at a glance'. Some features take a more sophisticated approach to the 'buy me now' strategy:

Say it with cashmere

Forget flowers. Say congratulations with Daniela Besso's Baby Hamper Service, already a hit with the likes of Claudia Schiffer, Kate Moss and Sadie Frost. Expectant mums deserve a little luxury, and these hampers with their range of cashmere blankets, teddies, cardigans and matching bonnets – all in soft blues, pinks and yellows – are perfect for any special baby occasion. (*Pregnancy*, September 2004)

Here, the appeal relies upon an up-market sensibility and taste signified by the exclusivity of cashmere baby products with celebrity endorsement. In *Junior Pregnancy and Baby*, a magazine aimed at the top of the market, exclusivity, designer labels and personalised products, gift wrapped and delivered to your door, become hallmarks of the special and extraordinary commodities marketed for pregnant women. The 'stylish capsule maternity wardrobe' by Hommemummy, for example, offers women a coordinating shift dress, trousers and a ballet cardigan, available in black only, in a 'beautifully designed gift box' for £275 (*Junior*, March 2005). In a deft elision between buying a bag and giving birth, the same magazine promotes a designer handbag as 'life changing':

Life changing

A lovely way to celebrate the birth of your new baby is
to own this gorgeous Tree of Life embroidered Mother's
Bag with the mother-of-pearl button detail £220. It's
the latest design by Pink Lining, who make some of the
yummiest bags for mummies. Start hinting now ...

In many other features, consumption is implicit, associated with life-
style, desire and taste rather than the direct need to buy. In a special
feature on baby showers in *Junior* magazine Grace tells her story
of organising a party for her friend and soon-to-be mum of twins.
Narrating in diary form, Grace documents the arrival of helium
balloons, roses, pink champagne, strawberries, cream scones and
glamorous guests. For her friend's special send-off Grace has booked
her into 'the spa of the moment' for 'some self indulgent "me" time'
followed by lunch at Harvey Nicholls, then the baby shower back
at her house later in the afternoon. The event is described as 'a big
girls' tea party' and a 'rite of passage for new mothers'. The essential
ingredients combine organised, baby-themed games with gossip, fine
food and tasteful gifts:

> Welcome to the celebration of an event that's yet to
> happen ... The baby shower is the new hot invitation....
> 'Demand is very much on the increase,' says Hilary Lewis,
> director of Babylist, a London-based baby equipment
> company whose client list includes Gwyneth Paltrow and
> Elizabeth Hurley ... And this season's hot gifts? Hilary
> says you can't go wrong with the classic Bill Amberg
> sling, linen and Swiss pique bedding personalised with
> the baby's name or initials, or a cashmere blanket. (*Junior*,
> April 2005)

The acquisition of life-style-choice commodities and the high
spending incited by these texts must be partly understood as a
counter-narrative to the selfless maternal subject found elsewhere
and associated with the past. Consumer culture invites mothers-to-be

to immerse themselves in the market, demanding active engagement, decision making and social positioning. Part of the work of pregnancy involves making sense of the commercial culture of motherhood by negotiating a path through the blizzard of products and signifiers that anticipate readiness for birth.

Maternal economies

Most women we interviewed appeared keen to distance themselves from the consumer world of celebrity-endorsed luxury items as presented by the magazines, and only one woman reported having a baby shower. They recognised the temporary and quickly fleeting nature of pregnancy and infancy, and expensive maternity wear and cashmere for babies appeared absurd and ridiculously out-of-step with their current priorities. The folly of excessive or inappropriate spending underlined their accounts as they elaborated upon their estrangement from the me-centred spend-thrift of representational forms. Interviewed in late pregnancy, women stressed the need to be *practical*, to take stock and to spend sensibly on the things that mattered. A couple of women reported buying 'nice' things for themselves, such as designer garments, massage oil and body lotion; most women, however, focused on the baby's needs as the motivating force for 'grown-up' acts of consumption. Across the sample, an emerging consensus suggested that 'essential' purchases include a cot, a pushchair, a set of baby clothes and nappies. The aesthetics of these items, their ergonomic qualities, how and where they were bought or acquired, can be seen as a site of diverse and contested personal investments.

Age, ethnicity and socioeconomic circumstances provide some indication of women's relationship to the commercial world and to each other. Women prepare for the arrival of their baby in contrasting situations, with different life experiences and with limited or more extensive resources to draw upon. Some women had just a corner of a room in which to create a new world. A 16-year-old living in her parental home was keeping her baby things in a suitcase under her bed. Other women expanded the project into large and newly acquired homes. While all women appeared to recognise first-time motherhood as a time for re-evaluation and life-style change, the form and texture of the change was contoured by age and social class. Younger and mainly working-class first-time mothers in the study (age 15–25) expressed a need to make small but significant personal changes that signalled a shift in thinking and a reformulation of priorities:

> "I feel like I've changed already, I've sort of become more responsible and just like little things like not spending so much money in a day or putting off getting a manicure and stuff like that. I know it sounds silly but just little things, it makes you think, you're not going to be able to do that when the baby comes … I want to start buying the baby some stuff, like teddies, picture frames and lamps." (Cody, 20)

> "You do feel a lot more confident. I do anyway, in myself. I feel like I've got this thinking cap on where it's made me grow up all of a sudden. Before I was rubbish with money and now I have to budget … It [pregnancy] does make you rethink everything cos you can't be selfish knowing you've got a little baby and its needs are more important than your needs are." (Sophie, 17)

Pregnancy for these women engaged them in a thoughtful and productive dialogue with themselves, a re-examination of who they are and how to live. Early pregnancy signalled an end to 'me-time' and the beginning of responsible adulthood (Ponsford, 2011). The imagined audience for this internal conversation may be the shapeless and nameless onlookers whose definition of 'good mother' is unlikely to embrace the idea of youth. Aware of how others may see them, young women demonstrate their fitness for motherhood by amply providing for their baby in selfless ways:

> "It might change your whole aspect of everything around you that (.) now I've got my child, everything I do would have to be for my child, and you've gotta give everything

you have, or any last thing you have, it will have to go towards the child. Because it's not just about you any more, it's about your child, so whatever you have you've gotta give it to your baby." (Lorraine, 21)

Our findings confirm Lustig's (2004) account of the ways in which young mothers, largely from ethnic minority communities in the US, demonstrate their commitment to parenthood by having professional portraits of their children taken. Baby pictures in this context assert the normalcy of young motherhood and attest to women's status as good mothers and good consumers. Professional, studio-based photographs make babies visible in a lavish way and can be seen as a riposte to educational settings that attempt to marginalise young motherhood. Additionally, the circulation of baby photographs within the family helps to build kin relations and contributes to a culture of care in which childhood is idealised through a specific practice of consumption.

Ethnic-minority subjects in our study tended to combine western-style practices of consumption with traditional cultural practices of their heritage. This was especially true of recent migrants, whose originary memories of home were *live* and closely connected to family and community through telephone, satellite television and internet. Sri Lankan-born Kanru has lived in the UK since her marriage five years ago. Pregnancy has prompted a growing awareness of the differences between western culture and her own across a whole range of fields: medical care, infant care, baby naming, attitudes to discipline and behaviour, food and eating. Kanru describes living in England as "making compromises" while positioning her culture as the "most important thing". Buying in preparation for the baby, Kanru and her husband present themselves as enthusiastic consumers, proudly announcing they have "bought everything" for the baby, as observed in field notes:

A new Mothercare pushchair, still in its box stood by the settee … Half of Mothercare was in their spare room. There was also a sarong sent by Kanru's mother that is customary for her to wear, for comfort, once she has had the baby. (MJK field notes, 11 August 2005)

Embracing the 'stuff' of western motherhood through consumption inflected with the continuation of practices from her Sri Lankan heritage, Kanru occupies a third space (Bhabha, 1994) common to diasporic subjects whose experience of moving and being is shaped

Consuming and maintaining traditional cultural practices – Kanru's preparations

by a prior history of colonial and postcolonial relations. Blending, compromising and marking difference, the couple's in-between status as migrants mirrors the in-between state of pregnancy that is lived in a finely grained way through consumption and the materiality of the domestic. Opposite their bedroom is a cupboard that they have turned into a Hindu shrine. Kanru feels it is important to be able to see this from the bedroom, and will not move to the bigger room for this reason. On their bedroom wall are two glossy and colourful pictures of babies, brought from Sri Lanka; they are idealised babies, looking happy, cute, angelic and a little dreamy/unreal. Kanru's husband tells us that this is a common cultural practice – not religious, but about the pregnant woman surrounding herself with images of beautiful babies, like the one she hopes to have.

In contrast to the self-reflective style of younger women discussed above, respondents in our middle and older age group (26–49), a wide range of upper working class, lower middle to middle class, tend to turn introspection outwards. Seemingly sure of themselves in subjective terms, taking on motherhood as an identity involved them in developing a particular relationship to consumption that was premised upon *getting organised*, doing the research, buying the right products and being prepared. Preparations, for these women, commonly take on the character of a baby audit, applying work-based skills to the personal project of motherhood. Here Belinda, a 42-year-old administration manager, explains her approach:

> "I sat down at the computer at work when I was bored one day and did a list initially of all the things that I could remember from years ago, of things that I used when I was nannying, and all the things that I thought were absolutely essential. And then I kind of flicked through magazines and looked at new ideas and things that people were marketing and thinking, 'Oh that might be quite good,' or, 'No I'm not going to bother with that,' or whatever. So I had quite a big shopping list. And then I started sort of pricing things up and just reading things about safety as far as car seats and cots and mattresses and things were concerned – not to the point of boring the pants off people but, you know, just asking friends what they used, what they liked, what they didn't like. That was quite helpful. You know, a couple of people have said with the little car seats that you carry them around in to start with, you know, 'Get one that isn't too heavy. Because you don't realise how much you cart it around, and some of them are really quite heavy.' You don't think about things like that probably, unless you've spoken to someone. And so that was quite helpful. And I went into John Lewis or Mommas and Papas saying, 'How much does it weigh? How does it fit into the car? Is it going to be easily adaptable for like if my Mum's going to have the baby for a weekend, if my partner and I want to go away or something, can I easily change it from my car into her car without too much drama?'"

Beginning with a list, supplemented by ideas from magazines, then seeking the advice of friends, Belinda turns shopping for baby into an accomplished consumer practice. Demonstrating expertise and using personal resources, women customise their spending to suit their life-style, buying products which fit with the kind of mother they seek to become. For most women in this age group the emphasis is on competence and functionality rather than economics, as explained by Alex (32), whose demanding job left her no time for shopping, encouraging her to register with the nursery shopping service at her local department store:

> "I thought, it doesn't cost any money, I can just write a list of stuff and get it. For me, it had to be done efficiently because I don't have time to spend ages trawling round the shops … we have the money to buy whatever we want really but it was a question of being reasonable about it. And it's not in my personality to go crazy."

Quality and value for money were important and recurrent themes. In this respect John Lewis[2] stores became a key reference point in identifying products and price range. Women scoped the nursery department of John Lewis – a brand dedicated to inspiring consumer confidence across the lifecourse – for ideas and information, though the final purchase might be made elsewhere, often on eBay. Some women did confess to the guilty pleasure of spending more than they were comfortable with, in accounts such as, "We started off quite good but then we just went a bit mad. We bought a wooden crib AND a Moses basket." Most women, however, narrate their purchasing practices as an exercise in restraint underpinned by good judgement. A few women in the older age group expressed anti-consumerist tendencies, questioning the commercialisation of motherhood, especially the need for so much baby stuff that proliferates in the confusion between commercially generated products and what newborns actually need. Echoing the values of the sling brigade, Melina and Hilary try to create a personal oasis amidst a sea of baby products:

> "I tried to stay away from the whole paraphernalia of motherhood, because the market is particularly targeting women. I tried to keep things minimal." (Melina, 32)

"Important things for baby are: comfort, warmth, knowing where her parents are, feeling safe, fed. What cot she's in, matching things, self-rotating mobiles, the perfect toy – not important.... Spending money on things like new mattresses – yes, because it's a safety issue.... But STUFF. STUFF for babies, you could spend thousands. You don't need it.... my big bugbear is baby baths – you don't need a baby bath, you need a bath, you need something to put water in to bathe the baby, and you need to be careful that it's the right temperature. I HAVE got a baby bath thermometer, for example." (Hilary, 39)

Developing strategies of consumption and 'bugbear' products illustrates how the market incites women to take a position on consumer practice; to draw a line and discipline desire while developing a way of communicating to others who they are. It is productive to ask what anti-consumerism means in this context. As preparations for birth involve women in total immersion in the products and values of the market, even when they are resisted, anti-consumerism appears to create another site for consumption as a politically generated alternative to the mainstream. Anti-consumption practices are born out of encounters with the market and would not exist without the market as the central reference point, despite their radical appeal. Buying the baby-bath thermometer but not the bath can be seen as a knowing act of consumption that may resonate with other mothers' sensibilities, yet leaves the market intact as the provider of 'all your baby needs'.

Baby things

For many women in our study, baby things have an appeal that takes on different forms, indicative of the kind of *work* the objects do in relation to maternal subjectivity. A teenage mother we spoke with found herself staring at baby clothes when she first became pregnant: "They're really cute and they smell nice." Another young mother reported buying baby clothes and toys before she became pregnant, indicating that the endearing quality of the objects resonated with her desire to become a mother. In keeping with Layne's (2000) study of pregnancy loss, respondents constructed themselves as mothers through the acquisition of baby things. Buying things for the baby prepares women for motherhood and consolidates a sense of the baby as 'real'. Layne explicitly draws our attention to the evocative quality of baby things; being small, soft and delicately put together, baby clothes in particular conjure up an emotional zone of precious other-worldliness, resonant of respondents' accounts:

> "I've got two drawers of brand new stuff. (laughs) It's just they're so sweet ... In Mothercare it's like, 'Oh look at all these little things, let's get this', you know, and I just couldn't resist it ... I get really emotional when I go (laughs) – it's just like, 'Oh GOD', you know ... Oh I just keep imagining them in this little outfit ... I've bought ridiculous amounts of little vests ... And I've washed them all as well, because I've heard you're supposed to wash off the chemicals. And when I had them like hanging on the line it was just amazing, like soon there's gonna be a little person in there ... And I think I just imagine them wearing it, and I want to have enough to keep it warm and nurture it, you know." (Kate, 31)

Laughing at the intensity of her emotional response to small things, Kate enjoys the pleasure of shopping for her unborn baby as a practice that brings the baby into being. Alongside the preparatory work, Layne points to the gift-giving network opened up by pregnancy (baby clothes remain the most popular gift for mothers-to-be in the US), charting the web of relationships and obligations that criss-cross friendship circles and the extended family. A small number of women in the study resisted buying things before the birth. In some cases this was part of a cultural tradition, for others it was linked to a previous miscarriage, but commonly the accumulation of baby things provoked superstition by "tempting fate". As one woman expressed it, "It's a bit scary. And it's just weird buying stuff for somebody who isn't even here yet." Across the study as a whole, the preparatory work of shopping for baby could begin before, during or after pregnancy, establishing patterns of consumption that played a significant part in the emotional realisation of the baby as a 'little person' in the making. Preparatory collecting of baby things also provided women with a bridge into new terrain and can be seen to take on the qualities of ritual as a significant ceremony for the self.

The market aimed at new mothers appears to acknowledge and amplify the emotional needs of parents by expanding the range of baby things available. The baby market aimed at pregnant women and new parents provides marketers with an expanding canvas for the promotion of new products. The logic of niche marketing suggests to companies that they pursue an incessant search for ever more specialised and unusual products to appeal to a designated consumer cohort as a necessity for economic survival. The widely promoted idea that maternity provides women with a special shopping opportunity is enhanced by the marketisation of Romantic ideals, particularly that children are a gift from God (Rousseau, 1979). From this perspective, children have an inherently endowed spiritual status, placing them close to God and Nature as the embodiment of innocence, virtue and hope. The religious aspect may have faded; however, the legacy of the Romantic movement appears to haunt the present period, particularly in the promotion and marketing of new products.

Tiny toes

> You'll be amazed at how quickly your baby's tiny tootsies will grow, but with an extra special memento from Wrightson and Platt you can keep them mini forever!
>
> Using unique techniques, the UK's leading lifecast sculptors will create a perfect cast of your little one's feet in bronze, silver, gold or even glass. The casts are incredibly detailed and will certainly be a talking point with visitors. To make things easier you don't even have to travel as the artists will come to your home. Prices start at £360. (*Pregnancy*, September 2004)

The explicit sentimentality of this artefact, suggesting to parents that they can keep their baby's feet 'mini forever', points to infancy as a desirable and endearing state to be preserved. Gillian Rose's (2004) study of middle-class mothers and their family photographs considers the ways in which photographs carry the 'trace' of the child's body that is both emotionally charged and embarrassingly trivial for mothers. Despite the paradox, women in her study felt compelled to take photographs and organise them. Whereas photographs, digital film and baby books become tools to document the child's journey from birth through key events in childhood, the lifecast sculpture appears to capture the trace of infancy in stasis. Unlike the baby, the bronze feet won't wear shoes, walk, kick or run away, making them simultaneously a preserved memento of babyhood and an object of immobilisation and truncated growth. The preservation of childhood, in this case, falls to parents whose desire to capture the symbolic innocence of their baby's physicality is working in tandem with creative and highly personalised commercial forces.

The increased commodification of pregnancy, birth and parenting has extended to areas previously untouched by the commercial sphere. The antenatal scan, for example, once limited to part of the medical assessment process in early pregnancy, has become a commercial venture promoted by several companies as a pre-birth bonding experience for parents-to-be.[3] Widely advertised in the classified pages of all the pregnancy magazines, a typical issue will include three to four advertisements from different companies offering 3-D and 4-D non-diagnostic ultrasound scanning at around £100 per session. The companies' promotional material used in ads suggest that they are 'scanning to nurture', offering parents-to-be the opportunity to 'capture precious moments' when their baby may be 'smiling, yawning, blinking, scratching their nose and sucking their fingers' in the womb. The largest company, with branches throughout the UK, is Babybond. Providing scans for different stages of pregnancy, Babybond claims to be the creator of the 4-D scan 'bonding experience' for women in their 24th to 32nd weeks of pregnancy. Babybond and other ultrasound scanning companies appear to blend romanticism with advanced new technology by suggesting that scans are provided for the purposes of 'bonding, reassurance and foetal wellbeing' (www.babybond.com). Like the capsule maternity wardrobe, Babybond products come as a complete package,

> DVD in sleeve, 1 x A4 colour gloss 3D enlargement in photomount, 6 x A6 colour gloss 3D prints, CD-ROM in white, blue or pink Babybond bag, **to take home:** **£230** (www.babybond.com)

Taylor (2004) comments on the increased visibility of foetal images in entertainment, advertising and anti-abortion campaigns. Her analysis of this phenomenon alongside the burgeoning practice of sonography argues that the foetus is fetishised as an object endowed with powers it does not have. Specifically, Taylor suggests that the foetus is seen as a life in itself, detached from its source, the mother. The commodification of ultrasound scanning may support the idea of fetishisation; however, the practices of women in our study suggest that images of the scan are more commonly used to celebrate and memorialise pregnancy and birth. Interviewing women in their home in late pregnancy, we found the scan displayed on mantelpieces, fridges and kitchen notice-boards. A woman working in a professional setting pinned the image on her office door as an 'announcement' to colleagues, and for many other women the image became the first item in the baby book. Collectively, these practices can be seen as anticipating the arrival of a new generation and a subsequent shift in status for the mother-to-be and the community of family and friends who support her (Layne, 2000).

A further example of the blending between romanticism and science can be seen in advertisements and features on stem-cell research. Though not as prominent or widely available as ultrasound scanning, stem-cell retrieval at birth appears to offer parents the hope of being the protectors and saviours of their children. The unspoken subtext is that these cells are more likely to save parents from disease than children, making the child's body a rich and valuable resource that marketers handle with caution. Saving and storing your baby's umbilical cord blood is promoted in the pregnancy magazine feature as a 'natural life insurance' against leukaemia and other related blood diseases. But more than this, stem-cell research promises to be a potential panacea for the treatment of many other diseases currently under investigation by leading scientists around the world. Investing in stem cells can be seen as a powerful act of faith, a belief in scientific progress combined with the parental desire to protect children from the foreseeable and unforeseeable risks of life. Smart Cells International advertises in pregnancy magazines as the UK's 'leading provider of safe storage of umbilical cord stem cells':

> **We've got you covered**
>
> Thankfully, the odds of your baby being attacked by a life-threatening disease are small, however, the existing treatments and promising research associated with umbilical cord stem cells, offers families extra peace of mind … an extra layer of coverage so to speak. (*Pregnancy*, September 2004).

Stem-cell storage claims to give children a future while also underlining the idea that children *are the future*. A feature on the 'stem cell debate' in *Junior* magazine indicated that the total cost of retrieval and storage of new-born stem cells is £1,250. One parent had the stem cells from her first child's umbilical cord stored two years ago and is planning to do the same for her second child. She justified her decision as a form of insurance, acting on knowledge that positions herself and her partner as informed and responsible parents:

> My husband and I felt that as we knew about it we couldn't not do it. We just hope it will be a waste of money. The way we looked at it is that the cost is roughly the price of a holiday – I'd rather not go on holiday and be safe in the knowledge that I could be helping my children and possibly other members of the family in the future. (*Junior*, February 2005)

Informal economies

The choice between new, second-hand and home-made items for your unborn baby remains significant as women begin to establish a maternal identity and simultaneously differentiate themselves from other mothers. In practice, most women do a mixture, combining new items with second-hand and hand-me-down goods, using an evolving narrative to explain and justify their choice. Heirlooms feature as highly prized items in collections, especially if they are associated with a woman's own childhood. Emergent patterns from the data suggest that age and social class play a part in decision making in this field of consumption. In general terms, young women expressed a preference for buying new, while older mothers were happy with second-hand items. However, within this general trend we found diverse practices and complicated rationales. Many women reported that the announcement of their pregnancy heralded the arrival of bags of baby stuff from relatives who were moving into the next phase of child rearing. Commenting on inheriting a mountain of toys and clothes from her sister-in-law, 26-year-old self- employed Eleanor says, "I'm not sure how much of it was altruistic or how much she just wanted to get it out of the house (laughs), practically everything he wears is a hand-me-down from her." As her baby was in most clothes for "all of ten minutes" she was very happy to give them a second outing, but would not buy baby clothes from a second-hand shop. The provenance of second-hand items was important to Eleanor, and in this she echoed the views of many women in the study. Other patterns of consumption point to the role of grandparents in the preparatory process. Many women reported that grandparents were keen to be involved and often sought to establish their connectedness before birth by buying a key item such as the pushchair or cot. For other parents, not being in a network meant buying everything from scratch and served as a reminder of their isolation in unknown territory.

Younger women in particular felt that it was important to buy new as a demonstration of their commitment to parenting:

> "Mum said we can get second hand but I said to her and I'm saying to everyone, this is my first (laughs) baby, I'm not having second-hand or car boot-sale things. Second hand is like using someone else's things. I don't like it … I don't want my sister's stuff, no, I wanna buy my OWN baby stuff." (Farah, 23)

Buying new from reputable high street stores and paying for it themselves can be seen as a matter of pride for some young women and also as a way of taking charge of a situation that risks being taken over by family and friends. The indignation of one young woman was very clear: "IT'S MY BABY but they've gone out and done the baby shopping." Taking control of preparations for themselves, many young women sought to create an ideal environment for their babies by embracing the familiar motifs of babyhood: pink and blue baby clothes, soft toys and products adorned with Disney characters and Winnie the Pooh. Younger mothers tended to choose expensive, top-end brands as a form of display, particularly evident when making larger purchases such as the pram:

> "I'm gonna buy the nicest pram, my pram has to be wicked. I don't wanna be walking down the street with a bad pram. Don't want people to think, you know, I can't provide for my baby. Oh my God, of course I can provide for my baby." (Mumtaz, 23)

However, initial intentions to provide babies with the best of everything were not necessarily sustained. For example, 26-year-old unemployed Anastasia shifted from a preference for designer brands to a habit of Primark over the first year of her child's life, as the costs of parenthood became apparent. Devoid of the need to showcase their fitness for motherhood, older first-time mothers were generally more relaxed about blending new with second-hand and hand-me-downs, often favouring new items with a distressed look that had a fashionable retro appeal. Following through on the desire to be sensible, many women in the 36+ age group had a developed, but not necessarily straightforward narrative on the preparatory process. Women in more comfortable socioeconomic circumstances bought many second-hand items from NCT sales, held regularly at local centres. This form of consumption was widely regarded as ethically sound because it supported the exchange of goods within a peer community of *mothers-like-me*. One woman on the fringes of an NCT network and with ambivalent feelings about belonging disparagingly referred to women in the group as "the sling brigade", a term that neatly caricatures the consumption patterns and parenting styles of a certain group of women. Generally associated with attachment parenting (see Chapter Five), the sling brigade represent a small but growing niche market in slings and accessories, mostly online, linking like-minded mothers in the US, Europe and Australasia. Women in this group tend to reject traditional baby products as unnecessary and, as they advocate sleeping with your baby when it's not in a sling, nurseries, cots and buggies become redundant.

A high proportion of women in the 36+ age group embraced the idea of second-hand consumption in an ironic inversion of what the young mothers told us:

> "I don't feel the need to do extravagant over-the-top purchasing ... I don't feel, you know, if I don't have it I'm not prepared or I'm not a good mother if I don't have Winnie the Pooh all round the walls. But I think that all comes with age too, and the security that, you know, actually that's not the most important thing." (Clara, 40)

Women like Clara, and Valerie below, formed alliances with other first-time mothers and drew upon friendship networks to "save" and pass on baby stuff for use among themselves:

> "And I really LIKE that thing about this sort of economy of babies that people just donate stuff to each other and it kind of circulates kind of outside the capitalist economy."

For women who have moved from a position of *new is not necessarily practical/value for money* to *second-hand is better* the internet offers much scope for recycling, bargain hunting and ethical purchasing. A website called Freecycle enables people to pass on things to others willing to pick them up. Many women reported taking full advantage of eBay, enjoying the virtual scramble for bargains and "saving" vast sums of money, especially on more expensive branded items such as cots and pushchairs. Customising patterns of consumption to suit ethical and eco-friendly agendas engaged women in attempts to find a space outside the market for the exchange of goods and could lead to Mumtrepreneur enterprises, turning bright ideas into business ventures. NCT second-hand sales created a new arena for consumption and a new network of mothers who developed a refined vanguard consumerism that, as Valerie intimated, created further patterns of inclusion and exclusion between women.

Buggies and nappies

The constant acts of discernment and interpretive meaning-making that accompany maternal consumption practices suggest a troubled and unresolved relationship both to baby things and to other mothers. Baraitser (2008) refers to the tendency to characterise commercially produced goods as despised substances, tainted by consumerism. Existing as an aside to the main drama, the relational dyad between mother and baby, the stuff of motherhood conventionally takes on a mediating or symbolic role in mother–child relations. Baraitser (2008) encourages us to rethink the relationship between maternal subjectivity and the objects women use in their mothering practice. Seeing maternal objects as furnishing the mother's workplace, Baraitser suggests that they can be seen as part of the 'ergonomics of motherhood' (Baraitser, 2008, p 127), shaping the contours of what women do and how they do it. Mothering engages women in multiple encounters with objects. The changing scale of baby things, from tiny buttons to heavy prams, recreates Alice-like experiences with the material world. Simultaneously, the experience of time may be differently felt, disrupted and in slow motion as women's bodies are literally encumbered by baby and baby stuff. Tuning in to the altered state of mothering, as a subjective site that resides within the body as well as the consciousness, Baraitser imaginatively suggests thinking about motherhood from the perspective of the object rather than the mother and child. Drawing upon Actor Network Theory, she proposes that objects are both ethical and social. Human sociality is held together by non-human elements that form part of the social in ways that make no distinction between human and non-human 'actors'. From this perspective, mother and child can be seen as appendages to the buggy, collectively generating a flow of action as they negotiate their way through their local environment.

Mothering engages women in efforts to release the ethical capacity of objects, to enable them to share the nature of their work. In this respect, material culture is far from trivial; advances in product design incorporate thoughtful and clever features that imbue the object with 'something of the hero' (Baraitser, 2008, p 225). In generating flow between actors, the mother is relieved of something by the object which appears to recognise the ethical nature of her work. Mother-and-baby objects encapsulate the thought that goes into creating them. In turn, this helps women to think about the thought that goes into marketing in general. Although women may be dancing on the edges of the market, playing catch-me-if-you-can, the fact that the market is so attentive and responsive is extraordinary – a form of attention that acknowledges the hidden work of mothering. This is alluded to by grandmothers in accounts that capture how alone and ignored they felt boiling nappies.

The ethical and social quality of objects is made explicit in the marketing of products themselves. Bugaboo, the popular and fashionable buggy manufacturer associated with celebrity mothers, 'yummy mummies' and famously making an appearance on the television series *Footballers' Wives*, advertises its range as 'the definition of mobile comfort' (www.bugaboo.com, accessed 5 August 2010).

The buggy as object of maternal practice

The range of buggies available points to the complex and fashion-prone needs of the modern mother. Women commented on the signs and signifying practices that proliferate in the market:

> "It took me ages to work out what sort of pushchair to get and I feel trapped by the way that everything makes a statement, you just can't get a neutral pushchair, it's all a statement about big wheels and going jogging and how much money they cost." (Laura, 35)

"Just how evolved does a pram need to be?" remarked another participant in a wry response to the widely promoted branding of buggies as 'multifunctional transportation systems'. In a Bugaboo campaign that draws inspiration from car advertisements, an ensemble of fathers and buggies perform a choreographed Busby Berkeley-style show of symmetry, precision and excellence (www.bugaboo.com, accessed 5 August 2010). Human and non-human combine to create a confident and visually compelling display of creative cool and functional brilliance. On the website, Bugaboo profiles its buggies as 'multi terrain', 'modular' and flexible. 'Frog-like suspension' enables the pushchair to glide over all surfaces, ensuring easy navigation through sand and snow. The 3-in-1 design offers the magical gift of versatility, transforming the buggy into a car seat and carrycot as required, and as demonstrated in the performance ad. The heroic design comes at a price, the cheapest and most basic model retailing at £749. Returning to young mothers and their desire for new and expensive buggies may point to their capacity to recognise the *flow* between objects and themselves. Seeing mother, baby and buggy as fused into one suggests an openness to absorbing the property of things and to considering what it means to be closely aligned with material objects. The conjoined action of mother and buggy may generate a 'new kinetic experience' (Baraitser, 2008, p 259) with the environment as well as a way of avoiding the embarrassment of looking poor. In choosing expensive buggies, young women demonstrate a knowingness and a familiarity with their locality and, consequentially, an awareness of their place within it. For some young mothers, investing in a buggy can be seen to inspire confidence, facilitating a way of being in the world in which they feel equipped to traverse the environment beyond the home. Mother, baby and buggy can become intrepid adventurers, able to handle anything and everything they encounter.

While buggies can be seen as objects of desire for mothers, nappies, in a literal sense become abject objects as repositories for the expelled waste cast off by babies. Two generations ago women used terry towelling nappies, which, to ensure hygiene, had to be washed at a high temperature. Some grandmothers in the study recalled nappies being boiled in a bucket on the stove as a familiar

Practising natural nappies

feature in family kitchens, prior to automatic washing machines becoming widely available. Now 95% of mothers in Western Europe use disposable nappies, which, aside from convenience, raises environmental issues as landfill sites become overloaded with non-biodegradable plastics largely from nappies. As cloth nappies use hot water, electricity, detergents, physical labour and, often, the fee of signing up to a washing service, the decision over nappies always involves consumption. Like the acquisition of baby things, preparing for motherhood offers no neutral territory. Attempts to act ethically, doing things differently and bypassing the market, appear to produce more networks and sites of potential division between women. Asking new mothers about their choice of nappy invites them to comment on their relationship to domestic waste, eco matters and global concerns. Most women positioned themselves as "green", expressing an interest in responsible consumption and a strong commitment to recycling; however, the practical appeal of disposables was overwhelming:

"I have thought you see, I like the idea of having er … cloth nappies and that's what I was determined what I was going to do, but I'm not sure with a baby in childcare whether that's really a very realistic idea. The idea of being given a whole bag of crap-filled nappies at the end of the day when I get back from work, I don't know, I haven't got a tumble drier at the moment, I don't know. I might give it a go and see how I get on, I mean then you've got the nappy service thing where they'll come and clean them for you so maybe that's the best way. I am very kind of anxious about the whole nappy thing I mean in environmental terms, just because its horrifying how many nappies babies get through it really is and like … 10 a day, more … just frightening amounts. And so I recycle everything, I have a compost bin you know, and it's just the idea of you know chucking these plastic things away constantly is just horrifying so er … we'll see but again I feel, like with the labour thing, that would be a nice way but actually if it's too much stress or whatever then I'm not going to beat myself up about it." (Orla, 42)

Rather than making a heart-felt decision, most women suggested that they were slipping into the idea of using disposables to save time and make life easier. New parenthood was demanding, it was important to be practical and, if necessary, to compromise on ideals and personal values. Using cloth nappies was not only less convenient, it involved dealing with urine and faeces, a thought that generated laugher and disgust in equal measures:

"I recycle everything, I really do … my partner says that I'm a hypocrite, we're having a little thing about it now. Because I've got boxes of everything, we've got compost, we do all of that, but I just draw the line at that [reusable nappies] (laughs). Sorry, I just can't … I just know I just don't want to even go there, you know … So I've got Huggies and Pampers at the moment, and I'm just gonna see which ones are best." (Elaine, 39)

Most women had bought disposable nappies in preparation for the birth even when they expressed a preference for cloth nappies. This purchase was made easier by the promotional offers of manufacturers. Pampers' website, for example, was widely used by women as a source of information on a diverse a range of matters on pregnancy and child development. The company sent vouchers for its products and free samples to new mothers who registered with the site. The introduction of biodegradable disposables provided a compromise position that was readily embraced by women looking for an eco-friendly solution to the nappy dilemma. Only one woman in the study appeared committed to "keeping the faith" at the risk of boring her not-so-principled friends:

> "It's OBVIOUSLY got to be reusable nappies. And I'm just AMAZED that friends don't go for reusable nappies. You know, I mean I've always been a bit of a kind of obsessive about my recycling and you know, friends find me quite sort of tediously self-righteous about these things. So kind of, yes of course I'd try, you know, reusable and washable nappies as a first." (Valerie, 42)

The nursery

A further area for maternal preparations and the marketing of products focuses upon the home as a transformative site of consumption as domestic space is rearranged to accommodate the new baby. In this respect popular culture tends to profile the creation of a nursery as the room in the house that marks the shift from couple to family. Decorating the nursery is treated as a venture into the future, a space that can be filled with the desires and imaginative projections of becoming new parents. In pregnancy magazines, features on creating a nursery are high on aesthetic appeal, usually filled with an abundance of photographs and little textual commentary. In keeping with magazines in the interior design and home make-over genre, features on the nursery commonly conclude with a 'get the look' guide to products and suppliers. Recurrently fashionable themes for nursery décor include white furniture, natural fabrics, pastel and neutral shades and a less-is-more approach to the display of toys, artefacts and childhood memorabilia. Clutter is out – making it a difficult look to maintain for anyone with young children and limited space. Decorating the nursery highlights parental sensibilities and aspirations: the room itself can become an idealised expression of their tastes and values, told through the lens of the environment they choose for their children. The following feature on decorating a boy's nursery points to the significance of style and taste and the ways in which parents draw upon a form of aesthetic capital to respond to the gender of their child and the circumstances of his birth.

> ### *A sea and sky theme, illuminated by fairy lights, creates the perfect boy's nursery*
>
> After indulging in everything pink and floral for their daughter Isabella-Rose, Grace and Michael Saunders decided to opt for classic French antiques for their second child, Gabriel Sky, adding a nautical theme … Gabriel was born at the peak of a summer heatwave so the aim was to create a room that exudes calm and cool … It retains a masculine feel, with a boat-shaped bookshelf, roughly-hewn boat ornaments and collection of *Tim at Sea* classic stories …
>
> Classic antique pieces are another important element. Key features include a vast French armoire found at a Paris flea market and a charming turn-of-the-century rocking horse, which Grace and Michael spotted – and bartered for – on Portobello Road. And the finishing touch? A watercolour of flowers painted by Gabriel's grandmother. (*Junior*, April 2005)

Interestingly, the tasteful cosmopolitan couple introduce an intergenerational element into their son's nursery as a 'finishing touch' – a reminder of their creative lineage that is present but not integral to the overall design.

The nursery offers parents-to-be a space to create a special place within the home for the new baby. We did not encounter any nurseries as self-consciously chic as those featured in the magazines. Women in our study presented this space in various states of 'readiness', from bare walls splurged with paint-pot colours and decorating mess to pristine and beautifully finished rooms. The new baby's room usually spoke, consciously and unconsciously, to the desires of the maternal as women sought to surround the child with the things that appeared important to them as a new family. While some women took the view that the child is entering our world as a couple, others worked to create a unique environment for their baby. Choosing primary colours or pastels, gender-specific items or neutral pieces, purpose-made nursery furniture or customised pieces all pointed to the significance of the maternal project as an investment in shaping the world of the baby in ways that are imbued with emotional connections. Carly spoke of decorating the nursery as a way of displaying the things that were important to her and, she hoped, would become important to her child. Working to create family bonds and maintain intergenerational connections became integrated into the preparatory project of decorating the nursery (see Chapter Three for a full discussion).

Access to space, and socioeconomic circumstances, could constrain or enhance the baby-room project. Young mothers living in the parental home or in local authority residential facilities were most restricted by limited resources. Interviewing women in these situations could leave a lasting, physically bounded trace of the social divisions that emerged between the women in our study:

> Sophie meets me and takes me to her unit in the mother and baby centre. It is very small – a kitchen/lounge and one bedroom with room for a single bed, a chest of drawers and nothing else ... I felt that the unit was compact and had everything she needed but that it was also an infantilising space for a young mother-to-be. The bedroom in particular seemed to emphasise her youthful status as a child who was expecting a child. It was a girl's room, there was a cartoon motif on her duvet – it's not *My Little Pony* but it reminds me of that. A Moses basket

on a stand and a baby relaxer lined the corridor-like space next to her bed. (MJK field notes, 22 August 2005)

For women in more privileged situations, decorating the nursery presented a fun activity that can be seen in Bourdieuian terms as an exercise in taste and discernment. Choice of colours, furniture, decorative motifs and artefacts structure the aesthetic domain as expressive markers of taste, as these contrasting accounts reveal:

"Well it's probably not so much colours, I'll probably go more *theme* if you see what I mean, if it's a girl it probably would be pink but I wouldn't go in and paint it pink I'd probably just keep it magnolia and just bring in all girly things do you know want I mean, rather than being pink, but have girly stuff in there and equally if it's a boy the same thing, I wouldn't paint the room blue but I would bring stuff in that's for boys really … we're having a mural painted at the moment, a friend is a really good artist and we're looking at fairy tale-type pictures, but soft, not scary ones." (Sharon, 29)

"I'd got a fair idea of what I wanted the nursery to be like. I knew I didn't want it to be all pastels and sort of soppy baby colours, I wanted it to be really vibrant and sort of stimulating and bright colours and things. So when I was looking at stuff I suppose I had that in my head all the time, you know, and was going for bright yellows and oranges and things, rather than pinks and soft colours." (Belinda, 42)

In terms of décor and room dressing, differences between women remain highly personal and often articulated as 'what I don't like/don't want for my baby'. Some women do not want a room that is 'too babyfied', while others create a baby heaven in cloud-like shades of white and cream. The two most-mentioned decorative themes were Disney characters and Winnie the Pooh, cited as examples of what women would not use or have used to decorate the baby's room.

Both figures can be seen as constitutive of a commercially saturated childhood, creating different fantasy worlds and peddling different kinds of 'cute' (Cross, 2004; Casey and Martens, 2007). Appealing to both children and adults, Disney characters conjure up a knowing, clever and magical landscape, while Pooh Bear lives in a benign world of bumbling and lovable silliness. In preparing the nursery, first-time mothers draw upon material culture to work with and realise the act of mothering. Developing an aesthetic sense in relation to baby products may appear individualistic, steeped in consumer culture and the repertoire of late-modern choice; however, as Clarke (2004, p 71) points out, 'commodities and infants are inextricably bound through the social processes and networks of consumption: they are "made" though a multitude of objects and exchanges'. In the accumulation of baby things, receiving gifts and hand-me-downs, and the purchase of key items, women act out and take on forms of connectedness and belonging integral to the construction of a maternal identity.

Conclusion

In this chapter we have explored the place of commodities in the transition into new motherhood, doing work that is preparatory, expressive and identity producing. In this chapter and elsewhere we have suggested that new motherhood may be a moment in which women are repositioned in relation to the market, operating not simply as consumers in their own right but as mediating a family economy and the relationship between the market and the child. We have noted the ways in which the mode of address to expectant mothers seeks to bridge some of the divides between the needs and desires of the child and the mother, forging a notion of pregnancy as 'me-time' that is entertaining yet which bears little relationship to the kinds of practices engaged with by women in our study.

We continued our exploration of the ways in which age and biographical stage structure the situation of mothering by considering the distinctive ways in which women of different ages orient towards the material and commercial culture of motherhood.

For the youngest women in the study, pregnancy signals the demise of their teen status, and with it, teenage consumption. In becoming mothers these young women are able to express their maturity by privileging the needs of their child over their own and displaying this to potentially judgemental others. Younger women were keen to demonstrate their ability to provide for their baby and their commitment to motherhood by buying new. They were the group most invested in material culture and most open to merger with objects in the recognition that a pushchair, for example, could become part of them rather than an object they used.

Women aged between 26 and 35 had timed the birth of their first child to fit around an established career that it was possible to 'break' without significant loss of status, the 'right' moment in their personal relationship and the necessarily capital resources. In their accounts of consumption these women also emphasised 'grown-up' acts of consumption, being practical, making life easy. Their accounts were redolent with a functional yet highly individualistic approach to objects – they work for me. This is the group of women who are most clearly targeted by advertising and whose aspirations and desires are reflected back through popular cultural imagery. Often living a version of the 'pure relationship' (Giddens, 1992) consuming for motherhood appealed to them as resourceful women who had embarked upon pregnancy as a beautiful big adventure that could be customised to suit their unique style and tastes. These women enjoyed pregnancy as a project of self-expansion and increased attention.

Yet there was also a group of first-time mothers who were not so ready to be wowed by the pleasures of consumption. These women came from across the sample, were predominantly middle class and often in the older age group. Commonly taking a discerning view of products as full of hype and froth, these women expressed a desire for alternatives to the market, positioned themselves as knowing consumers, creating a new arena for exclusionary vanguard consumerism. In some cases these women were actively involved in circumventing market processes, for example, sharing or swapping goods informally. Yet attempts to collectivise tended not to cross boundaries of class and culture, as women shared and swapped with others like them.

Our research has captured a particular historical moment in time as well as a shared biographical moment as women anticipate and move into new motherhood. Much of what we have explored in this chapter is anticipatory, revealing how women engage with a common culture of commodities, advertising and products in order to imagine and enact a new identity. Much of this is also aspirational, involving ideas about who we think we are, what we want to be and what we are afraid of being. As time passes, practices and, increasingly, habits set in that are constrained by the concrete realities of our situations. Certainly we found that a year after the birth of a child, women had very different feelings about some of the objects that they had invested so much hope in when eight months pregnant. What our findings presented in this chapter suggest is that new mothers encounter the market in very different ways and immediately begin a process of participation (however complicated and ambivalent) that involves them in distinctive cultures of consumption and parenting. Research with families of toddlers and school-age children suggests that class-based consumption practices are a critical vehicle through which inequalities and privileges are reproduced, with the middle classes engaging in 'concerted cultivation' and working-class families consuming for both survival and pleasure (Lareau, 2003; Vincent and Ball, 2007).

Notes

[1] Splash mats, baby cutlery, name books, T-shirts, story-book CD, baby blanket, teat and soother set and baby bath puppet are just some of the freebies collected over the study period.

[2] John Lewis is a UK department store chain that claims to be 'Britain's favourite retailer'. The store has a significant online business and, as at November 2010, a policy of being 'never knowingly undersold', meaning that it will match the price of any item that you find cheaper elsewhere.

[3] In one of our research sites the local hospital had an official policy of refusing to tell expectant parents the sex of their baby. This had significant consequences in this research site, as many mothers held back from buying clothes or decorating nurseries. The only mothers in this site who knew the sex of their child were those who had paid to have 3-D scans.

EIGHT

Birth

Jade's hospital bag

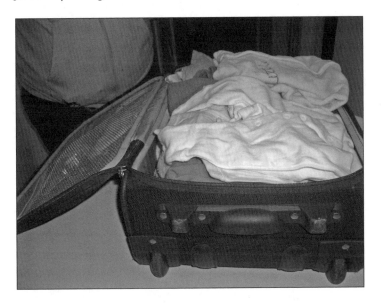

We now turn to the final chapter in women's journey of becoming mothers: anticipating, planning and experiencing birth. The temporality of the pregnant body and the nearness of its conclusion was an inevitable aspect of the dynamic within our interviews with the women in our study. For some women, such was the discomfort of sitting for long periods that the interviews were carried out with women perched on their shiny rubber birthing balls. Carefully packed hospital bags and TENS machines could be spotted in corners of rooms. On a few occasions interviews that were set up for a particular date were cancelled because the onset of labour came earlier than expected, while other interviews were followed by e-mails exclaiming that the birth had occurred not long after the interviewer had left.

The hospital bag visually represents this journey, and women were happy to reveal its contents for us to record with our cameras. Nappies, a night shirt and slippers, for one woman a pair of flip-flops on the advice of a friend to avoid soggy feet, and other somewhat alien items such as incontinence pads, all served as a stark reminder of the physical journey the body was about to endure – with a full set of baby clothes for the return journey home, materialising the objective of one becoming two. Like the other 'props' of birth, the hospital bag is both enormously poignant (capturing the human drama and danger of birth) and potentially comic (revealing disparities between expectations and realities and between feminine and maternal identities). The latter is captured in the 'labour bag' list of celebrity mother Jules Oliver (Oliver, 2005), which includes a very long list of what she packed her first time round (including hairdryer, straightening balm, under-eye concealer, fashion magazines and lip gloss in three colours). She then reveals a much shorter list of those items she actually *used*: clothes, pads, nappies, toiletries, fan and face spray. The underlying message communicated is that birth is a serious business which undoes the body work of frivolous femininity and somehow remakes the woman as a mother.

In this chapter we explore how women anticipate and subsequently make sense of an experience that is, for most, previously unknown. We focus on the way in which birth stories circulate within maternal cultures, asking how birth is made intelligible and noting the cultural silences that continue to exist around it. The chapter begins by situating the contemporary practice of 'birth planning' within a longer history of childbirth, contrasting the current consensus around 'normal birth' within a medicalised framework which provided the context for the birthing experiences of a previous generation. Age and social class have been recognised as key factors impacting upon women's capacity to make informed choices about birth, with certain birthing bodies in danger of being excluded from normative ideals. We will introduce the way in which older, mid-age and younger women drew on their position within a common culture of motherhood to understand birth, and within this the role of bodily and cultural capital. We then go on to explore the ways in which the 'scary bits' of birth are encountered and digested by women, focusing on television as a resource and the stories of other women – including grandmothers. We attempt to capture the significance of generation at the moment of birth, with women both seeking out and rejecting connection with their own mothers, balancing allegiances within the family. Throughout, we counterpose women's expectations of birth with evidence from case studies of how these translated into practice. We end with a detailed account of how one couple made sense of their experience, and in doing so bring together many of the themes explored in the chapter, revealing birth as an emotional, embodied, inter-subjective, scary and altogether messy experience.

The cultural context of birth

Melanie's birthing ball

The period during which we conducted our research was characterised by a maternity policy agenda dominated by ideas of 'informed choice' and increasing the capacity for 'normal birth'. At the same time, the rates of home births have declined and those of caesarean sections had reached record highs, leading to speculation as to whether 'choice' is an illusion in the context of increased intervention and stretched resources. It has also been a period when women's birthing bodies have become more visible and subject to normative ideals about what constitutes a healthy and responsible birthing body. But is birth planning a rational individualistic activity in which women armed with the 'facts' are empowered to 'choose' birth options? In our interviews we invited women to reflect on their deliberations in relation to imagining and planning childbirth. Many had been encouraged by health professionals to make a 'birth plan' and had already done so or were planning to do so soon. Most had some idea of where they would like to give birth, whom they would like to be present and the 'type' of birth they would like to have, including levels of medical intervention and pain relief. As discussed in Chapter Three (Body), the 'birth plan' lies at the centre of contemporary antenatal care within the NHS: the idea that all women can actively make decisions and make choices about their birth and are empowered through antenatal education and midwife support to do so in an informed way. While many have argued that this conception of choice is an 'illusion', given that it is constructed within a medicalised framework, it does constitute a different context to that which shaped the experience of birth for a previous generation.

Although the grandmothers interviewed in our study did not belong to a single age cohort, many talked about going into childbirth with an element of naivety about what to expect, taught only about basic breathing techniques and experiencing birth within a largely medicalised context, often without the support of birthing partners (including fathers). While there might be continuities of experience between the youngest of our grandmothers and their daughters, those who gave birth in 1960s and early 1970s witnessed a significant shift in the social context of birth – from home-based midwife care to a hospital-based approach. Within the UK, this shift took place largely between1963 and 1974, during which time the percentage of births at home fell from 30% to 4.2% (Nove et al, 2008). Within this new 'medical model' childbirth was reconstructed as a condition that demands expert monitoring, regulation, control, supervision and intervention. Women's knowledge, experience and management of birth had been subsumed in the name of expert knowledge of risk prevention and 'safety' (Oakley, 1979; Davis-Floyd, 1992; Jordan, 1993; Cahil, 2001).

The fear and experience of pain and danger in childbirth, and women's right for control over this through pain relief and medical intervention, was a focus of first-wave feminist activism. (Reissman, 1983). In pre-modern Europe, death was closely associated with images of childbirth, 'the mother's womb could become the baby's tomb and the mother gave the child life at the risk of her own' and '[death's] 'fearful prognostication was never absent: it was part of the order of nature' (Gelis, 1991, p 238). It is easy to dismiss this 'pre-modern' experience of birth as the stuff of rural peasant life, but we need only go back to the experiences of the great-grandmothers of the women in our study, to a time of high maternal mortality rates, which dropped from 86 deaths per 100,000 total live births in 1948 to just 6.2 per 100,000 in 2008.[1] The use of technology and medication became a focus for second-wave feminist critique, which argued that medicalisation devalued women's own knowledge of their embodied experience of pregnancy and birth, making 'women's labour in bearing children invisible' (Oakley, 2005, p 119; Young, 1990).

Contemporary third-wave feminist positions take a more ambivalent position to the critique of technological birthing, suggesting that the promotion of 'natural' childbirth may result in women's feeling guilty about medical intervention while also portraying an essentialist view of the female (Annandale and Clark, 1996; Crossley, 2007; Woolf, 2001). While expert medical knowledge remains a dominant discourse within contemporary society, there have been a number of challenges to its hegemony, including interventions by natural childbirth campaigners and midwives who, particularly in the UK, have continued to advocate for birth that is safe and satisfying. As indicated in Chapter Five, increasingly, maternity care is subsumed within consumer approaches to healthcare, where different approaches to birth are presented as equally valid options which may be chosen to suit a woman's broader life-style and sense of self. For example, the NHS website and resource *Emma's Diary* explains: 'It's a good idea to make a birth plan early on in your pregnancy to help you decide how you would like your labour and birth to be managed. One of the things you will need to think about is how you want to give birth.' It then goes on to provide a description of four birth choices ('active birth'; 'natural birth'; 'water birth'; and 'hi-tech birth') before providing a list of considerations for inclusion in the birth plan.[2]

Informed choices: anticipating birth

In 2006 only 2.7% of births took place at home, the majority of them being to mothers over the age of 30 not giving birth for the first time (Nove et al, 2008). Between 2006 and 2007 the caesarean rate stood at 24.3%; 11.5% of births were instrumental deliveries; and over 20% of labours were induced. Only an estimated 52% of births were normal deliveries (NHS IC, 2008). The caesarean section rate is relatively low among young mothers; the highest percentage of caesarean sections were in the cases of older women in the context of 'high risk' (POST, 2002). Older mothers (40+ years old) were found to have an increased risk of having a stillbirth, and the risk is regarded in relation to physical complications such as pre-eclampsia and gestational diabetes (CMACH, 2010). The stable rate of maternal mortality within the UK has been attributed to the increase in older-age mothers giving birth. The increasing caesarean rate has also been attributed to an increasing number of multiple births, resulting from increased use of assisted conception.

During the course of our research there was mounting activity, and pressure on the government, from the midwife movement to improve maternity services, which cumulated in the publication of the *Maternity Matters* White Paper in 2007 (DH, 2007). This document proposed that there should be equality in birthing, with all women given the right to informed choice about the location of birth (including home and midwife-led birthing centres), type of birth and birthing attendants, with an emphasis on access to a 'normal birth' – defined as birth without surgical intervention, use of instruments, induction, epidural, spinal or general anaesthetic. In 2008 an estimated 2,500 couples in Britain spent between £500 and £1,000 hiring a 'doula' from a fast-expanding industry, and it is estimated that this figure has quadrupled in the past five years (Donnelly, 2009). One mother was quoted in the *Telegraph* as saying:

"The birth experience was something that was really important to us; there are people who spend more on a buggy" (Donnelly, 2009). In the context of stretched maternity services, it appears that the message of 'equality' in *Maternity Matters* is becoming somewhat skewed, with relative privatisation of aspects of support enabling the privileged few greater chances of telling successful birth stories.

Most of the women in our study were aware of these challenges to a certain extent. Monica (39), who was planning a home-based water birth, explained:

> "the impression I'm getting – is that there was a bit of a – not a backlash as such, but women sort of asserting their rights a bit more and saying, 'No, I'm not going to be lying flat on my back'. And they seem to be very keen on having natural birth."

Regardless of age, women tended to aspire to a birth that was "as natural as possible". There were, of course, exceptions where, for different reasons, women elected for or had to come to terms with the idea of caesarean section delivery following medical advice. These exceptions included cases where the baby was in breech position, multiple births and previous experience of stillbirth or miscarriage. They also included an older mother who felt that her age made natural birth too risky and a woman who became a mother through surrogacy. Deliveries were most often planned to take place in hospital, although a small minority of women had opted for a midwife-led birthing unit. Eight of our 62 interviewees expressed the desire for a home birth, including a few who opted to locate the birth process at home for as long as possible, entering hospital only for the later stages.

The potential for realising 'informed choice' and capacity for 'normal birth' have remained the subject of much debate and speculation. During the period of our research there was a wealth of media coverage about the NHS's stretched resources and incidences of MRSA within hospitals, which led to questioning as to whether choice was actually possible (Franklin, 2008). Many of the women in our study recognised that their choices were limited according the resources available within their area, in particular the allocation of water-birthing pools on a 'first come, first served basis'. In addition, the practice of rotating midwives made it difficult for some women to get consistent support in birth planning (see Hadfield and Thomson, 2009 for further discussion).

Previous research has highlighted the way in which social class can be implicated in how women exercise control in their planning of the birth, with middle-class women feeling more activist, and working-class women more fatalistic because of their trust, familiarity and relationship with health professionals (Zadoroznyj, 1999). Inequalities in relation to maternal care were a key feature of the *Maternity Matters* White Paper, with the recognition that certain groups from deprived areas were failing to have their needs met, and consequently experienced higher rates of mortality. In particular, the White Paper highlighted increased likelihood of maternal death for single mothers, the unemployed, those living in deprived areas and those experiencing domestic violence. Similarly, infant mortality was linked to women in routine and manual socioeconomic groups, black and ethnic populations and single-parent families (DH, 2007). Mothers under 20 years old have the highest neonatal mortality rate, linked to social deprivation and delays in seeking maternity care (CMACH, 2010). To rectify this issue, the White Paper suggested that efforts be made to investigate what prevented these women from seeking or maintaining contact with maternity services, and adjusting maternity services to meet the needs of women from disadvantaged backgrounds.

For many of the younger teenage mothers in our study it was the perceived 'judgement' of midwives accessed through their GP surgery that restricted conversations about birth choices. Those with access to specialist parenting education centres valued having a space in which they felt able to ask midwives questions about birth and to learn from the experience of peers, exploring a range of 'normal' birthing options, including home birth and water birth. Securing comfort and privacy were key objectives in their birth plans, particularly for the two women who opted for a domino and home birth. In talking to these young women, we gained a sense of their desire for birth to reflect as much as possible a familiar and familial surrounding that protected them from their overriding fears of being judged or 'looked at'. The presence of family members, partners and, particularly, their own mothers at the birth was a recurrent theme in the narratives of younger mothers. As we will explore, it was through this intergenerational support that some of these young women were able to make successful interactions with health professionals and medical intervention in the face of perceptions of incompetence and irresponsible mothering.

Older women's preoccupations around birth tended to be very different. Usually birth was envisaged as a private couple experience, although there were examples of relatives being present at the birth. Older mothers (aged 36+) tended to undertake serious research when planning the birth, were often sympathetic towards natural birth literature and were most likely to plan for home births.[3] They were also least likely to prioritise a fear of pain in their consideration of birth options, perhaps reflecting the messages of the natural birth texts. Yet birth plans were often made tentatively with the recognition that, as older mothers, they might be more high-risk and susceptible to medical intervention. Women accepted that putting the safety of the baby before their own desire for a particular kind of birth was part and parcel of being a 'good mother', a compromise heightened if, like Clara, they felt that this might be their last chance for parenthood.

> "Other people on my antenatal class they have no fear that anything will be wrong with their baby, or that anything will go wrong. They're scared about labour, and are not scared about the baby. I'm not scared about labour at all … I think that maybe there is a factor of age in it. Because (.) I feel like this is a real last chance saloon for me." (Clara, 40)

Women in the middle age group (26–35) perceived themselves as having babies at the 'normal' time and appeared to be deeply implicated in cultural discourses about normal birth. As we have discussed in other chapters, these women are the target audience of a plethora of life-style magazines, television programmes and 'factual' advice literature, and they tended to be highly attuned to the ideas of informed choice in childbirth. Mid-age mothers generally anticipated giving birth with their partners, with childbirth symbolising a key moment in the romantic couple experience. As good biographical planners, mid-age mothers tended to have confidence about their physical condition in relation to the risks of pregnancy and childbirth. There were, of course, exceptions within our sample where women were regarded as a high medical risk. Generally, however, the potential for birth without intervention was left relatively open, with 'back-up' plans for pain relief. Yet women were reluctant to wed themselves to ideas of 'normal birth' in the face of the unknown. One woman described birth without intervention as "going all hippie", and the idea of giving birth for the first time outside the hospital context was juxtaposed with the idea of being a good mother ("who are you doing it for, at the end of the day?"). There was also the sense that women felt pressure to have a 'natural birth', which could result in feelings of being a 'failure' if intervention did occur; several drew on a popular counter-narrative citing the advice of friends to "take the drugs if you need them". Hannah, aged 32, who was expecting to have a caesarean because of her baby being in breech position, frames her explanation in terms of conflicting cultural discourses:

> "It's the first baby and I just don't want to risk anything, you know. Um I'm actually really quite relieved. (laughs) I feel – I feel guilty that I feel relieved, which is bizarre. Because I think, deep down, it kind of makes you feel less of a woman.... Oh God, are people going to think I'm too posh to push? (laughs). Um yeah I think women are a bit down on other women about that, aren't they?"

In general, women's anticipatory accounts of birth planning were characterised by flexibility and uncertainty. Among the middle and older age groups of women in particular, perceptions of risk were highly developed and there was a willingness to entrust one's own safety and that of the child to the 'experts', with risk awareness and avoidance becoming 'a moral enterprise relating to issues of self-control, self—knowledge and self-improvement' (Lupton, 1999, p 91). Previous research on middle-class women's anticipatory narratives has demonstrated the way in which these women seek out and prioritise expert knowledge, placing trust in experts, and are 'seduced' by formal medicalised preparations for birth (Miller, 2005). This study suggests that perceptions of risk may play an important role in the 'self-surveillance' practices of middle-class mothers, constructing certain 'choices' as being wayward or potentially selfish (Lawler, 2000; Ribbens-McCarthy et al, 2002). The counter discourses identified by Miller, in which notions of natural bodily capacity are moralised (the 'good mother' will give birth naturally whereas the 'guilty' mother may give birth with assistance), were also evident in our research.

Uncertainty was primarily articulated in relation to the impossibility of imagining birth, how one's body would react to birth, what pain in birth is like and, for some, a general sense of 'fear' about the unknown. In order to make informed 'choices', women needed to have a sense of what birth would actually feel like, and as first-time mothers this understandably posed a challenge. We found, however, that this fear and uncertainty could also be seen to be rooted in a much deeper social construction of birth. Whilst consultation and reliance on expert knowledge was a clear feature of most women's accounts of birth, women's birth planning was underpinned by embodied, emotional and inter-subjective experience of birth.

The 'scary bits' of birth

Interviewer: So have you read the whole thing then?

Jessica: (laughs) No. Some bits, which are too scary, I just leave out.

Interviewer: Which bits are the scary bits?

Jessica: Um, I suppose looking at things like – er when you get to the actual birth. And you sort of think, well (laughs) I think I'll just let that happen and – and – you know.

Interviewer: So you've tried not to focus too much on the birth?

Jessica: Um (.) yeah not – I haven't dwelled on it. Because, you know, you know it's inevitable, you know one way or another you're going to give birth. And I mean I like to – I'm quite – I like – I do like lots of information, so I do like to sort of know. But I don't – I don't think it's necessary to know absolutely everything. Because it's happened for so many (laughs) thousands and thousands of years and people have coped.

In *Telling Bodies: Performing Birth*, Della Pollock (1999) argues that the 'progressive' construction of pregnancy and birth in antenatal teaching and literature encourages a narrative structure in birth stories in which 'planning becomes conception becomes pregnancy becomes ten fingers and toes birth – the nine months and counting model of birth telling' (Pollock, 1999, p 4). As documented in Chapter Three, these narratives circulate in magazines, websites and pregnancy advice literature, inciting readers to map their own progress with glossy illustrations of the growing bump. Yet, like Jessica, some women navigated these texts carefully, avoiding descriptions of birth, not wanting to tempt fate by planning too soon or scaring oneself about what could go wrong. Some, like Jessica, deliberately choose not to have a birth plan.

In 1976 US feminist Adrienne Rich wrote about women's need 'to understand the extremity and meaning of the "transition stage", and the "psychic" as well as physical dimensions of labour' (Rich, 1976, p 185). Yet such accounts continue to be marginal. Women in our study who were interested in natural birth invested more time in reading and thinking about birth, drawing on authors such Grantly Dick-Read (first president of the National Childbirth Trust) and Sheila Kitzinger, whom 35-year-old Faye describes as writing "proper sensible birth books", enabling women to "know all the options, empowering women to make the right choices". Yet even where women were committed to as natural a delivery as possible, they still could, like Alex, experience the natural birth literature "a little bit beyond, a little bit too way out". Knowing the 'facts' can help women to think about the type of birth they would like and to understand the implications, benefits and drawbacks of different options while in labour, if those options are available. But, as Pollock argues, the construction of birth as a linear progressive process produces a narrative space that leaves little room for the messy, laborious, spiritual, emotive, euphoric, dramatic, violent – at times horrific and for the fortunate few orgasmic – experience of birth. Death, stillbirth, disability, illness also become an unspoken taboo that is put aside, absent from the casual chat that draws in expectant mothers about due dates, baby names and the sex of the baby. Expectant parents, according to Pollock, became 'locked' into a narrative script which looks for a happy ending. Birth stories, in turn, are expected to confirm this expectation through what she terms a 'comic-heroic' narrative construction:

> Stories with dire conclusions are often simply prohibited, either by doctors who warn prospective mothers off anecdotes and lore for fear of panic or non-compliance or by the generations of mothers who feel that they're doing newcomers a favour by not revealing the secret. (Pollock, 1999, p 5)

No all women took this happy ending for granted. For example, Leyla (30) (who had come to the UK seven years previously as a political asylum seeker from Turkey) explains through an interpreter that her mother had died during the birth of her second child: "She was young but had diabetes, and in those days they didn't place much importance on it. In those days ... she died on the operating table from loss of blood." Leyla's account emphasises her perception of equity in UK maternity services where "there are many cultures but the system treats them all the same", contrasting this with Turkey where "they support their own and don't treat us well. And if you have money you get better treatment and they'll put you in the front of the queue." The following extract, taken from her interview, reveals much about her own ambivalent feelings about birth and represents an interesting cultural exchange between interpreter, interviewer and interviewee.

Interpreter: Have you thought about a birth plan? You know here they ask you about how you would like to give birth? Using gas, at home, in hospital ...?

Leyla: Yes, (laughs) I'd like to have a caesarean.

Interpreter: Why?

Leyla: Because you don't have any pain that way. Isn't that true?

Interpreter: Yes but in this country there is a popular school of thought that says if you don't give birth naturally you have not experienced the 'real' thing. Did you know that? That's the thinking here.

Leyla: I just want the easy way! I'm a bit scared you know? Because it's my first.

Interpreter: (to the interviewer) I'll explain.

Leyla: And if I had given birth before it would be easier, but I haven't so I don't know.

Interpreter: You can't choose of course, can you? [Bit of a mix-up here as choose and vote are the same word in Turkish]

Leyla: Oh, no. They said [at the hospital] if you are healthy you can't have a caesarean. I asked them. If there is no problem you have a normal birth. They said if there is a problem they would do a caesarean. Of course! That was just my thinking.

Where women had experience of more than one country to draw on, the specificity of the UK birthing culture was brought into relief. In most cases women felt that the UK compared favourably, although their reasons for this differed. For example, Australian Heather liked the British midwife-led approach to birth that minimised intervention, encouraged a quick return home and provided follow-up health-visitor care. She contrasts this with the private healthcare experience reported by her sister back in Australia, who was provided with a private room, pampering and a candle-lit dinner for two, yet for whom support ended at the hospital door. Heather's mother was much less positive about the state of hospital hygiene in the UK when she came to visit her pregnant daughter, expressing concern that she would not get a proper rest if sent home the day after giving birth.

'True life' birth stories

Reading birth

The reluctance to engage with birth expressed by Jessica and others is not just a concern with a future event that is as such unknowable, but can be seen in relation to particular societal norms of what is speakable and unspeakable about women's birthing bodies. Anticipating the unknowable – how one's own body and the body of one's baby will respond to the inevitable physical experience of childbirth – many of the women in our study described a tension between opting to 'try not to dwell on' the 'scary bits' and, conversely, seeking out birth stories and the experiences of other women through vignettes found in the advice literature, pregnancy magazines, televised births and the birth stories of friends and relatives.

In contrast to their accounts of learning about birth through literature and antenatal teaching, women's accounts of watching dramatised and televised births were associated with an engaged discussion of the 'scary bits' of birth – the psychic, embodied and emotional dimensions of labour. Our findings support Lomax and Fink's contention that the visual may 'facilitate the narration of accounts ordinarily stigmatised and silenced' (2010, para 9.1), as well as Jensen's (2010) argument that televised forms of expert advice may operate in completely different ways than traditional texts. For first-time mothers, birth is a mediated event that is only knowable through representations generated by others. Women of all ages engaged with visual images of birth through programmes on the UK satellite Discovery Health and Leisure Channel, the BBC documentary *Desperate Midwives* and through the videos of birth shown in antenatal classes. Not all women in the study watched televised births – some were restricted by having only terrestrial television or through a rejection of watching television in general.[4] But many women actively sought out these visual representations as a way of imagining and engaging with the meaning of birth. Several described their viewing as "obsessive" and "compulsive", with one woman commenting "you don't want to watch it but you have to see the end bit". Words such as "amazement", "emotional" and "miraculous" were used to describe the visual drama of birth. Mary (33) found that in watching these programmes, "it's almost like you're with these women it's absolutely amazing".

Other members of the family were also drawn into this compulsive viewing, particularly siblings and partners. For example, 33-year-old Deborah described "white knuckling it" with her sister while watching a medicalised hospital birth on the BBC3 programme *Desperate Midwives*. This shared viewing appeared to bring a point of connection for significant others around the experience of birth. Vickie (33) described returning home to catch her partner watching it:

> "The voice-over went, 'And it's the first time the baby looks into the Mummy's eyes', and he went, 'oh I couldn't bear it' ... He was so emotional. (laughs)"

For Mary, the British documentary *Babes in the Woods*, set in a birthing unit in the New Forest, was particularly powerful. When we met her, Mary had recently been told that her baby was breech and she might have to forgo her planned natural vaginal birth for a caesarean section, something that caused visible emotion during her interview. Mary explains that watching the documentary enabled her to see other women whose plans for natural birth had "failed", licensing the view that "it doesn't always happens, all you can do is give it your best you know". Other women saw the benefits of watching televised births to visualise the different types of birthing options (both natural and medicalised versions) they had read about and different settings for birth. Elaine (39), for example, who was planning a hospital birth, comments: "I've seen the forceps and thought – they're just barbaric". And Melody (28) attributes her belief in her own capacity for a "normal birth" in a midwife-led birthing centre to watching births on television, explaining that:

> "It is just how people react and how they seem to be in each different experience and it just seems far more relaxed ... what I really want in terms of the intervention ... more natural and ... easier and the people seem far calmer ... more ideal to me than being strapped to a bed."

Yet these visual birth stories, while representing the 'mess and gore' of birth still appeared to confirm the reassuring 'happy ending', where "no matter how painful a labour may be or how gruesome it looks at the end of the day all these mothers forget the pain and they've got their babies in their arms" (Karen, 30). The happy endings of these true-life stories are more reassuring than the portrayal of birth in some hospital dramas, in which death in childbirth and the loss of babies made gripping viewing. Although televisual birthing was generally looked to as a source of realism, it could also offer escapism. For example, Louisa (35), told us how much she had enjoyed the programme *Portland Babies*, based on birth in a private hospital, "seeing how rich people do it". Louisa recognised that her NHS experience would, if she was lucky, include a water pool, but was unlikely to include "a private room with nice curtains". Others were more circumspect about "real life" birth stories, avoiding those on television and elsewhere on the grounds that "you can know too much" and "lull yourself into a false sense of security" (Charlotte, 32).

Intergenerational birth stories

Although we explored the birth plans of over 60 women, we know about what subsequently happened with only our 12 case studies. Table 8.1 attempts to trace some of the contradictions and continuities between women's reported plans and their subsequent accounts of their experiences. Three women had the birth that they planned, at least in terms of location and levels of intervention (Alex, Deborah, Tina). Several who had hoped for a water birth did not get it. Three who had planned home births ended up in hospital (Monica, Nadia, Kim) and two had unplanned emergency caesarean sections (Anastasia, Sofia). In this section we explore women's accounts of their births, drawing on the case-study data, which includes interviews with grandmothers about their own experience of birth a generation before and, where possible, interviews with partners and significant others. The picture that emerges is very different from the rational discourse of informed choice that characterised the antenatal interviews, constituting a messier, more embodied and relational perspective in which bodies are connected over time and space.

Table 8.1: Planned and reported births of case-study women

	Planned birth	Reported birth
Alex, age 34	Natural, limited intervention, birth centre, partner present.	Natural, limited intervention, birth centre, partner present.
Anastasia, age 26	Hospital, prefer natural but leaving it open. Water, gas and air, maybe epidural, partner and neighbour present.	Hospital, caesarean, epidural. Bad experience with long birth, partner and neighbour present.
Cody, age 20	Hospital, water, gas and air, epidural, partner, mother and sister present.	Hospital, not water, pethidine, no time for epidural and gas and air, partner, mother and sister present.
Deborah, age 33	Home, natural, partner and friend present.	Home, natural, partner and friend present.
Heather, age 27	Hospital, natural in water, partner present.	Hospital, natural, birthing ball, gas and air, asked for epidural but advised could do without. Not water birth, partner present.
Kim, age 16	Home, natural, mother and grandmother present,	Hospital, natural, mother and grandmother present.
Lorraine, age 21	Hospital, natural, gas, air and water, mother, aunt and sister present,	Hospital, natural, gas, air. Not water birth, mother and sister present.
Marion, age 48	Home or hospital and epidural, partner present.	Epidural and caesarean, partner present.
Monica, age 39	Home, natural in water, partner present.	Hospital, gas and air, pethidine, wanted epidural but no staff to administer, partner present.
Nadia, age 36	Home, natural in water, partner present.	Hospital, epidural, forceps delivery, partner present.
Sofia, age 24	Hospital, natural in water, midwife-led, partner and mother present.	Hospital, caesarean and epidural, partner and mother present.
Tina, age 36	Hospital, natural, tens, partner present, possibly mother present.	Hospital, natural, gas and air, partner and mother present.

Not all the women in our study knew about their own mothers' experiences of labour and birth. Women like Carly and Gail, whose mothers had died, could experience an acute longing for this knowledge during their own pregnancies. Some women, like Anastasia, reported that their mothers withheld accounts of their own birth, and stories could also be 'blocked out' by daughters. Yet, where they were known, birth stories could be well worn, the subject of family humour and bravado, actively used to structure relationships within the family. Cody told her interviewer that she was mistaken for a stomach "ulcer" in pregnancy, a story her mother still enjoyed to tell. Cody explains that her mother's "favourite" daughter was also her "favourite birth" because of the way she just "slipped out". Evidence of a family narrative around birth was also evident in the Thompson family when 16-year-old Kim proclaimed "My story is the best!", prompting her mother to share with the interviewer an account of her daughter's birth that involved "becoming as large as an 'elephant'". Kim jumps in to finish the story: "when it came to my due date I just didn't come ... they said my mum wouldn't have a Christmas if they didn't induce her".

A resource drawn on by women to imagine birth (regardless of social class or age) was their mother's own birthing body. For many there seemed to be an implicit reading into our questions "Do you know about your mother's birth or can you tell us of any birth stories in your family?" that the embodied experience was likely to be replicated. Their narratives highlighted how birth can become the site for intense intergenerational traffic of emotion in which both mother and daughter became increasingly aware of each other's embodiment and connection, what Pines (1997) describes as a moment of 'reawakening' for both parties. Mumtaz and Deborah are typical in their comments:

> "She's had all natural births. So HOPEFULLY, hopefully I'm hoping I'm gonna be taking after her ..." (Mumtaz, 17)

> "Mum, I am the same shape as you, I hope it is going to be the same!" (Deborah, 33)

This could also translate less positively in terms of a communication of anxiety and apprehension in relation to the pending birth. One woman talked about needing to "block out" her mother during pregnancy and birth, and some grandmothers kept a deliberate distance from their daughters until the birth was over. Establishing a connection between generations of birth can be complicated and uncomfortable. One teenage mother reported noticing that her mother turned her back, hiding her face when responding to her cousin's question about whether birth hurts. Women described their mothers' "tentative" questions enquiring about how they felt, often over the telephone. This anxiety could be magnified by geographical distance, as in the case of 27-year-old Heather, who recounted a telephone call with her mother in Australia:

> "'Darling, I JUST am SO worried about you, I'm SO worried. I just DON'T want you to be in pain, you know, during that birth …' And I was like, 'Mum, for goodness sake, women have been doing this for THOUSANDS of years, you know, everyone'll be fine.' And she was like, 'But you're MY little girl, and I don't want YOU in pain.' …. I said to her, 'Do I need – do I need to be worried? … Is something bad GOING to happen?'"

This searching anxiety and protectiveness prompted some mothers to invite themselves to the birth of their grandchild or to offer their services as birthing partners. This could pose a problem, particularly for those women who envisaged their birth as a private couple experience, finding themselves mediating between two forms of intimacy.

In talking with expectant mothers and grandmothers it became clear that women's earlier childbearing experiences were reawakened by their daughters' pending labours. Jessica, whose fear of the "scary bits" of birth we learned about earlier in the chapter, was well aware of the story of her own birth. She explains that her mother refers to "a passing of souls", with her own birth coinciding with her grandfather's death and a period of grief and depression. For Jessica. growing up with this legacy was difficult: "as a child you don't always want to hear that".This spectral theme is extended in Jessica's account of sharing the news of her pregnancy with her mother, who claimed that she already knew because she had a "strange feeling in [her] belly, like something was moving". Jessica reports powerful feelings of guilt when she decides to reject her mother's offer to attend the impending birth, explaining that her presence would make the couple feel "uncomfortable".There is a sense then that the "scary bits" of birth hold a deep and troubling meaning for both mother and daughter.

Painful themes of loss and bereavement could be encoded and preserved within birth stories, to be unlocked again in a new context. For one mother-in-law, the imminent birth of her grandchild appeared to re-invoke memories of the loss of her only daughter, whose brain was irrevocably injured in birth. Her unexpected outburst of emotion and anxiety in the present caused the expectant couple concern for her health and well-being. Her daughter-in-law, Melina, observes, "I can see her worrying a lot about it. Everything is coming back to her."

Birth stories can also operate as historical artefact, providing accounts of the birthing practices of the past – sometimes anachronistic and out-dated, often unreliable, yet providing clues about a distant drama. Kate (31) carefully recites the story of her own birth as a record of a trauma that precipitated her mother's severe post-natal depression, an account that reveals the painful way in which our stores are shared.

> "This is in my Mum's words – and she was given a pill to slow the – to slow me down ... But I've never come across that in anything ... my Dad doesn't like to talk about the past, and thinks it should be left where it is. But um I have thought about asking him, but I always sort of bottle out (laughs) at the last minute ... it was a big red pill, sometimes she tells me, but then it changes colour and it's a white pill, or a blue pill ... she blames it more on this pill she was given and – and her hormones, which is why she had the breakdown." (Kate, 31)

Fearful of these "big red pills" and the they effects had on her family, Kate had omitted pethidine from her birth plan, hoping for as natural birth as possible, and had approached a Chinese herbalist for some "stuff to burn" if she became overdue, to avoid being induced. These glimpses into the emotional, embodied intergenerational versions of motherhood remind us that, while we may expect or desire to hear or tell the 'linear', 'happy-ending', neat and tidy birth story, alternative images of birth, the messy, sometimes spiritual, embodied and emotional 'stuff' are never far from the surface. Such images get caught up in anticipatory narratives in a seemingly un-linear manner, revealing the coexistence of the present and the past, which is largely unconscious as births become entangled.

Narrating intergenerational embodiment

The majority of the grandmothers whom we interviewed gave birth to their first child in a significantly different cultural context, although the contrast was less for those who were younger. Not all gave birth within the UK, nor within the publicly funded NHS. Most had experienced hospitalised birth, usually in the presence of a male doctor. For some it also involved pethidine and medical intervention in the form of forceps or episiotomies. Most of the grandmothers had endured a solitary first labour, either because of unreliable couple relationships or single motherhood or because men at the birth were either not accepted or expected in "those days". In some cases, because of staff shortages they also gave birth without continuous support from either midwife or doctor. Some of the grandmothers shared very difficult stories of first births with interviewers and we were unsure as to whether these were stories that they had shared with their daughters. The worst of these stories were characterised by broken narratives of a loss of innocence, drugged confusion and memory loss. Youthful inexperience and subservience to doctors are combined with glimpses of the violence of birth, with women describing not knowing what "hit them", feeling like they were "on a conveyor belt" and "being kept on the bed". In sharing these difficult birth stories with interviewers, grandmothers constructed their younger birthing selves as both naive and stoical: "I didn't utter a sound", "the usual tough old thing", "you just got on with it", "I just thought it was normal".

In some families there were strong affinities between the generations, and grandmothers had a significant influence on (and in) their daughters' birth experiences. Not surprisingly this was associated with generational proximity and relationships between younger mothers whose own mothers tended to be relatively young themselves. Lorraine, aged 21, told us that her own mother had given birth to her first child in 1979, 16 years old and alone in a Caribbean hospital. Lorraine described her mother as "very brave", yet failing to do what "the doctor told her to do – they sewed her up without any drugs". Lorraine expects her own experience of giving birth in the UK to be "totally different", yet she is determined to do as the doctors tell her and to "push push". She had been disappointed by the lack of opportunity to discuss birth options with her midwife and to attend antenatal classes. Despite some differences of opinion between them over her marriage and pregnancy, she accepted her mother's proposal to be with her at the birth. When we interviewed Lorraine's mother, Beverley, now aged 42, we were told a more graphic account of this first birth in which we got a glimpse of her younger self and her deference to medical authority.

> *Beverley*: I was in pain and pain and pain, and then the pain went away. And um the doctor said to me, 'Push, push,' and I'm pushing with my throat, as you do, 'urgh, urgh'. And he said, 'No, no, no you have to push below.' And I said to myself, I'm going, 'Yeah right.' So he said, 'No, no you have to push, you have to push.' And I'm like 'urgh'. And um I heard him say to the nurse, 'Bring' – whatever it was, I can't remember the word that he said – and I saw the nurse bringing a scalpel. (laughs) WELL did I start to PUSH, (laughs) but it was TOO LATE, by that point it was too late. And um I had three (.) she cut me three times. And every time she cut it was on the doctor's orders to cut – no anaesthetic, nothing.

> *Interviewer*: So she was cutting you inside?

Beverley: No, she was slitting my vagina, making it wider. There was no gas and air, cos this was in the Caribbean, and everything's got to be done natural, you know what I mean. And she cut me three times. And I was like, 'I'm sorry I didn't push.' (laughs)

Interviewer: Wow I bet you were screaming, weren't you?

Beverley: I didn't, you know. I didn't, I didn't, I didn't. Because at the time I thought, you know, it was normal, and this is what everyone did, and de-de-de-de-de. And um (.) the baby came out, and I had 16 stitches, I had 9 inside and 5 outside. And (.) they took the baby away.'

The birth story that Lorraine subsequently shared with us could not have been more different to that of her mother.

"They started to tell me to hurry but I was taking my time as I wasn't in no pain … they rushed me into the labour ward, they had to break my waters, they put tube on his head because they said he was distressed … came straight on the bed I didn't have to push, three pushes and he came on the third push. … the doctor wasn't ready [mum and sister] were in the room when I was giving birth. My sister came round to the front when I was pushing and she's going ooh I can see lots of hair, and everyone's like laughing and then my mum said oh yeah can see hair."

Here we gain a sense of how a family script might be rewritten, with Lorraine asserting her own embodied knowledge over panic of the delivery room, with the support and presence of her sister and her mother.

Normal birth and normalising birth

Monica's birthing pool

Storying a difficult birth can be understood as playing a part in normalising the experience, creating and sharing a narrative through which unbearable and stigmatising feelings can be aired and gain recognition (Lomax and Fink, 2010). Here we focus on the birth story of Monica, drawing also on interviews with her partner, Jamie, and her mother, Erica.

Monica (39) had approached the birth of her first child in a quietly confident manner. She has always enjoyed the story of her own birth: at home, her father present and over in 45 minutes. She hoped to replicate something of the same, planning a home birth with a midwife and her partner, using a water pool that she had purchased because of the lack of availability of those to borrow or rent. Monica's mother Erica explained that she was careful not "interfere", believing that, as in her own experience with her mother, her daughter would not wish to discuss birth with her, and drawing on Monica's extensive research as adequate preparation to justify this. We subsequently discovered that Erica's first birth had been "horrific,

I think Monica found this too", in a hospital setting ("like a conveyor belt" and something she claims to "barely remember".

Monica's birth story is a narrative of disenchantment. After going overdue she had to forgo her plans for a home water birth and was induced in hospital, which she described as "not a clean nice environment, different people, you didn't know what was happening". Alone for the beginning of labour after her partner was asked to leave, Monica describes feeling like a "nuisance ... you know how polite we are ... I didn't want to make a lot of noise". The account that we built of how the labour progressed is narrated from two positions, Monica's own hazy "hard to remember", and through the eyes of her partner, who came "hurtling back" to the labour ward. Monica's attempts to negotiate pain relief fell on deaf ears and she was unable to get the epidural that she wanted, managing on gas and air and pethidine. The labour progressed quickly, but in the final stages the baby became stuck and Monica was given an episiotomy. Her partner, Jamie's, account captures the visceral shock of birth for those observing as he moves from tiptoeing round the ward to pick up Monica's things, to the labour unit:

> "When I got there she's strapped onto this thing with a mask on, going ... Have you seen *Blue Velvet*? That's the image that came into my mind really. I was just going to start singing some sort of Bobby Vee song and then you'd have had the complete picture. They were just like really medieval and just ... not how it's portrayed in NCT antenatal classes as this lovely natural moment ... they ripped her ..., slashing ... And then to see her afterwards ... you know, it was all ... it was just like the movie! But fortunately she didn't really know ..."

It was only at the end of the birth, when she was stitched up by the midwife who had treated her before the birth with acupuncture, that Monica felt that someone was "looking her in the face – cared about me as a person". A year on, when she shares this story with the interviewer, Monica is "glad for the distance" and has accepted that she did not get the "magical moment people talk of". She continues to be "upset thinking about how things had gone", especially the way she was treated by hospital staff, and is resolved that with a second birth she would be "more selective about where I went and I'd a bit more active". Monica continues to suffer from complications arising from the episiotomy and she jokes that the birthing pool taunts her from the spare room: "got to sell that thing, got to get rid of that". Yet Monica has also forged a positive account of her experience in relation to ideas of good mothering, noting that "when you think what could go wrong. I just count myself lucky." She and Jamie share a heroic couple narrative of birth where they are joined in the "wide-eyed" shock of becoming parents, even though "it was me going through the physical side of it I felt as if it was both of us delivering him and having him". Monica explains that she has learned much from her experience and aims to have a second birth story that she can pass on to the next generation.

Conclusion

The idea of creating a birth plan, in which a woman anticipates birth and makes choices about location, care and pain relief, grew out of the natural birth movement of the 1960s and 1970s and the attempt to empower women to take back control of childbirth from obstetric medicine. Yet the purpose of informing women about normal birth and choice was not intended to be the whole picture; structural factors need to be in place to support women to realise choices. In the words of pioneering campaigner Sheila Kitzinger:'It is not only a matter of giving women choice, but about assessing the risks and benefits for different settings for birth and the quality of relationships that are created between caregivers and the women they serve' (Kitzinger, 2008, p 78). Yet questions of 'risk' and 'benefit' continue to be contested, with outcomes for mothers and babies increasingly distinguished and the relative safety of different settings shaped by investment. An editorial in the *Lancet* published in 2010 asserted that 'women have the right to choose how and where to give birth, but they do not have the right to put their baby at risk. There are competing interests that need to be weighed carefully' (*Lancet*, 2010). The politics of childbirth are far from over.

In this chapter we have explored the ways in which the women in our study were preparing themselves for the birth of their first child. Although these women were all at the same stages of pregnancy at this same historical moment, drawing on many of the same cultural resources, their situations also differed in radical ways – not least shaped by their ages and the biographical stages at which they were becoming mothers. We have attempted to show how the women in our study anticipated giving birth to their first child in a cultural context that constructs notions of informed choice and birth planning, promoting women's capacity for normal birth. By and large, women adopted this framework for imagining birth, constructing plans while also accepting the need for flexibility in the face of uncertainty. Women were preparing for birth in a context where maternity services were financially stretched and where birth plans might operate primarily as reassuring fictions. Alongside this rational planning we also observed women engaging in other kinds of emotional preparations which sometimes involved collective viewing of visual media and connecting with 'real life' stories. The importance of supporting first-time mothers as they negotiate this unknown territory is confirmed by a report by Royal College of Midwives in 2010 which reports an 'alarming' rise in birth trauma, associating increasingly requests for caesareans with mothers who are 'too scared to push' after difficult first births (Campbell, 2010).

By drawing on case-study interviews we developed a richer understanding of how stories of birth circulate and operate within families. Interviews with grandmothers give us access to birth stories from a different historical moment, retold within a research relationship and a changing family dynamic. Through these intimate family portraits we gain insight into how communication within families does and does not take place, and how birth becomes a moment of intensive intergenerational traffic. Women in our study had very different relationships with their mothers and we have explored examples of intergenerational proximity as well as distance, including examples of labour that are primarily family affairs and those that are experienced through the couple relationship. The very different accounts of birth that we gathered from the women in the study suggest the vital importance of consistent support, care and advocacy for the labouring woman and how a breakdown in care can result in a traumatic experience. First birth continues to operate as an initiation into motherhood which is only partially narrated within the common culture of motherhood.

All of the women interviewed in our study were planning to give birth within the NHS provision, although several expressed interest in employing 'doulas' as a strategy for securing consistent midwife care. At the time of writing, the UK Royal of College of Midwives declared that the UK faced a crisis in public maternity services, with resources overstretched by a rising birth rate and the organisation and funding of services uncertain in the face of NHS reform. It is easy to take for granted the existence of a 'common culture' of maternity services, shaped by a partnership between midwifery and obstetrics and providing a consistent ideology of 'choice' and 'equity' as well as joined-up provision of antenatal and post-natal care. The evidence that we have captured in this chapter suggests that securing this service has been a significant historical achievement for women, yet it is fragile, undermined by inadequate resources. The logic for those who can afford to 'buy' an enhanced standard or style of care is compelling yet, would have potentially devastating consequences for the provision of a common maternity service.

Notes

[1] www.independent.co.uk/life-style/health-and-families/features/the-birth-of-the-nhs-856091.html.

[2] These include: Where are you going to have your baby? What kind of birth do you want? Who do you want to be with you as your birth partner? Do you have any special requirements to help you through labour? What is your ideal method of pain relief? Do you want your waters broken or to wait for it to happen naturally? Would you rather tear naturally than have an episiotomy? Do you want your partner to cut the cord? Would you like your baby to be given to you immediately after being born? Do you want to breastfeed your baby as soon after the birth as possible? Do you want your baby with you all the time? Would you like the placenta to be delivered with the aid of drugs, or naturally? Are you happy to have student midwives or medical students

present at the birth? (www.emmasdiary.co.uk/giving_birth/article/plan, accessed 10 November 2010).

[3] In a US context it has been established that three groups of women are more likely to have home births: upper middle-class college-educated women who are critical of medicalisation; conservative or religious women invested in the privacy of the family; and extremely young women who have little pre-natal care (Michie and Cahn, 2005).

[4] None of the women reported watching birth films on *YouTube*, a cultural phenomenon that appears to have developed since our original fieldwork (Longhurst, 2009).

NINE

After birth

We approached the making of modern motherhood study with apparently simple yet ambitious objectives, to ascertain what first-time motherhood means to women; to discover the significance of intergenerational and generational narratives and identifications; and to explore whether and how being a mother changes women's identities. In the course of the study women and families gave us privileged access to their intimate worlds during an important period of their lives, the transition to first-time motherhood and the arrival of a new generation. Our methodology has shaped the knowledge that we have produced. Over the course of this book we have explored different dimensions of this process, drawing on interviews with expectant mothers, analyses of the cultural and material contexts that frame contemporary motherhoods and case studies of how families respond to the experience. The book has been organised to capture something of the temporal process of transition, beginning with stories of conception and culminating in stories of birth, yet we have also drawn on our rich case-study material to suggest how narratives may echo through generations within a family and the ways in which expectations may be confounded, confirmed and reframed by experience.

The transition to motherhood is also an arena where differences between women are defined and compounded through the creation of distinct cultures of child rearing (Clarke, 2004; Byrne, 2006; Tyler, 2008). In previous generations, mothers worked and/or looked after their children, depending on social class and income. Today there are a range of different maternal identities to 'choose' from or be positioned by. Some present fantasy images, like celebrity mothers with their perfect bumps who regain their pre-pregnancy bodies in a matter of weeks. Other mothers are identified by the media as 'yummy mummies', 'teenage mums' or 'older mothers'. Policy discourses identify working mothers as 'heroic', doing their best for their families, while 'stay-at-home mums' have 'chosen' to look after their children themselves. Other groups of mothers identify with certain kinds of parenting styles. Generally, women with similar ideas about motherhood are drawn together in friendship networks, increasingly through internet message boards.

The different chapters of the book have focused attention on aspects of the maternal experience that we felt demanded extended discussion – because they were issues that both preoccupied mothers and were salient to a wider popular culture and policy agenda. A distinctive contribution of this book has been to bring together the reflexive relationship between the biographical and its cultural context, and we have consistently sought to counterpose the ways in which women talk about their lives with reflections on how motherhood is represented in popular culture and how these representations in turn contribute to the biographical challenges faced. The process of dissecting and aggregating women's accounts in order to explore different dimensions of motherhood enables us to gain a sense of diversity, as well as insights into how experiences may be patterned. So, for example, we gain much by isolating and pooling women's accounts of birth or the body. Yet this process also fragments accounts from their original context within an individual or family biography, resulting in a loss of meaning. By using and returning to case studies we hope to have both mapped the contours of contemporary motherhoods and revealed the particularity of each mothering situation, including the psychic complexity of the unfolding drama of family life. In this final chapter we review the work undertaken in the book, reflecting first on the theoretical concepts employed before returning to our data set to engage with the core question of our study: whether and how motherhood changes women's identities. Finally, the chapter explores the ways in which themes that arise across chapters can be understood to inform a maternal politics.

Situations and the practices of mothering

> ... this simultaneity of the historical-cultural
> determination of what it means to be a mother and the

unique first-timeness of the experience means that new motherhood identities should not be simply understood as pre-given and externally produced, but as developed and creatively made by mothers themselves out of the social, material and psychic resources available in their external settings, their relationships, their life histories and current experiences. (Elliott et al, 2009, p 19)

In Chapter One of the book we set out a broad conceptual framework that has helped us to think through our rich and diverse data set. We have drawn heavily on the ideas of the 'situation' taken from the existential feminism of Simone de Beauvoir, which allows us to think about the temporary state of pregnancy at the same time as holding in tension the specificity and commonality that women experience as they are positioned in and through institutional and cultural processes. The situation can be simultaneously embodied, biographical and specific, yet also understood as produced and constrained by historical circumstance and social patterning. Our situation orients us towards distinct cultures of mothering, realised both in terms of local values, practices and resources and in the way we encounter shared cultural resources and representations. The concept of the situation encompasses the biographical and lets us move beyond it in order to think about how a coincidence of situations may constitute a generation, within which there is diversity, complexity and potential solidarities. If we think of motherhood as a situation our attention is not consumed by questions of being, but rather oriented towards questions of doing – what does this situation allow and how are we placed (Wetherell, 2009, p 5)?

As a thread within feminist thought, this existential and contingent approach solves many of the problems associated with thinking about women as simultaneously the same and different, and as both socially located yet active and creative (Howie, 2010). Yet the concept of 'the situation' also has weaknesses. By definition, the idea of the situation draws our attention to the individual biography, and although we might engage with coincidence we are not encouraged to think about complicity, dependencies and entanglements, or how one situation may be dependent on another. In an attempt to respond to this we have drawn on a complementary concept for our study, this time taken from the work of Norbert Elias, that of the 'configuration'. For Elias, individual situations constitute nodes within a configuration. For our purposes in this study, a configuration could be a family or community, defined at any moment in time by the relationship that exists between situations. The family looks different from the perspective of each of these positions, and as situations change, so family relationships reconfigure. The arrival of a new generation within a family generally constitutes a significant moment of change and realignment, which remakes situations, relationships and perspectives.

The third key term that we have worked with is 'narrative', encompassing both the shared 'canonical narratives' that are available within the culture and the smaller narrative claims through which selves are brought into being and remade continually. This focus is partly as a consequence of the centrality of talk to our method, but also because we are interested in the work that stories do in making experiences intelligible and available for representation and response. Chapters on Conception and Birth demonstrate the important role that story-telling plays in connecting the situation of the individual to that of a couple and a wider network of family, friends and professionals. These chapters also capture the echoes of earlier stories that continue to circulate within families, as well as revealing the absence of stories about more difficult and embodied experiences. By building family case studies and returning to participants over time we also build up a picture of the iterative character of narrative, with what are apparently the same phenomena revisited in new circumstances and the passage of time giving rise to the most radical perspective on difference in which the past is remade within a constantly changing present (Deleuze, 1994). Popular culture can also be understood in narrative terms, as existing in conversation with this dynamic personal and family trajectory, which coincide to form generational units, potential audiences and market niches. For a new product or a kind or mode of advice to resonate with an audience, it must establish recognition: a knowingness about the inner world and desires of its audience. This is a process shaped both by conservatism (the reflecting back of what is and has been) and by innovation (the imagination and invention of what could be).

Yet the term 'narrative' also has limitations, failing to capture more visual and embodied processes of meaning-making and affective exchange. In an increasingly visual and mediated culture different conceptual and methodological tools are needed to explore the operations of gender (Coleman, 2009), the mediation of expertise (Jensen, 2010) and encounters between mothers, others and the environment as they read each other's bodies, kit and styling in knowing ways and play a part in assembling connections between things, places, people and feeling. Although we have tried to capture something of the embodied practices associated with mothering, our approach has been shaped and constrained by our methodology. Ideally, practices are documented through observation, and we have had the opportunity to explore this in further research not reported here (Thomson et al, forthcoming). Practices appear to be critical in the ways that mothers distinguish themselves from each other with particular commodities, styles of use and embodied practices (breast/bottle feeding) communicating social class and ethnic identifications. Practices are also central to the ways in which intergenerational connections are experienced, with embodied memories and physical styles of parenting evoked in practice,[1] as well as the ways in which women learn to perform motherhood, partly through mimesis and repetition and partly through taking on ritualised intergenerational practices.

Self, identity and change

We now return to our data and the women in our study in order to think about the ways in which becoming a mother may change us. We interrogated mothers about change when we met with them a year after the birth of their child. Most drew in some way on a shared narrative about the transition to motherhood curtailing fun and sociality, signifying a shift from pleasing oneself to pleasing another – what Hollway describes as the 'ordinary conflict between individuality and intersubjectivity' (2010, p 26). In some cases mothers in our study drew on this narrative to negate it – explaining how surprised they were that this had not in fact happened, or explaining that they had already changed their life-style some time previously. In distancing themselves from 'what people say' women were also personalising their experience. Where they were invested in securing connection between pre- and post-birth life-style, they tended to claim continuity – seeking to get back to usual as quickly as possible. For surgeon Alex, it revealed the intensive organisational labour involved in this process, pragmatically embracing it to ensure that career momentum was not lost. For 16-year-old Kim, continuity is a luxury afforded by an involved mother who, by incorporating her daughter into the extended family, allows Kim to go on being a teenager. Others embraced the potential to be changed by the experience of motherhood. For example, 49-year-old Marion, who initially struggled with "not feeling her old self", presented motherhood as changing her outlook and her "sense of priorities.... Things that always seemed superficial now seem quite irrelevant ... I think with either birth or death you get a real immediate sense of priorities." Heather, whose pregnancy had been unplanned, subsequently reworked her pre-pregnancy self as ready, and suggested that the perceived significance of identity change might itself act as a disincentive to motherhood:

> "I almost think Ben happened for a reason ... I wonder if we would have, I think we would have kept putting it off, I don't know when we would have ever, it's quite a scary to think of having a child, and I wonder when we would have gone right enough's enough, I think we might have kept putting it off, so yeah, ...30 was the plan to a degree, but it was so the right time, it really really was the right time of our lives, it was time to grow up and move on and go the next step, you were meant to be in there weren't you baba-cake? Are you still a bit tired cheeky-chop? Yeah you might have a little cuddle angel-cake."

If the cultural narratives about readiness for motherhood focus on ideas of maturity, adulthood and the ability to be selfless, the accounts that women provided as to how motherhood might actually have changed them in practice were rather different. Here we quote the account of Kay, whose partner Nadia had given birth to their son, Gabriel, a year previously. Kay's account pays little attention to identity per se, focusing much more on activity, routines and practices.

Interviewer: Do you have an identity that's slightly different?

Kay: It's really odd isn't it, I do and I don't, I feel I have an 'in' to a whole routine of conversation that I could never ever imagine before, I can talk endlessly about prams and Moses baskets and all that, and what you wipe their bottoms with and all those things ... and you can immediately have an entirely you know four-hour conversation with somebody and its mostly taken up with children and stories and this that and the other so there is a kind of huge other part of the identity that happens because you can engage in that suddenly where you haven't really been able to, well you've been able to talk to people, but you've never been able to engage at the same level. ...

I use to be a stickler for time, time keeping and time keeping is just something you've got to sort of say, you've got to give yourself an hour leeway on a lot of things, so you know apart from appointments obviously with doctors and things. Everybody else it's like well we hope to be there about 7pm but probably 7 to 8 it's those sort of things that we can't ... cos things just take a lot longer, you're all ready to go out and then he'll have a poo, and then you've got to change him and everything, or he'll pour half a tin of yoghurt over him so you know all those things ...

It's like all those really big step changes in your life that sort of, you can remember ... after my dad died, of course I had 36 years of my father being alive but once he was dead you know you just change it and you can't although

you know rationally what it was like before, because it's
not part of your day-to-day existence any more ...

Here Kay is able to conjure, in the form and fluency of her talk, so
much about the disjunctures associated with significant life events. It is
the very texture of her life, the minute-by-minute being in the world
that has changed, and keeps changing, whether you are the parent,
the child or both. Becoming a parent and losing a parent are intense
emotional events that take Kay to a different place with distinctive
before and after zones. Her emergent practices as a new mother can
be seen as a response to her changing emotional landscape and an
attempt to create harmony between the intensity of her emotions
and the routine practices of daily life. Through accommodating
highly charged feelings within the seemingly banal activities that
give shape to the everyday, Kay is active in the accomplished project
of transition, a state that moves towards forms of settlement between
past and present while anticipating new deals between the present and
the future. These themes of connection, transition and a transformed
temporality were expressed by women in a range of ways.

Monica reports a similar shift in the fabric and texture of her world:

"It's surprised me just how interesting it is and I suppose
how enjoyable it is ... every day is interesting, isn't it, the
things that come out, his humour ... when he does new
things, like when he started to crawl and he can make
his feelings known I think, that's what's interesting now.
Is ... he obviously can't speak yet but he can make his
feelings known quite clearly you know and I do find,
I mean you have these ideas of yourself as a parent that
you're going to be, not strict, but you're going to do it
alright and you're not going to have kind of a spoilt baby
or a spoilt child and I find myself thinking, 'oh god, he's
got me wrapped round his little finger' you know, and
just how subtle it is and how clever it is. But not in a
knowing way, just how, that's how babies are made and
it's just quite clever, I think how cleverly designed they
are and they're so cute and so fascinating and you know,

and even the things that would be horrible in an adult like going for a poo, in a baby it's not offensive and it's not horrible and they're just … it's very clever the way that you're hooked in to it."

She explains that since having Lucien she has lived much more "in the moment" and experiences "a really profound change of who I am and how I feel, connected to the world I suppose. I feel er … I don't know, I feel much more aware of the fact that everybody you see is somebody's son or daughter or that they were a baby once." Occupying a different emotional space, Monica deftly describes her changed sense of self as significant, all-encompassing and not necessarily aligned with expectations or formulations created in the before-birth era. Birth as a temporal and emotional disruption that changes women's way of being in the world emerges as a subtle but significant finding of the study. Passing through the time zone from single woman to maternal subject has a seismic impact on all aspects of women's lives, potentially re-orientating approaches to work, relationships, modes of empathy and the organisation of everyday activities. This small-scale personal revolution is rarely commented on in public discourse. Nor do we know whether the shifting temporality of new motherhood remains a feature of women's lives – or do the clocks go back at some point, at the end of infancy/on returning to work or at some other unmarked and unspecified moment? To what extent are contemporary experiences shaped by situational cues and to what extent by the relatively enduring demands of a new-born child? Viewing motherhood as an in-between state, with reverberations beyond the mother–child relationship, calls for an approach that incorporates an understanding of the temporal and affective registers that may be interwoven into the transitional journey of becoming a mother, sometimes in unacknowledged or under-reported ways.

Maternal publics

In this final section we turn our attention to motherhood and the domain of the political. Aware of the legacy of second-wave feminism outlined in Chapter One, we are keen to consider the ways in which our data speak to ideas of women's activism and the potential for collective formations aimed at effecting social change. We have privileged age as an analytic category within the study: framing the research through divergent demographic trends towards older and younger motherhood, structuring our sample to represent this range and exploring the salience of age as a way of structuring our findings. Yet we want to clarify that age operates as an organising category through which normative discourses on good mothering operate, rather than as a thing in itself. The findings laid out in this book point to the salience of age in women's accounts of their experiences, both because social class is encoded within the temporal shape of the female biography and because of the subversive part that physical capital plays a within this process, with younger bodies potentially more fertile and elastic than older ones.

In this respect, the age at which motherhood is encountered (if at all) is a key defining factor in the distinction between the androgynous choice biography of late-modern theory and the gendered 'normal biography' of those seen to lag behind (Du Bois-Reymond, 1998; Henderson et al, 2007), which in turn becomes the medium through which social class is remade in the neoliberal economy. The flexible-choice biography promises educational and professional success, and potential social mobility to all prepared and able to meet the exacting and inflating standards of extended dependency and higher education. Young women on this trajectory are required to compete as equals, trading their right to have their gender recognised with the privilege of access (McRobbie, 2007; 2009). It is only at the point of motherhood – which is most often delayed until education, career and couple are suitably synchronised – that the full penalty of motherhood (and being female) is encountered, and these costs are experienced as the consequence of choice, with the market positioned as the 'public' through which solutions may be provided. For working-class women there may be a different kind of settlement between motherhood and work, the projects understood as complementary in different ways: with motherhood providing motivation for work, breadwinning demonstrating maternal competence, or mothering providing an attractive alternative to low-paid, insecure work.

Countries differ significantly in terms of how the task of caring for and educating children is approached, and the extent to which this is seen to be within or outside the collective responsibility as constituted within the welfare state (Abrahamson et al, 2005). Conservative commentator Sheila Lawler has argued that the welfare state is the last site of institutionalised gender difference within the UK – treating women as having different needs to men, expressed specifically in benefits and provisions in relation to motherhood – but also in recognition of the impact of caring on the female biography (Radio 4, 2010). The UK is increasingly moving towards a model in which responsibility for social reproduction is privatised with the welfare state, providing a safety net for only the most impoverished. As the state withdraws from the provision and regulation of education, social insurance and care, the gap is filled either by the market or by unpaid labour. It is in this context that Arlie Hochschild suggests that the market has an interest in inflating standards, ensuring that it can outperform the stay-at-home parent, grandparent or home-schooling network.

Yet the state is not simply a provider of care, it also operates as an employer, especially for women. As we found in Chapter Six, on work, the extent to which employers recognise and accept some responsibility for the work of mothering varies considerably across and within sectors. As public sector jobs are remade within the market, it is likely that the responsibility for social reproduction will be shifted further towards the individual and the family. In recent years it has become fashionable to ridicule middle-class parenting as increasingly 'paranoid' (Furedi, 2008) and 'intensive', drawing attention to an inflation of parental expectation and the proliferation of interventions aimed at improving children.[2] The contemporary critique of intensive mothering rearticulates the two hate-figures of the rejecting and the overprotective mother that Ehrenreich and English find in the advice literature of the post-war years. Rather than focusing on parenting styles and subjectivities, we suggest that it may be more accurate to think in terms of an intensification of responsibility taking place, with middle-class anxiety expressing an increased perception of insecurity. With the break-down of the social contract through which state institutions mediate life chances (however clumsily) in 'good enough' public childcare, education and health services, families experience themselves as fully responsible for securing their children's future, by any means necessary and available. It is in this context that questions of intergenerational justice begin to be articulated, and whole-family economic strategies will no doubt begin to radically change the shape of biographies across the life course.

In Chapters Six (Work) and Eight (Birth) we reveal something of the ways in which women negotiate maternity and fairness in relation to the welfare institutions. Yet, as the state retreats as a site of citizenship and the arbiter of what is fair and just, important questions arise as to where and how other forms of 'publicness' might be brought into being, and the part played by the maternal in these formations. As we have explored in this book, motherhood not only intensifies the meanings of the home (with ideas of 'stay-at-home mothering', 'home birth' and 'home-made' gaining power and significance) but also brings women into a heightened relationship with the market and into new forms of publicness. In Chapter Three (Body) we explored how the visibility of pregnancy reconstitutes relationships, inviting dialogue and rendering the self as public property in new and sometimes uncomfortable ways. Lisa Baraitser has conceptualised this in terms of the task of mothering being the creation of the 'specific' (an individual) from the 'generic' (children), which inevitably demands that she engage in practices of citizenship which are watched by others, who in the process of watching become the 'public'. Baraitser illustrates this through the example of a child deconstructing an elastic barrier shaping an airport check-in queue. That the child deconstructs the temporary order of the queue is inevitable. And the members of the queue do not step in but wait for the mother 'not only to make a citizen of the child, but to do so publicly – to voice on behalf of everyone, nice and loud, just why we have a barrier, and why it must be maintained' (Baraitser, 2009, p 21). Baraitser's choice of the airport is deliberate: along with supermarkets, car parks, and hotels it is one of the 'non-places' of supermodernity, places that appear to be without history or civic tradition. These are forms of the public constituted in and through the market and are places that women may find themselves, either as low-paid workers or as doing their mothering with an audience. Baraitser's message is both that the work of the mother is always a collective and civic project, even if it is not recognised as such by the state, and that 'publicness' is created by performances of mothering in view of others.

Baraitser's account of the ethically agentic mother negotiating the spaces of the city is very appealing, yet does it adequately acknowledge and span social divisions? We hoped to have brought into the frame accounts of other kinds of mothers as ethical civic actors – young mothers who negotiate public spaces, constantly in fear of judgement, incited to display their maternal competence. Not all mothers can or do replace the barrier, explaining why it must be maintained. Such acts also bring publics into being, yet these publics are less benevolent and reassuring. Our explorations of representations of mothering within popular culture suggest that idealised images of mothering are widespread and diffuse – employed as vehicles for the incitement of consumption. Images of bad mothering are much more condensed: Jordan and Vicky Pollard carried much of this weight at the time of our fieldwork, instantly recognisable caricatures of the boundaries of public tolerance. Chapters on the body, expert advice and commodities have all drawn attention to the importance of popular culture as a site of publicness through which maternal identities are mediated. Imogen Tyler captures this 'deeply incoherent' discursive field by juxtaposing the 'terrorizing maternal figurations' (the feckless young mother, the perverse older mother and the child-failing working mother and the self-failing stay-at-home mother) with 'an unending parade of images of beautiful, young, white, tight pregnant and postpartum celebrity bodies' (Tyler, 2009, p 5). She argues that although maternity has 'never been so public', 'only certain kinds of maternal experience can be communicated and heard' (Tyler, 2009, p 5). In this context, the task of representing maternal diversity outside of a deficit model is incredibly important.[3]

So what can we point to in this book as examples of maternal politics? And how might notions of 'progressive' or 'transgressive' be constituted? Is the middle-class lesbian couple who negotiate donor insemination within a legal and bureaucratic framework more or less normative than the transnational couple who must organise their parenting through the nexus of immigration regulation? Can any two teenage mothers be assumed to be the same? How can we compare the parenting practice that allows a child to remain sleeping in the morning when his mother leaves for work with the Sunday-night preparation of a week of home-cooked food for the daughter entrusted to the child minder? What does it mean to defend Jordan or to laugh hysterically at Vicky Pollard? One of the things that we have discovered in undertaking this research is the power of the 'terrorizing figurations' described by Imogen Tyler. It took us a long time to listen to and recognise what we were told by certain women – it is all too easy to dis-identify with the ambitious working mother who pragmatically delegates care, or the attachment parent who dedicates her education to the project of parenting. It is also easy to romanticise the heroism of the full-time father or the teenage mother.

When we shared our data with other researchers, and increasingly with journalists and policy makers, we again recognised the power of these figures as well as the cultural dominance of middle-class narratives. We were asked to verify the existence of 'disapproving and disappointed grandmothers', 'paranoid parents', 'intensive mothering'. We hope the picture that actually emerges from this data set is more mundane, ambiguous and balanced, with most mothers reporting intense moments, which might be considered to be 'political', where they were forced into uncharted ethical territory and had to make quick yet consequential decisions about how to live and who and what to defend. Some of these took place in encounters with experts and institutions, some in relation to the market and consumption, some in relation to family, friends, strangers and other children. Paradoxically, new parenthood is a highly privatising moment where individuals, couples and families see themselves as having heightened responsibility for their destinies. Yet it also reveals our dependency on others and our investments in shared spaces and institutions such as the street, neighbourhood, nursery, school and clinic. The welfare settlement that shaped our own childhoods (and the inequalities of our generation) appears to be on the verge of transformation. 'Parenting' may have proved to be the Achilles heel of progressive politics, yet if we accept the inherently political character of mothering (and the idea that small acts of mothering bring small kinds of publics into being), then it is possible to imagine a maternal politics that does not depend on the state to organise and express solidarity.

Our research suggests that there are boundaries that seem to matter and arenas of activity that are morally dense and emotionally charged. Beginning with the body as the first boundary, the maternal subject is commonly read as the carrier of a developing foetus. Her body invites public scrutiny through well-established aesthetic, moral and medical frameworks offering different but consistently normative ways of appraising and judging a 'successful pregnancy'. The pregnant woman, however, may not feel quite herself as the embodied experience creates physical disturbances that blur distinctions between inside and outside. Presenting a challenge to the integration of the body, the pregnant subject has been described as, 'decentred, split or doubled in several ways … I literally do not have a sense of where my body ends and the world begins' (Young, 1990, pp 162–3). The physicality of pregnancy as personally disorientating and publicly evaluated may offer some explanatory power in conceptualisations of pregnancy as a uniquely individualised experience, popularised by the birth plan and pervasive notions of pampering, indulgence and 'me-me time'. Living the in-between state of impending motherhood, the selfhood of the maternal subject is compromised by its status as both one, not one – a condition that may inhibit connections and collectivities based upon the unitary self of active citizenship. Other boundaries, it appears, are drawn up in the weeks after birth as new mothers reconfigure bodily boundaries once the baby is in the world. During this period of emotional adjustment and practical demands, women begin to reconcile the emotional intensity of birth with the mundane and repetitive practices of child care. As Marion, Monica and many others reported, this period also sets in train a range of parenting styles and approaches that give babies a character and women a developing sense of themselves as mothers. Establishing an ease of fit between the feelings and the practices becomes the ongoing work of new motherhood as women find pathways back to being in the world that dissemble the Moebius-like bodily flux of pregnancy. As our respondents reveal, this entails renewed forms of evaluation and the emergence of new practices that may involve moments of recuperation, fissure and continuity as new mothers seek to integrate the trauma of birth with their pre-pregnant, present and future selves.

Notes

[1] See Elliott et al (2009) for an extended discussion of how women may access 'dormant infantile experiences' on becoming mothers, as well as Stern (1998) for a critique of the idea of maternal regression.
[2] The Mamsie network provides a space for academics, artists and writers to collaborate in the representation of motherhood, http://mamsie.wikispaces.com/.

APPENDIX 1

The study design, methods and sample

The research questions for the Making of Modern Motherhood study were:

- What does motherhood mean to first-time mothers? Are there differences between women relating to age, social class, ethnicity and sexuality?
- What are the intergenerational narratives concerning motherhood? How do they resonate with theories of individualisation or shifting patterns of interdependence?
- How does being a mother change women's identities? What forms of entitlement (or loss) does it bring and what social practices/ actions and forms of solidarity does it incite?
- How have women of different generations imagined and practised motherhood? What resources and advice do they draw upon (texts, people, products, community) and how does this fit with other identities, life plans?
- What part do men play in influencing women's expectations and experiences of motherhood?

In addressing these questions we combined longitudinal and cross-generational research designs, enabling us to capture an interplay of historical, generational and biographical processes.

Questionnaire

A pre-selection questionnaire was developed, piloted, refined and distributed through settings in a new town and inner-city research sites, including: Mothercare shops; public and private antenatal classes; Sure Start; young mothers' projects; and specialist networks aimed at disabled and lesbian mothers. The primary aim of the questionnaire was to assist us in identifying a diverse interview sample of expectant first-time mothers. In addition to demographic data and a basic reproductive history, we also collected information concerning the respondents' mothers, preferred sources of advice, media consumption, antenatal activity, birth plans and feelings about pregnancy. In total 144 questionnaires were completed and data was coded and inputted into SPSS, and basic descriptive statistics were run on an initial sample of 131. The resulting report guided our analysis of media texts and informed our selection of interviewees.

Interviews

From the volunteers we identified a sample of 62 expectant mothers for interview. Volunteers were followed up fulfilling the requirements of a quota sample constructed primarily in relation to age, but providing diversity in terms of social class, ethnicity, work status, living situation and proximity to family support. An interview schedule seeking to capture biographical narratives was generated, piloted and refined. We sought different forms of data from the different stages of the interview. An initial invitation to respondents to tell the story of their life and pregnancy was followed by a discussion of the resources that they drew on in preparing themselves for motherhood. By inviting uninterrupted life narratives at the start of the interview we attempted to capture something of the narrative form that is the basis of the biographical narrative interpretive method (Wengraf, 2001) and the idea that in constructing a story of their lives research subjects will provide insight into both the social and psychic conditions of their lives (Hollway and Jefferson, 2000). We deliberately sought to capture the ways in which women might be storying their pregnancies, inviting them to retell family stories of their own births and accounts of 'conception' that must be produced for family, friends and professionals (Thomson et al, 2009). Visual prompts were then used to facilitate an exploration of sensitive issues including sexual relations, body image, breastfeeding and dis-identifications with other mothers on the basis of social class, age, ethnicity and disability. The final section of the interview involved discussion of the respondents' expectations of motherhood and their birth plans. Interviewees were also asked about preparations for the arrival of the baby and, with their consent, photographs were taken to record these.

Consents for recording and archiving were negotiated before and after the interviews, which were generally conducted in women's homes and recorded digitally. A coding frame was generated through an analysis of a sub-sample of interviews and an agreed approach was established before the full sample was coded using computer-based qualitative analysis software. After the interviews, detailed reflective field notes were made documenting access, setting, appearances, emotional dynamics and emergent themes. Our style of recording field notes was guided by ethnographic note taking and the use of case profiles in qualitative longitudinal research (Thomson and Holland, 2003; Thomson, 2007, 2010b). Our approach recognises the subjective feelings of the researcher as data in their own right, and these are documented within the field notes in order to enhance meaning (Lucey et al, 2003). Field notes were shared and interrogated at research team meetings and group analysis events alongside transcripts and visual data (see Thomson, 2010b, for overview).

Case studies

Twelve women were invited to take part in case studies. In making our selection we sought a diverse sample as well as considering the resilience and enthusiasm of potential participants. Case studies included interviews with grandmothers, great-grandmothers and 'significant others' and were completed with a second interview with the expectant mother at least one year after birth. Interview schedules were generated through a combination of standard questions and themes identified from the expectant-mother interviews. Grandmothers and great-grandmothers were asked to recall what they knew of their own mothers' experiences of pregnancy and birth before providing a detailed account of their own first pregnancies and commenting on their daughters' experiences. They were also asked to share images and objects from their own mothering, and photographic records were made with their consent. In most cases all stages of data generation in case studies were undertaken by a single researcher. Multi-disciplinary analysis workshops were enormously productive in helping us to create a common framework for the analysis and representation of case-study data.

Our case-study mothers ranged in age between 16 and 48, born between 1956 and 1989, grandmothers ranged in age from 78 to 39. The two great-grandmothers were aged 83 and 59. In Figure A.1 we map the age ranges of mothers, grandmothers and great-grandmothers included in the 12 case studies. The maternal span of case-study families can be measured as the gap between the grandmother's date of birth and date of daughter a becoming mother. The widest maternal span was found in the Woolfe family, where the 78-year-old grandmother was born in 1928 and the daughter became a mother at 43. The shortest maternal span can be seen in the Thompson family, where the 39-year-old grandmother was born in 1966 and the daughter became a mother at 16.

Cultural analysis

Ongoing forms of cultural analysis were carried out throughout the study period, contributing to both the research methods used in fieldwork and the analysis of data. As mentioned above, the initial questionnaire identified media consumption, books and popular texts that women had consulted during the course of their pregnancy. Interviews built upon this knowledge in follow-up questions and discussion. Visual prompt materials drawn from pregnancy magazines and other media sources were also used in interviews to facilitate discussion. Digital photographs recording the ways in which women had prepared for the birth provided a social document of the materiality of impending motherhood. An analysis of popular representations of contemporary mothering was undertaken in parallel with the interview study. We also carried out a focused analysis of magazines aimed at new mothers during the period September 2004–April 2006 (Kehily, under review). Collectively, a cultural approach can be seen as a strand running through the study, building a rich archive of motherhood as a cultural project, seen most clearly in women's engagements with media forms, expert advice, practices of consumption and materiality. Recognising the importance of visual culture as a feature of the cultural approach appears most critical in relation to issues of embodiment. We found the pregnant body to be a particularly dense signifier of meanings encoded in cultural texts and decoded by women themselves. Across the chapters we engage with these meanings as the pregnant body is made sense of in the different domains of the aesthetic, the moral and the medical.

APPENDIX 2

Description of the sample

Adwin Friend Amelia Neighbour Jill 50 Mother Marica 58	New town, 26, postgraduate student, married, lmc, black African
Alex CALDER Mother Barbara 65 Friend 38 Baby Sian	City, 34, surgeon, married, umc, white British
Alice	City, 32, fundraiser, married, lmc, white British
Amber	City, 18, student, single, wc, mixed race (African Caribbean/white)
Anastasia ARBEN Partner Richie 46 Neighbour Mother Marica Baby David	City, 26, unemployed, married, wc, Romanian/Russian
Anna	City, 36, secondary teacher, lmc, cohabiting, white British
Belinda	New town, 42, administrative manager, cohabiting, lmc, white British
Carly	New town, 28, sales, married, wc, white British
Carol	New town, 39, customer service training, married, lmc, white British
Cathy	City, 38, youth worker, married, surrogacy arrangement, lmc, white British
Chantel	City, 16, unemployed, lives at home (boyfriend will move in), wc, mixed race(white/Caribbean)
Charlotte	City, 32, events manager, married, umc, white British
Clara	City, 40, researcher, married, lmc, white American

Clarissa	City, disabled network contact, 40, helpline advisor, lives alone with support of carer, lmc, white British
Cody SHAW Friend Maxine 22 Mother Jackie 55 Baby Alisa	City, 20, shop assistant, single, living at home, wc, white British
Deborah RICKARD Mother Judy 58 Friend Saskia 38 Baby Ruby	New town, 33, information officer, married, lmc, white British
Donna	New town, 17, unemployed, cohabiting, wc, white British
Elaine	City, 39, sales, married, lmc, white British
Eleanor	City, 26, self-employed IT, married, lmc, white British
Emily	New town, 33, early years teacher, married, lmc, white British
Farah	City, 23, supermarket worker, married, wc, British/Turkish
Faye	City, 35, primary teacher, married, lmc, white British
Fiona	New Town, 15, student, living at home, wc, white British
Gail	City, 28, unemployed, cohabiting, wc, white British
Hannah	City, 32, practice nurse, cohabiting, lmc, white British
Heather CHAPMAN Partner Andy 30 Mother Matty 58 Baby Ben	City, 27, primary teacher, married, lmc, white Australian
Hilary	City, 39, gallery owner, married, umc, white British
Jade	New town, 17, student, single, mother and baby unit, wc, mixed white/African Caribbean
Jessica	New town, 32, teacher, married, lmc, white British
Karen	New town, 30, secondary school teacher, married, lmc, Asian British
Kate	City, 31, nursery teacher, married, lmc, white British

Kay	City, 44, executive voluntary sector, civil partnership, umc, white British
Kim THOMPSON Mother Gillian 39 Grandmother 60 Baby Tempest	New town, 16, student, single, living at home, wc, white African
Laura	New town, 35, lecturer, cohabiting, lmc, white British
Leyla	City, 30, student, married, wc, Kurdish
Lorraine HALES Mother Beverley 42 Sister Danielle 20 Baby Nkosi	City, 21, chef, married (currently living apart), wc, African Caribbean
Louisa	New town, 35, administrator in family business, married, lmc, white British
Lyn	New town, 31, waitress, married, wc, Chinese/British
Marion WEST Partner Richard 42 Sister 50 Baby Bethan	New town, 49, self-employed training consultant, cohabiting, lmc, white British.
Mary	New town, 33, administrator, married, lmc, white British
Melina	City, 32, postgraduate student, married, wc, Greek
Melissa	New town, 18, student, cohabiting, wc, white British
Melody	New town, 28, fundraiser, married, lmc, white British
Mercedes	City, 43, self-employed language teacher, married, lmc, Colombian
Minaal	New Town, 24, unemployed, married, wc, Asian Bangladeshi
Monica FORTUNE Partner Jamie 41 Mother Erica 67 Baby Lucien	City, 39, civil servant, married, lmc, white British
Mumtaz	City, 17, beauty therapist, married, wc, Asian Bangladeshi

Nadia WOOLFE Partner Kay 44 Mother Jean 65 Mother Avril 78 Baby Gabriel	City 2, 36, NHS manager, civil partnership, umc, white British
Nadire	City, 27, manager, cohabiting, lmc, British/Turkish Cypriot
Natasha	New town, 17, unemployed, cohabiting, wc, white British
Orla	City, 42, financial services, single, lmc, white British
Pauline	City, 40, manager early years, cohabiting, wc, white British
Sarila	City, 42, counsellor, married, lmc, British/Turkish
Sharon	New town, 29, administrator, married, lmc, white British
Serena	City, 17, unemployed, boyfriend – lives at home, wc, black Caribbean
Shoba	New town, 33, clerical worker, married, lmc, Sri Lankan
Sofia SEZGUM Partner Rifaat 26 Mother Selma 47 Baby Feyza	City, 24, beauty therapist, married, wc, British/Turkish Cypriot
Sophie	New town, 17, student, single, mother and baby unit, wc, white British
Tina WAGLAND Mother Patricia 60 Grandmother Rosie 82 Baby Saffron	New town, 36, accountant, cohabiting, lmc, white British
Tracey	New town, 17, student, single, wc, white British
Valerie	New town, 42, lecturer, cohabiting, lmc, white British
Vickie	City, 33, journalist, cohabiting, lmc, white British

Legend: lmc: lower middle class; umc: upper middle class; wc: working class

References

Abrahamson, P., Boje, T. and Greve, B. (2005) *Welfare and families in Europe*, Aldershot: Ashgate.

Adkins, L. (2003) 'Reflexivity: freedom or habit of gender', *Theory, Culture and Society*, 20(6): 21–42.

Adkins, L. (2009) 'Feminism after measure', *Feminist Theory*, 10(3): 323–39.

Adorno, T. (1991) *The culture industry: Selected essays on mass culture*, London: Routledge.

Ailwood, J. (2008) 'Mothers, teachers, maternalism and early childhood education and care: some historical connections', *Contemporary Issues in Early Childhood*, 8(2): 157–64.

Annandale, E. and Clark, J. (1996) 'What is gender? Feminist theory and the sociology of human reproduction', *Sociology of Health and Illness*, 8(1): 17–44.

Arai, L. (2009) *Teenage pregnancy: The making and unmaking of a problem*, Bristol: The Policy Press.

Arber, S. and Attias-Donfut, C. (eds) (2000) *The myth of generational conflict: The family and state in ageing societies*, London: Routledge.

Armstrong, J. (2010) 'Class and gender at the intersection: working class women's disposition towards employment and motherhood', in Y. Taylor (ed) *Classed intersections: Spaces, selves, knowledges*, Aldershot: Ashgate, pp 235–54.

Bailey, L. (1999) 'Refracted selves? A study of changes in self-identity in the transition to motherhood', *Sociology*, 33(2): 335–52.

Baraitser, L. (2008) *Maternal encounters: The ethics of interruption*, London: Routledge.

Baraitser, L. (2009a) 'A conversation with Lynne Segal', *Studies in the Maternal*, 1(1), www.mamsie.bbk.ac.uk/back_issues/issue_one/LynneSegal.html, accessed 29/08/2010.

Baraitser, L. (2009b) 'Mothers who make things public', *Feminist Review*, 93: 8–26.

Bartky, S. (1990) *Femininity and domination: Studies in the phenomenology of oppression*, New York: Routledge.

Bauer, E. and Thompson, P. (2006) *Jamaican hands across the Atlantic*, Kingston: Ian Randall Publishers.

Bauman, Z. (1988) *Freedom*, Milton Keynes: Open University Press.

Beck, U. (1992) *Risk society: Towards a new modernity*, London: Sage.

Beck, U. and Beck-Gernsheim, E. (1995) *The normal chaos of love*, Cambridge: Polity Press.

Bertaux, D. and Bertaux-Wiame, I. (1997, 2nd edn 2003) 'Heritage and its lineage: a case history of transmission and social mobility over five generations', in D. Bertaux and P. Thompson (eds) *Pathways to social class: A qualitative approach to social mobility*, Oxford: Clarendon Press, pp 62–97.

Bhabha, H.K. (1994) *The location of culture*, London: Routledge.

Bjerrum Nielsen, H. and Rudberg, M. (1994) *Psychological gender and modernity*, Oslo: Scandinavian University Press.

Bjerrum Nielsen, H. and Rudberg, M. (2000) 'Gender, love and education in three generations', *The European Journal of Women's Studies*, 7(4): 423–53.

Blackman, L. (2004) 'Self help, media cultures and the production of female pschopathology', *European Journal of Cultural Studies*, 7(2): 219–36.

Blum, L. (1993) 'Mothers, babies and breastfeeding in late capitalist America: The shifting context of feminist theory', *Feminist Studies*, 19: 291-311.

Bourdieu, P. (1977) (1984) *Distinction: A social critique of the judgement of taste*, Cambridge, MA: Harvard University Press.

Brannen, J., Moss, P. and Mooney, A. (2004) *Working and caring over the twentieth century: Change and continuity in four generation families*, Houndsmill: Palgrave Macmillan.

Breitenbach, E. (2006) *Gender statistics: An evaluation*, Working Paper No 51, Equal Opportunities Commission, available at www.equalityhumanrights.com/uploaded_files/PSD/wp51_gender_statistics_evaluation.pdf.

Bryceson, D. and Vuorela, U. (eds) 2002 *The transnational family: New European frontiers and global networks*, Oxford: Berg.

Butler, J. (1990) *Gender trouble: Feminism and the subversion of identity*, London: Routledge.

Butler, J. (1993) *Bodies that matter: On the discursive limits of sex*, London: Routledge.

Butler, J. (2004) *Undoing gender*, Boca Raton, FL: Routledge.

Byng-Hall, J. (1995) *Rewriting family scripts: Improvisations and systems change*, New York: Guilford Press.

Byrne, B. (2006) 'In search of a "good mix". Race, class gender and practices of mothering', *Sociology*, 40(6): 1001–17.

Cahil, H.A. (2001) 'Male appropriation and medicalization of childbirth: a historical analysis', *Journal of Advanced Nursing*, 33: 334–332.

Campbell, D. (2010) 'Too scared to push: big rise in reported birth trauma', *Guardian*, 15 November.

Carsten, J. (ed) (2000) *Cultures of relatedness: New approaches to the study of kinship*, Cambridge: Cambridge University Press.

Casey, E. and Martens, L. (2007) 'Introduction', in E. Casey and L. Martens (eds) *Gender and consumption*, Farnham: Ashgate.

Chambers, P., Allan, G., Phillipson, C. and Ray, M. (2009) *Family practices in later life*, Bristol: The Policy Press.

Charles, N., Davies, C. and Harris, C. (2008) *Families in transition: Social change, family formation and kin relationships*, Bristol: The Policy Press.

Chavkin, W. and Maher, J. (2010) *The globalization of motherhood: Deconstructions and reconstructions of biology and care*, London: Routledge.

Chodorow, N. (1978) *The reproduction of mothering: Psychoanalysis and the sociology of gender*, Los Angeles and London: University of California Press.

Clarke, A. (2004) 'Maternity and materiality: becoming a mother in consumer culture', in J. Taylor, L. Layne and D. Wozniak (eds) *Consuming motherhood*, New Jersey: Rutgers University Press, pp 57–71.

Clarke, D. and Haldane, D. (1990) *Wedlocked? Intervention and research in marriage*, Cambridge: Polity Press.

CMACE (Centre for Maternal and Child Enquiries) (2010) *Perinatal mortality 2008 Report*, 21 July.

Coleman, R. (2009) *The becoming of bodies: Girls, images, experience*, Manchester: Manchester University Press.

Connell, R.W. (2002) *Gender*, Oxford: Blackwell.

Couldry, N. (2010) *Why voice matters: Culture and politics after neoliberalism*, London: Sage.

Crompton, R. (2006) *Employment and the family: The reconfiguration of work and family life in contemporary societies*, Cambridge: Cambridge University Press.

Cross, G. (2004) *The cute and the cool, womdrous innocence and modern American children's culture*, Oxford: Oxford University Press.

Crossley, M. (2006) 'Childbirth, complications and the illusion of choice: a case study', *Feminism and Psychology*, 17(4): 543–63.

Cunningham-Burley, S., Backett-Milburn, K. and Kemmer, D. (2005) 'Balancing work and family life: mothers' views', in L. McKie and S. Cunningham-Burley (eds) *Families in society: Boundaries and relationships*, Bristol: The Policy Press.

Cunningham-Burley, S., Backett-Millburn, K. and Kemmer, D. (2006) 'Constructing health and sickness in the context of motherhood and paid work', *Sociology of Health and Illness*, 28(4): 385–409.

Cusk, R. (2001) *A life's work: On becoming a mother*, London: Faber and Faber.

Davies, H., Joshi, H., Rake, K. and Alami, R. (2000) *Women's incomes over the lifetime: A report to the Women's Unit*, London: Cabinet Office.

Davis, K. (2007) *The making of Our bodies, ourselves: How feminism travels across borders,* Durham, NC: Duke University Press.

Davis-Floyd R. (1992) *Birth as an American rite of passage*, Berkeley, CA: University of California Press.

de Beauvoir, S. (1997) [1949] *The second sex*, Paris: Gallimard/Vintage.

de Certeau, M. (1984) *The practice of everyday life*, Berkeley, CA: University of California Press.

Deleuze, G. (1994) [1968] *Difference and repetition*, London: The Althone Press.

Dermott, E. (2008) *Intimate fatherhood*, London: Routledge.

Dermott, E. and Seymour, J. (eds) (2011, forthcoming) *Displaying families*, Houndsmill: Palgrave.

DH (Department of Health) (2007) *Maternity matters: Choice, access and continuity of care in a safe service*, London: DH.

Donnelly, L. (2009) 'Doulas: meddlers in the maternity suite or a mother's best friend?', *Telegraph Online*, 12 December, www.telegraph.co.uk/health/6797264/Doulas-meddlers-in-the-maternity-suite-or-a-mothers-best-friend.html, accessed 21 August 2010.

Doucet, A. (2006) *Do men mother? Fatherhood, care and domestic responsibility*, Toronto: University of Toronto Press.

Douglas, M. (1966) *Purity and danger*, London; Routledge.

Du Bois-Reymond, M. (1998) '"I don't want to commit myself yet": young people's life concepts', *Journal of Youth Studies*, 1(1): 63–79.

Duncan, S. (2005) 'Mothering, class and rationality', *Sociological Review*, 53(1): 50–76.

Duncan, S., Edwards, R., Reynolds, T. and Alldred, P. (2003) 'Motherhood, paid work and partnering: values and theories', *Work, Employment and Society*, 17(2): 309–30.

Edwards, J. and Strathern, M. (2000) 'Including our own', in J. Carsten (ed) *Cultures of relatedness: New approaches to the study of kinship*, Cambridge: Cambridge University Press, pp 149–66.

Ehrenreich, B. and English, D. (1979) [2nd edn 2004] *For her own good: 150 years of the experts' advice to women*, London: Pluto Press.

Ehrenreich, B. and Hochschild, A. (2003) *Global woman: Nannies, maids and sex workers in the new economy*, London: Granta Books.

Elias, N. (1978) *What is sociology?*, New York: University of Columbia Press.

Elliott, J., Gunaratnam, Y., Hollway, W. and Phoenix, A. (2009) 'Practices, identifications and identity change in transitions to motherhood', in M. Wetherell (ed) *Theorizing identities and social action*, Houndsmill: Palgrave, pp 19–37.

Enright, A. (2004) *Making babies: Stumbling into motherhood*, London: Vintage.

Erel, U. (2009) *Migrant women transforming citizenship*, Aldershot: Ashgate Press.

Everingham, C., Stevenson, D. and Warner-Smith, P. (2007) 'Things are getting better all the time? Challenging the narrative of women's progress from a generational perspective', *Sociology*, 41(3): 419–37.

Featherstone, M. (1982) 'The body in consumer culture', *Theory, Culture & Society*, September, 1(2): 18-33.

Ferri, E. and Smith, K. (2003) 'Partnership and parenthood', in E. Ferri, J. Bynner and M. Wadsworth (eds) *Changing Britain, changing lives: Three generations at the turn of the century*, Bedford Way papers, University of London Institute of Education, pp 105–132.

Finch, J. and Mason, J. (1993) *Negotiating family responsibility*, London: Routledge.

Firestone, S. (1970) *The dialectic of sex: The case for feminist revolution*, New York City: Morrow.

Foucault, M. (1978) *The history of sexuality, vol 1*, trans. R. Hurley, Harmondsworth: Penguin.

Franklin, J. (2008) 'Mapping discourses of motherhood', unpublished working paper.

Fredriksen, E.H., Harris, J., Moland, K.M. and Sundby, J. (2010) '"A defeat not to be ultra-fit": expectation and experiences related to pregnancy and employment in contemporary Norway', *NORA – Nordic Journal of Feminist and Gender Research*, 18(3): 167–84.

Furedi, F. (2008) *Paranoid parenting: Why ignoring the experts may be best for your child*, Chicago: Chicago Review Press.

Gabb, J. (2005) 'Locating lesbian parent families', *Gender, Place, Culture*, 12(4): 419–32.

Gabb, J. (2008) *Researching intimacy in families*, Houndsmill: Palgrave.

Gatrell, C.J. (2005) *Hard labour: The sociology of parenthood*, Maidenhead: Open University Press.

Gatrell, C.J. (2011) 'Policy and the pregnant body at work: Strategies of secrecy, silence and supra-performance', *Gender, Work and Organisation*, 18(2): 158–81.

Gelis, J. (1991) *History of childbirth*, Oxford: Basil Blackwell.

Giddens, A. (1991) *Modernity and self identity: Self and society in the late modern age*, Cambridge: Polity Press.

Giddens, A. (1992) *A transformation of intimacy: Sexuality, love and eroticism*, Cambridge: Polity Press.

Gillies, V. (2006) *Marginalised mothers: Exploring working-class experiences of parenting*, London: Routledge.

Gillis, J. (1996) *A world of their own making: Myth, ritual and the question of family values*, Cambridge, MA: Harvard University Press.

Gramsci, A. (1971) *Selections from the prison notebooks*, London: Lawrence and Wishart.

Grosz, E. (1994) *Volatile bodies: Toward a corporeal feminism*, Sydney: Allen and Unwin.

Hadfield, L. (2009) 'Conviviality and maternity: anticipating childbirth and negotiating intergenerational difference', *Feminist Review*, Birth Special Issue, 93(1): 128–33.

Hadfield, L. and Thomson, R. (2009) 'The making of modern motherhoods', *Practising Midwife*, 12(7): 30–3.

Hadfield, L., Rudoe, N. and Sanderson-Mann, J. (2007) 'Motherhood, choice and the British media: a time to reflect', *Gender and Education*, 19(2): 255–63.

Hakim, C. (2000) *Work–lifestyle choices in the 21st century: Preference theory*, Oxford: Oxford University Press.

Hardyment, C. (2007) *Dream babies: Childcare advice from John Locke to Gina Ford*, London: Francis Lincoln Ltd Publishers.

Harkness, S. and Waldfogel, J. (1999) *The family gap in pay: Evidence from seven industrialised countries*, CASE paper 29, London: LSE.

Haug, F., Andresen, S., Bunz-Elfferding, A., Hauser, K., Lang, U., Laudan, M. et al (1999) *Female sexualization: A collective work of memory*, trans. E. Carter, London: Verso.

Hays, S. (1996) *The cultural contradictions of motherhood*, New Haven: Yale University Press.

Henderson, S., Holland, J., McGrellis, S., Sharpe, S. and Thomson, R. (2007) *Inventing adulthoods: A biographical approach to youth transitions*, London: Sage.

Hermes, J. (1995) *Reading women's magazines*, Cambridge: Polity Press.

Hochschild, A. (1997) *The time bind: When home becomes work and work becomes home*, New York: Henry Holt.

Hochschild, A. (2003) *The commercialization of intimate life: Notes from home and work*, San Francisco, Los Angeles and London: University of California Press.

Hockey, J. (2008) 'Lifecourse and intergenerational research', Paper presented at Timescapes Launch, University of Leeds, 31 January.

Hoddinnott, P. (1996) 'Why don't some women wnat to breastfeed and how might we change their attitudes?', MPhil thesis, Cardiff, University of Wales.

Holland, J. and Thomson, R. (2009) 'Gaining a perspective on choice and fate: revisiting critical moments', *European Societies*, 11(3): 451–69.

Hollway, W. (2010) 'Conflict in the transition to becoming a mother: a psycho-social approach', *Psychoanalysis, Culture and Society*, 15(2): 136–55.

Hollway, W. and Jefferson, T. (2000) *Doing qualitative research differently: Free association, narrative and interview methods*, London: Sage Publications.

Howie, G. (2010) *Between feminism and materialism: A question of method*, Houndsmill: Palgrave Macmillan.

Hummel, C. (2008) 'Intergenerational relationships in a migration context', in E. Widmer and R. Jallinoja (eds) *Beyond the nuclear family: Families in a configurational perspective*, Bern: Peter Lang, pp 79–95.

Irwin, S. (2003) 'Interdependencies, values and the reshaping of difference: gender and generation at the birth of twentieth-century modernity', *British Journal of Sociology*, 54(4): 565–84.

Jensen, T. (2009) Book review of 'Queering reproduction: achieving pregnancy in the age of technoscience', *Feminist Review*, 93: 143–5.

Jensen, T. (2010) '"What kind of mum are you at the moment?" Supernanny and the psychologising of classed embodiment', *Subjectivity*, 3: 170–92.

Jordan, B. (1993) *Birth in four cultures: A cross-cultural investigation of childbirth in Yucatan, Holland, Sweden and the United States*, revised and expanded by R. Davis Floyd, Prospect Heights, IL: Waveland Press.

Kehily, M.J. (1999) 'More sugar? Teenage magazines, gender displays and sexual learning', *European Journal of Cultural Studies*, 2(1): 65–89.

Kehily, M.J. (2002) *Sexuality, gender and schooling, shifting agendas in social learning*, London: Routledge.

Kehily, M.J. (2008) 'From the margins to the centre? Girlhood and the contradictions of femininity across three generations', Special Issue of *Girlhood Studies*, 1(2): 51–71.

Kehily, M.J. (under review) 'Pregnant with meaning: pregnancy magazines and the encoding of the maternal subject', *European Journal of Cultural Studies.*

Kehily, M.J. and Thomson, R. (2011) 'Displaying motherhood: representations, visual methods and the materiality of maternal practice', in E. Dermott and J. Seymour (eds) *Displaying families,* Basingstoke: Palgrave

Kiernan, K. (2004) 'Redrawing the boundaries of marriage', *Journal of Marriage and Family,* 66(4): 980–7.

Kirkman, M., Harrison, L., Hiller, L. and Pyett, P. (2001) '"I know I'm doing a good job": canonical and autobiographical narratives of teenage mothers', *Culture, Health and Sexuality,* 3(3): 279–94.

Kitzinger, S. (2008) 'Letter from Europe: Home birth reborn', *Birth,* 35 (1): 77-8.

Kohn, M. (1963) 'Social class and parent–child relationships: an interpretation', *American Journal of Sociology,* 68: 471–80.

Kristeva, J. (1980) *Desire in language: A semiotic approach to literature and art,* trans. T. Gora, A. Jardine and L.S. Roudiez, ed. L.S. Roudiez, New York: Columbia University Press.

Lancet (2010) 'Home birth: proceed with caution', *The Lancet,* 376(9738): 303–31.

Lareau. A. (2003) *Unequal childhoods: Class, race and family life,* Berkeley: University of California Press.

Lawler, S. (2000) *Mothering the self: Mothers, daughters, subjects,* London: Routledge.

Layne, L. (2000) '"He was a real baby with real baby things": a material culture analysis of personhood, parenthood and pregnancy loss', *Journal of Material Culture,* 5(3): 321–45.

Layton, L. (1998) 'Performance theory act 3: the doer behind the deed gets depressed', in L. Layton, *Who's that girl? Who's that boy? Clinical practice meets post-modern gender theory,* Northvale, NJ, and London: Jason Aronson Inc, pp 207–39.

Liedloff, J. (1986) *The continuum concept,* Cambridge, MA: Da Capo Press.

Lesnik-Oberstein, K. (2008) *On having an own child: Reproductive technologies and the cultural construction of childhood,* London: Karnac.

Lewis, J. (1992) *Women in Britain since 1945,* Oxford: Blackwell.

Lomax, H. and Fink, J. (2010) 'Interpreting images of motherhood: the contexts and dynamics of collective viewing', *Sociological Research Online*, 15(3).

Longhurst, R. (2009) 'YouTube: a new space for birth', *Feminist Review*, 93: 46–63.

Lovell, T. (2000) 'Thinking feminism with and against Bourdieu', *Feminist Theory*, 1(1): 11–32.

Lucey, H., Melody, J. and Walkerdine, V. (2003) 'Project 4:21 Transitions to womanhood: developing a psychosocial perspective in one longitudinal study', *International Journal of Social Research Methodology*, 6(3): 279–84.

Lupton, D. (1999) *Risk*, London: Sage.

Lustig, D.F. (2004) 'Baby pictures, consumerism and exchange among teen mothers in the USA', *Childhood*, 11(2): 175–93.

Lyonette, C., Baldauf, B. and Behle, H. (2010) '*Quality' part-time work: A review of the evidence*, London: Government Equalities Office.

McIntosh, J. (1985) 'Barriers to breast feeding: choice of feeding method in a sample of working class primiparae', *Midwifery*, 1: 213–24.

McLeod, J. and Thomson, R. (2009) *Researching social change: Qualitative approaches to personal, generational and historical processes*, London: Sage.

McKie, L., Gregory, S. and Bowlby, S. (2002) 'Shadow times: the temporal and spatial frameworks and experiences of caring and working', *Sociology*, 36(4): 897–924.

McNeil, M. (2007) 'New reproductive technologies: stories of dreams and broken promises', *Feminist cultural studies of science and technology*, London: Routledge, pp 71–93.

McRobbie, A. (1978a) 'Jackie: an ideology of adolescent femininity', Occasional paper, Centre for Contemporary Cultural Studies, University of Birmingham.

McRobbie, A. (1978b) 'Working class girls and the culture of femininity', in Centre for Contemporary Cultural Studies, *Women Take Issue*, London: Hutchinson.

McRobbie, A. (1981) 'Just like a Jackie story', in A. McRobbie and T. McCabe (eds.) *Feminism for girls: An adventure story*, London: Routledge and Kegan Paul.

McRobbie, A. (1991) '*Jackie* magazine: romantic individualism and the teenage girl', in *Feminism and youth culture: From 'Jackie' to 'Just Seventeen'*, London: Macmillan.

McRobbie, A. (1996) 'More! New sexualities in girls' and women's magazines', in J. Curran, D. Morley and V. Walkerdine (eds) *Cultural Studies and Communications*, London: Arnold.

McRobbie, A. (2007) 'Top girls? Young women and the post-feminist sexual contract', *Cultural Studies*, 21(4–5): 718–37.

McRobbie, A. (2009) *The aftermath of feminism: Gender, culture and social change*, London: Sage.

Maher, J., Lindsay, J. and Bardoel, A. (2010) 'Freeing time: the family time economies of nurses', *Sociology*, 44(2): 269–87.

Mamo, L. (2007) *Queering reproduction: Achieving pregnancy in the age of technoscience*, Durham, NC and London: Duke University Press.

Mason, J. and Tipper, B. (2008) 'Being related: how children define and create kinship', *Childhood*, 15: 441–60.

Mauthner, M. (2002) *Sistering: Power and change in female relationships*, Houndsmill: Palgrave.

Michie, H. and Cahn, N.R. (2005) 'Closer to home; the domestic in discourses of upper middle-class pregnancy', in S. Hardy and C. Wiedmer (eds) *Motherhood and space: Configurations of the maternal through politics, home and the body*, Basingstoke: Palgrave Macmillan, pp 105–12.

Miller, D. (1998) *A theory of shopping*, Cambridge: Polity Press.

Miller, D. (2004) 'How infants grow mothers in North London', in J.S. Taylor, D.F. Wozniak and L. Layne (eds) *Consuming motherhood*, New Brunswick: Rutgers University Press, pp 31–51.

Miller, T. (2005) *Making sense of motherhood: A narrative approach*, Cambridge: Cambridge University Press.

Miller, T. (2010) *Making sense of fatherhood: Gender, caring and work*, Cambridge: Cambridge University Press.

Mitchell, J. (2003) *Siblings, sex and violence*, Cambridge: Polity Press.

Moi, T. (1999) *What is a woman? and other essays*, Oxford: Oxford University Press.

Morgan, D. (1996) *Family connections: An introduction to family studies*, Cambridge: Polity Press.

Morgan, D. (2011) *Rethinking family practices*, Houndsmill: Palgrave Macmillan.

Nayak, A. (2006) 'Displaced masculinities: chavs, youth and class in the post industrial city', *Sociology*, 40(5): 813–31.

NCT (National Childbirth Trust) www.nct.org.uk/parenthoodpolicy, accessed 29 September 2010.

NHS IC Report (2008), www.ic.nhs.uk/work-with-us/consultations/nhs-maternity-statistics-review.

Nordqvist, P. (2008) 'Feminist heterosexual imaginaries of reproduction: lesbian conception in feminist studies of reproductive technologies', *Feminist Theory,* 9(3): 273–92.

Nordqvist, P. (in press) '"I don't want us to stand out more than we already do": lesbian couples negotiating family connections in donor conception', *Sexualities*, 19.

Nove, A., Berrington, A. and Mathews, Z. (2008) 'Home births in the UK, 1955 to 2006', *Population Trends 133*, London: Office for National Statistics.

Oakeshott, I. (2010) 'The bullies hiding behind Mumsnet's skirts', *Sunday Times*, 14 February.

Oakley, A. (1979) *Becoming a mother*, Oxford: Martin Robertson.

Oakley, A. (2005) *The Ann Oakley reader: Gender, women and social science*, Bristol: The Policy Press.

O'Connor, H. (2011, forthcoming) 'Resisters, mimics and coincidentals: intergenerational influences on childcare', *Community, Work and Family.*

Oliver, J. (2005) *Minus nine to one: The diary of an honest mum*, London: Michael Joseph Ltd.

ONS (Office for National Statistics) (2009) *Who is having babies? 2008*, Statistical Bulletin, www.statistics.gov.uk/pdfdir/births1209.pdf.

Parker, R. (1996) *Torn in two: The experience of maternal ambivalence*, London: Virago.

Pettinger, L., Parry, J., Taylor, R. and Glucksmann, M. (2005) *A new sociology of work?*, Oxford: Blackwell.

Phoenix, A. (2008) 'Claiming liveable lives: Adult subjectification and narratives of "non-normative", childhood experiences', in D. Stauneas and J. Kofoed (eds) *Plays in power*, Copenhagen: Danmarks Paedagogiske Universitesforlag, pp 178–93.

Phoenix, A., Woollett, A. and Lloyd, E. (1991) *Motherhood: Meanings, practices, and ideologies*, Newbury Park: Sage.

Pines, D. (1997) 'The relevance of early psychic development to pregnancy and abortion', in J. Raphael-Leff and R.J. Perelberg (eds) *Female experience: Three generations of British women psychoanalysts on work with women*, London: Routledge, pp 131–43.

Plummer, K. (1995) *Telling sexual stories: Power, change and sexual worlds*, London: Routledge.

Pollock, D. (1999) *Telling bodies: Performing birth*, New York: Columbia University Press.

Pollock, G. (2009) 'Mother trouble', *Studies in the Maternal*, 1(1), www.mamsie.bbk.ac.uk/back_issues/issue_one/griselda_pollock_abstract.htm.

Ponsford, R. (2011) 'Consumption, resilience and respectability amongst young mothers in Bristol', *Journal of Youth Studies*, doi: 10.1080/13676261.2011.559217.

POST (Parliamentary Office of Science and Technology) (2002) *Caesarean sections*, No 184, October, POST.

Power, N. (2009) *One dimensional women*, Winchester/Washington: Zero Books.

Radio 4 (2010) 'Whatever happened to sisterhood?', broadcast 10 October, available at www.bbc.co.uk/programmes/b00v1nlk.

Radway, J. (1984) *Reading the romance: Women, patriarchy and popular literature*, Chapel Hill, NC: University of North Carolina Press.

Reissman, C. (1983) 'Women and medicalization: A new perspective', *Social Policy*, 14(1): 3–18.

Reynolds, T. (2006) *Caribbean mothers: Identity and experience in the UK*, London: Tufnell Press.

Ribbens McCarthy, J., Edwards, R. and Gillies, V. (2002) *Making families: Moral tales of parenting and step-parenting*, York: Sociology Press.

Riceour, P. (2004) *Memory, history, forgetting*, Chicago: University of Chicago Press.

Rich, A. (1976) *Of woman born: Motherhood as experience and institution*, London: Virago.

Rose, G. (2004) '"Everyone's cuddled up and it just looks really nice": an emotional geography of some mums and their family photos', *Social and Cultural Geography*, 5(94): 549–63.

Rose, G. (2010) *Doing family photography: The domestic, the public and the politics of sentiment*, Aldershot: Ashgate.

Rosenthal, G. (1998) *The Holocaust in three generations: Families of victims and perpetrators of the Nazi regime*, London: Cassells.

Rouse, J. (2010) 'Can they hang on while I give birth and breastfeed? Individualisation, agency and oppression in entrepreneurs' maternity experiences', Paper presented at Gender, Work and Organisation, 21–23 June, Keele University, UK.

Rousseau, J.J. (1979) [1792] *Emile, or on education*, trans. Allan Bloom, New York: Basic Books.

Rubin, R. (1977) 'Binding in the post partum period', *Maternal-Child Nursing Journal*, 6: 67-75.

Rubin, R. (1984) *Maternal identity and the maternal experience*, New York: Springer.

Ruddick, S. (1980) 'Maternal thinking', *Feminist Studies*, 6(2): 342–62.

Rudoe, N. (2011) *Young mothers, education and exclusion*, unpublished PhD thesis, The Open University.

Rudoe, N. and Thomson, R. (2009) 'Class cultures and the meaning of young motherhood', in H. Graham (ed) *Understanding health inequalities*, 2nd edition, Maidenhead: Open University Press, pp 162–78.

Sanderson-Mann, J. (2009) *The everyday activities of motherhood*, unpublished MPhil thesis, The Open University.

Schmied, V. and Lupton, D. (2001) 'The externality of the inside: body images of pregnancy', *Nursing Inquiry*, 8: 32–40.

Sharpe, S. (1984) *Double identity: The lives of working mothers*, London: Pelican.

Sharpe, S. (1994) *Fathers and daughters*, London: Routledge.

Shildrick, M. (2009) 'Becoming maternal: things to do with Deleuze', *Studies in the Maternal*, issue 3, available at www.mamsie.bbk.ac.uk/shildrick.html.

Shipman, B. and Smart, C. (2007) '"It's made a huge difference": recognition, rights and the personal significance of civil partnership', *Sociological Research Online*, 12(1).

Shirani, F. and Henwood, K. (2010) 'Continuity and change in a qualitative longitudinal study of fatherhood: relevance without responsibility', *International Journal of Social Research Methodology*, 14(1): 17–29.

Sichtermann, B. (1983) *Femininity: The politics of the personal*, Cambridge: Polity Press.

Silva, E. and Smart, C. (1998) *The new family*, Cambridge: Polity Press.

Skeggs, B. (2004) *Class, self, culture*, London: Routledge.

Skeggs, B. and Woods, H. (2009) 'The transformation of intimacy: classed identities in the moral economy of reality television', in M. Wetherell (ed) *Identity in the 21st century: New trends in changing times*, Houndsmill: Palgrave Macmillan, pp 231–49.

Smart, C. (1992) *Regulating womanhood: Historical essays in marriage, motherhood and sexuality*, London: Routledge.

Smart, C. (1996) 'Deconstructing motherhood', in E.B. Silva (ed) *Good enough mothering: Feminist perspectives on lone mothering*, London: Routledge, pp 37–57.

Smart, C. (2007) *Personal life: New directions in sociological thinking*, Cambridge: Polity Press.

Stacey, J. (1998) *Brave new families: Stories of domestic upheaval in the late twentieth century America*, Los Angeles: UCLA Press.

Steedman, C. (1985) 'The mother made conscious: the historical development of a primary school pedagogy', *History Workshop Journal*, 20: 35–149.

Stern, D. (1998) *The motherhood constellation: A unified view of parent–infant psychotherapy*, London: Karnac Books.

Strathern, M. (1992) *After nature: English kinship in the late twentieth century*, Cambridge: Cambridge University Press.

Taylor, J. (2004) 'A fetish is born: Sonographers and the making of the public foetus', in J. Taylor, L. Layne and D. Wozniak (eds) *Consuming motherhood*, New Jersey: Rutgers.

Taylor, Y. (2009) *Lesbian and gay parenting: Securing social and educational capital*, Houndsmill: Palgrave Macmillan.

Thompson, P. (1993/2005) 'Family myth, models and denials in the shaping of individual life plans', in D. Bertaux and P. Thompson (eds), *Between generations: Family models, myths and memories*, Oxford: Oxford University Press, pp 13–38.

Thomson, R. (2007) 'The qualitative longitudinal case history: practical, methodological and ethical reflections', *Social Policy and Society*, 6(4): 571–82.

Thomson, R. (2008) 'Thinking intergenerationally about motherhood', *Studies in the Maternal* 1(1), available at www.mamsie. bbk.ac.uk/back_issues/issue_one/journal.html.

Thomson, R. (2010a) 'Using biographical and longitudinal methods: researching motherhood', in J. Mason and A. Dale (eds) *Understanding social research: Thinking creatively about method*, London: Sage Publications, pp 62–74.

Thomson, R. (2010b) 'Creating family case histories: subjects, selves and family dynamics', in R. Thomson (ed) *Intensity and insight: Qualitative longitudinal research as a route into the psychosocial*, Timescapes Working Paper 3, available at www.timescapes.leeds. ac.uk/assets/files/WP3_final_Jan%202010.pdf.

Thomson, R. and Holland, J. (2003) 'Hindsight, foresight and insight: the challenges of longitudinal qualitative research', in R. Thomson, L. Plumridge and J. Holland (eds) *International Journal of Social Research Methodology*, Special Issue on Longitudinal Qualitative Research, 6(3): 185–7.

Thomson, R. and Kehily, M.J. (2010) 'Troubling reflexivity: the identity flows of teachers becoming mothers', *Gender and Education*, first published 19 October 2010 (iFirst).

Thomson, R. and Kehily, M.J. with Hadfield, L. and Sharpe, S. (2008) *The making of modern motherhood: Memories, representations, practices*, The Open University, available at www.open.ac.uk/hsc/__assets/ yqwnotatstun71rdbl.pdf.

Thomson, R., Kehily, M.J., Hadfield, L. and Sharpe, S. (2009) 'The making of modern motherhoods: storying an emergent identity', in M. Wetherell (ed) *Identity in the 21st century: New trends and changing times*, Houndsmill: Palgrave Macmillan, pp 197–212.

Thomson, R., Kehily, M.J., Hadfield, L. and Sharpe, S. (forthcoming) 'Acting up and acting out: encountering children in a longitudinal study of motherhood', *Qualitative Research*.

Tinkler, P. (1995) *Constructing girlhood: Popular magazines for girls growing up in England 1920–1950*, London: Taylor and Francis.

Turner, J. (2009) 'Yum yum! Delicious babies', *Guardian*, 1 August, www.guardian.co.uk/books/2009/aug/01/mummylit-daddylit-parenting-books, accessed 20 October 2010.

Tyler, I. (2001) 'Skin-tight, celebrity pregnancy and subjectivity', in S. Ahmed and J. Stacey (eds) *Thinking through the skin*, London; Routledge.

Tyler, I. (2008) '"Chav mum, chav scum": class disgust in contemporary Britain', *Feminist Media Studies*, 8(4): 17–34.

Tyler, I. (2009) 'Birth: introduction to the special issue', *Feminist Review*, 93: 1–7.

Van Every, J. (1995) *Heterosexual women changing the family: Refusing to be a wife*, London: Taylor and Francis.

Vincent, C. and Ball, S. (2001) 'A market in love? Choosing pre-school childcare', *British Journal of Educational Research*, 27(5): 633–51.

Vincent, C. and Ball, S. (2007) '"Making up" the middle-class child: families, activities and class disposition', *Sociology*, 4(6): 1061–77.

Volosinov, V. (1973) [1929] *Marxism and the philosophy of language*, trans. L. Matejka and I. Turner, London: Seminar Press.

Walkerdine, V. (2009) 'Steel, identity, community: regenerating identities in a South Wales town', in M. Wetherell (ed) *Identity in the 21st century: New trends in changing times*, Houndsmill: Palgrave Macmillan, pp 59–75.

Walkerdine, V., Lucey, H. and Melody, J. (2001) *Growing up girl: Psychosocial explorations of gender and class*, Basingstoke: Palgrave.

Weeks, J. (2007) *The world we have won: The remaking of erotic and intimate life*, London: Routledge.

Weininger, E.B. and Lareau, A. (2009) 'Paradoxical pathways: an ethnographic extension of Kohn's findings on class and childrearing', *Journal of Marriage and Family*, 71: 680–95.

Wengraf, T. (2001) *Qualitative research interviewing: Biographic, narrative and semi-structured method*, London: Sage Publications.

Wetherell, M. (2009) 'The identity/action relation', in M. Wetherell (ed) *Theorizing identities and social action*, Houndsmill: Palgrave, pp 1–16.

Wheelock, J. and Jones, K. (2002) '"Grandparents are the next best thing". Informal childcare for working parents in urban Britain', *Journal of Social Policy*, 31: 441–63.

Widmer, E., Castren, A., Jallinoja, R. and Ketokivi, K. (2008) 'Introduction', in E. Widmer and R. Jallinoja (eds) *Beyond the nuclear family: Families in a configurational perspective*, Bern: Peter Lang, pp 1–10.

Williams, R. (1961) *The long revolution*, London and New York: Columbia University Press.

Williams, R. (1989) *Resources of hope, culture, democracy, socialism*, ed. R. Gale, London: Verso.

Willis, P., Jones, S., Canaan, J. and Hurd, G. (1990) *Common culture: Symbolic play at work in the everyday cultures of the young*, Buckingham: Open University Press.

Wilson-Kovacs, D. (2007) 'Consumption and sexual intimacy: Towards an understanding of intimate cultures in everyday life', in E. Casey and L. Martens (eds) *Gender and consumption*, Farnham: Ashgate.

Woodroffe, J. (2009) *Not having it all: How motherhood reduces women's pay and employment prospects*, London: Fawcett Society.

Woodward, K. and Woodward, S. (2009) *Why feminism matters: Feminism lost and found*, Houndsmill: Palgrave Macmillan.

Woolf, N. (2001) *Misconceptions: Truth, lies, and the unexpected on the journey to motherhood*, New York: Doubleday.

Young, I.M. (1990) 'Pregnant embodiment', in I.M. Young (ed) *Throwing like a girl and other essays in feminist philosophy and social theory*, Bloomington, IN: Indiana University Press.

Zadoroznyj, M. (1999) 'Social class, social selves and social control in childbirth', *Sociology of Health and Illness*, 21(3): 267–89.

Postscript

In the short time between completing and finalising the manuscript for this book the politics of motherhood have continued to gallop along. In policy terms mothers and families have been hit hard. The proposal for shared parental leave was dropped soon after the Coalition came into government, and Child Benefit and Sure Start have been early victims of the austerity cuts. Within popular culture two very different books have made waves, both speaking to middle-class parenting. First the transatlantic hit *Battle Hymn of a Tiger Mother* by Amy Chua (Bloomsbury Publishing, 2011) reveals attachment parenting as a losers' game within a global context of growing competition and downward social mobility. While appearing to tell a comic story of cross-cultural confusion and teenage rebellion, the dominant message of tough love and private tutoring could not be clearer. The second book, *Shattered: Modern Motherhood and the Illusion of Equality* by Rebecca Asher (Harvill-Secker, 2011) also addresses the middle-class mother, yet within a more domestic context, objecting to the logic of unequal responsibility between the sexes, shaped by UK maternity leave policy and a long hours' presenteeism in professional employment. In the UK context the politics of mothering appears to have shifted away from questions of child poverty towards the centre and the troubles of the 'squeezed middle'.

Index

Page references for notes are followed by n